Abstracts of the

DEBT BOOKS

of the

PROVINCIAL LAND OFFICE OF MARYLAND

Volume I

St. Mary's County

Liber 39: 1753, 1754, 1755, 1756, 1757, 1758
Liber 40: 1759

By

V. L. Skinner, Jr.

CLEARFIELD

Printed for Clearfield Company by
Genealogical Publishing Company
Baltimore, Maryland
2013

ISBN 978-0-8063-5630-3

Made in the United States of America

Introduction

The Provincial Land Office of Maryland was responsible for the dispensing of land from 1634 to 1777. Land was initially acquired by a warrant and was then patented. Information concerning these documents are found in the Warrants and Patents series of the Provincial Land Office located at the Maryland State Archives and are indexed by Peter Wilson Coldham in his five-volume series *Settlers of Maryland*, published by Genealogical Publishing Company.

Land was patented according to the desires of the patentee, and the name given to a patent was not necessarily unique within any particular jurisdiction.

The Lord Proprietor's personal hold on land affairs was much weakened during the royal period from 1689 to 1715. However, it was immediately revived when his proprietary rights were restored in 1715 (Hartsook and Skordas, *Land Office and Prerogative Court Records*). Both the Rent Rolls and the Debt Books date from this restoration period.

The Rent Rolls and the Debt Books are the means by which the Lord Proprietor kept track of the rents due him. Each piece of land granted to a person was subject to a yearly rent according to the terms of the patent.

A Rent Roll consists of entries for each tract of land patented, plus the name of the person for whom it was originally surveyed, the present owner, the acreage, and the rent. Alienations, or subsequent sales and leases of the piece of land, are also included.

A Debt Book consists of a list of persons owning land with the names and rents of each tract that he or she owned, all listed in one place under his or her name.

The Debt Books

The Debt Books are arranged by county, by year, and then by the name of the person paying the rent. There are a total of 54 libers, covering all of the counties. The extant Debt Books for the Western Shore counties are essentially annual, dating from 1753 to 1774. (The Debt Books for 1750 for five Western Shore counties–Anne Arundel, Baltimore, Charles, Prince George's, Frederick–are found in the Calvert Papers, located at the Maryland State Archives.) The extant Debt Books for the Eastern Shore counties are also essentially annual, dating from 1733 to 1775.

Each liber contains information for only one county, but for multiple years. For purposes of identification, each section (i.e., year) of any particular liber is given the denotation of the specific year.

Tracking land ownership over various years is particularly important for intestate estates, land inherited by women, and land that is not specified in a will.

The information in this series is presented in a tabular form:

- liber and folio citation, with any pertinent date.
- name of the person paying the taxes.
- name of the tract of land.
- acreage.

Notes to Reader

The following conventions are used in this book:

1. "The" at the beginning of any tract name has been omitted.
2. The index contains both tract names and surnames, sorted together.
3. "Crossed out" entries in the original libers have been included, as such.
4. Names have been transcribed as they are written; no attempt has been made to standardize any spelling.
5. Introduction and index pages of the original libers have been omitted.

Abbreviations

AA	Anne Arundel County	o/c	overcharged
ACC	Accomac County	p.	perches
a/s	alias	PA	Pennsylvania
BA	Baltimore County	PG	Prince George's County
CE	Cecil County	PW	Prince William County
CH	Charles County	p/o	part of
cnp	name continued on next page	QA	Queen Anne's County
CR	Caroline County	SM	St. Mary's County
CV	Calvert County	SO	Somerset County
DE	Delaware	SU	Sussex County
DO	Dorchester County	s/o	son of
FR	Frederick County	<t>	torn
h/o	heirs of	TA	Talbot County
KE	Kent County MD	tbc	to be charged to
KEDE	Kent County DE	<unr>	unreadable
n/a	not available	VA	Virginia
n/g	not given	WO	Worcester County

Contents of this volume

This book is the first of three volumes for St. Mary's County, an original county formed in 1637. It is also a "burned county", i.e., the courthouse burned and no probate or land records exist prior to 1777.

The debt books for St. Mary's County cover the following years: 1753, 1754, 1755, 1756, 1757, 1758, 1759, 1760, 1761, 1762, 1763, 1764, 1765, 1766, 1767, 1768, 1769, 1770, 1771, 1773, 1774.

From the Debt Books entries, two interesting facts are evident: (1) St. Mary's County had a Free School established by 1753; and, (2) Leonard Town was an established community, with numerous lots already occupied. James Heath is the largest landowner, with 5500 acres. Thomas Reeder is the landowner with the greatest number of tracts of land. Some St. Mary's County landowners are cited as inhabiting the following jurisdictions: Prince George's County (MD), Charles County, Patuxent, Benedict, Portobacco, London, Bermuda, and Virginia.

39:1753:1-1 ...		**Acres**
Daniel Clocker	"Lewis Neck"	30
	"Clockers Freehold"	50
Elisabeth Clocker	"St. Anns Freehold"	70½
	"Clockers Fancy" a/s "Clarks Fancy"	56
Thomas S. Waughop	"Hunting Quarter"	150
	"Poney Point"	750
	"Smoot"	150
Nicholas Sewall	pt. "Little Eltonhead Manor" ("Rich Neck")	1590
Edward Digges	pt. "Little Eltonhead Manor" ("Rich Neck")	300
William Price	"Brick Hill"	217
Edward Horne	pt. "Half Head Folly"	100
Ignatius Taylor	pt. "Little Eltonhead Manor" a/s "Governors Gift" ("Rich Neck")	60
James Dafforen	"Cole Harber"	150
George Asquith	"Stinmore"	100
	"Inclosure"	30
	"Thomas & George in Company"	4
John Rodes	"Jesbury Plains"	330
Isaac Prevatt	"<t> Ridg"	50
	pt. "Cross Mannor"	150
Robert Pearce	pt. "Cortany Fancy"	60
	pt. "Price's Chance"	25
39:1753:1 ...		
Thomas Thorpe	"Strife"	50
John Milburn	"Surgesons Folly"	50
	"Wills Swamp"	50
James Styles	pt. "Styles Chance"	59
	pt. "What Care I"	28
	pt. "Chance"	6
	pt. "Elisabeth Mannor"	43
John Price	"Grove"	50
	"Farnhans"	83
Robert Greenwell	pt. "Back Land"	70
	pt. "Quaintons Pleasure"	117
	pt. "Greenwells Marsh"	49

h/o Richard Debutts	pt. "Massom"	200
	pt. "Hopewell"	100
	"Strife"	100
	"Itchcombs Freehold"	340
	"Chockers Marsh"	100
	"Dunbare"	100
John Stevens	"Wellclose"	200
James White	pt. "Fresh Pond Neck"	150
William Morgan	"Hazard"	73
	pt. Partrick Hills"	15
	"White Burch Freehold"	100
39:1753:2 ...		
Richard Barnhouse	pt. "Cross Mannor"	1000
	pt. "Elisabeth Mannor"	1000
John Cole	pt. "Revells Backside"	50
	"Nobles Victor"	50
	"Harberts Grief"	43
	pt. "Shock Parke"	24
John Mitchell	"Mitchells Choice"	47
Cornelius Barber	pt. "Luck Land"	470
	"Nicholas Hope"	135
Baptist Barber	pt. "Wast Ham"	250
	pt. "<t> Land"	200
	pt. "<t>	100
Mrs. Donalson	pt. "Mitcham Hills"	200
Phillip Key, Jr.	pt. "Mitcham Hills"	100
George Leatham	pt. "Mitcham Meadows"	100
Luke Russell	"Brough"	50
James Gough	"Barnerds"	100
	pt. "Margertts"	200
	"Bacon Neck"	200
	"Proprietors Gift" or "Lordships Favour"	50
	"No Name"	50
	"St. Teratia"	100
39:1753:3 ...		
William Sissell	pt. "Cadle"	50

Thomas Sissell	pt. "White Aker"	50
	pt. "Addition to White Aker"	18
John Thompson	pt. "Daves's Forris"	50
Mary Greenwell	pt. "Green Hill"	221
John Bap. Carberry	pt. "Honton Parke"	1189
George Bouth	pt. "Norton Parke"	56
Athan. Nottingham	"Knevetts St. Ann"	100
Clement Stranford	"Leith"	100
Thomas Hatton Combs	"Hattons Rest"	250
	"Addition to Harts Delight"	152
John Heard	pt. "St. Lawrences Freehold"	193
	pt. "Heards Security"	43
	pt. "Hannover"	350
Francis Spink	"Shercliff"	300
Peter Howard	pt. "Twitnam"	100
Benjamin Jarbo	pt. "Heard Security"	70
Marke Jarbo	pt. "Heard Security"	40
39:1753:4 ...		
Mathew Heard	"Pole"	120
	"William Heards Purchass"	115
	"Ashmans Freehold"	150
	"pt. "Hannover Addition"	123
	"Heards Choice"	100
	pt. "Heard Security"	263
Marke Heard	"Thirds"	425
James Tayler (St. Mary's)	pt. "Snow Hill Manor"	100
Mathew Hebb	"Small Hopes"	56
William Hebb	"Gardinners Purchass"	100
	"St. Williams"	114
	"Freehold"	75
	"Causeen"	50
	pt. "Geo. Point"	50
	"No Name"	50
	pt. "Hidden Hole"	280
	"Mackeys Point" pt. "Mackeys Neck"	50
John French	pt. "Honton Parke"	160

Arthur Thompson	"Thompsons Expence" or "Thomas Expence"	125
John Norris	pt. "Wheatleys Content"	95
	pt. "Heard Choice"	57
John Hammond	pt. "Lewgroes Plains"	200
William Watts	"Bushels Rest"	150
	"Timber Swamp" & "Addition to Timber Swamp"	160
39:1753:5 ...		
James Thompson	pt. "Small Hopes"	100
	pt. "Swamp & Iland"	120
	"Farthing Fortune & Addition"	60
	"Mills Meadows"	150
	pt. "Howns Low"	50
	"Prattle Well"	100
	"Small Hopes Addition"	78
	"Divided Hills"	51
Richard Brewer	pt. "Howns Low"	50
Nicholas Mills	"Strife"	200
	"Strifes Addition"	109
	pt. "Wheatleys Chance"	150
	pt. "Squable"	50
	pt. "Medley"	300
h/o James Blomfeild	"Coles Addition"	50
	"Roberts Freehold" or pt. "Roberts Neck" a/s pt. "Medley"	90
John Sanders Power	pt. "St. Barberys"	200
Mrs. Neale	pt. "St. Winefreits Freehold"	250
h/o James Neale	pt. "St. Winefreits Freehold"	30
h/o Oswell Neale	pt. "St. Winefreits Freehold"	220
	pt. "St. Winefreits Freehold"	452
Robert Cole	"Coles Purchass"	209
Phillip Tippett	pt. "Suttles Range"	154
39:1753:6 ...		
John Suttle	pt. "Suttle Range" a/s "Rest"	136
Andrew Mills	"Wolverhamton"	150
William Ward	"Quainton"	100
Thomas Mattingly (cnp)	"Mount Missery"	100

	pt. "St. Thomas"	150
Vincent Taylor	pt. "St. Tiratia"	100
	"Plains"	150
	"Ensgelath"	300
	"Ensgelath Addition"	140
Jos. Guibert	pt. "Dynard"	100
John Thompson	pt. "Susquahanah Point"	100
	"Smiths Discovery"	258
	"Susquehannah Point" & "Edloes Addition"	195
	"Parks Addition"	110
	pt. "Cross Mannor"	170
Aben Simmons	"Stratford"	100
	"Trophey"	100
James Wood	"Disert"	125
	"Arabice"	76
William Mackin	"Beards Choice"	50
	"St. Margretts Fields"	100
	"St. Margretts Forrest"	100
	"Shirwell"	100
39:1753:7 ...		
Charles Suall	pt. "St. Margretts"	66
John Hilton	pt. "Honewill"	146
John Edwards	"Price Lott"	100
	"Plains Treeho"	93
	"Buck Parke"	100
Thomas Asquith	pt. "St. Richard Mannor"	350
	pt. "Hamsfield"	100
	"Hunting Neck"	200
	"Hickory Hills"	100
Cornelius Maning	pt. "Neale's Lott"	209
	"Broad Neck"	83
	"Rednor"	404
Elizabeth Hopwell	"Hopewells Chance"	170
	"Gardiners Neck"	200
	"Hogpen Neck"	150

Joseph Hopwell	pt. "Massom"	300
	"Asquith Defence"	122
Elizabeth Wiseman	"Batchellors Hopewell Rectified"	374
	"Force Put"	100
	"Hopewells Delight"	200
	"Back Acres Begining"	100
William Stone	pt. "Graden"	100
Cutbert Fenwick	pt. "Fenwick Mannor"	147
39:1753:8 ...		
John Price Williams	pt. "Kith & Prices Rest"	190
James Heard	pt. "St. Clement Mannor"	150
	pt. "Fenwick Manor"	175
	"Hardship"	147
	"Renevetts Beginning"	100
	"Two Friends"	131
John Sanner	pt. "Fresh Pond Neck"	150
Thomas Rablin	"Best Land"	50
John Thorne	pt. "Disert"	62½
	pt. "Jesham"	50
James Keth	pt. "Kith & Prices Rest"	200
	"Town Neck"	200
	"Satisfaction"	580
	"Remainder"	19
Abso. Tennyson	"Phenisfort"	700
	"Johns Fourtune"	61
	"Gilberts Folly"	36
	pt. "Partrick Hills"	13
	"Inclosure"	62
Mvl. Lock	"Walston"	100
	pt. "Trumans Lodge"	150
	pt. "Kith & Prices Rest"	58
Mary Clarke	"Addition"	100
39:1753:9 ...		
Hugh Hopewell	"Hopewells Adventure"	95
	"Addition to Hopewells Adventure"	52
John Arthurs	pt. "Underwoods Choice"	100

Anthony Smith	pt. "Underwoods Choice"	100
John Wilkinson	"Industry"	153
William Harrisson	pt. "St. Margretts"	100
	"Wards Addition"	36
h/o Charles Ganyott	"Ganyotts Lott"	50
	pt. "Yoake by Chance"	41
Mary Edwards	"Damonds Adventure"	110
	"Edwards Back Land"	52
Thomas Shanks, Jr.	"Shanks Adventure"	101
	pt. "Clarker"	100
	pt. "St. Oswell"	100
	pt. "Cole Parke" a/s "Clarks Wesdiscovery"	50
	"Shanks Risque"	102
John Morgen	pt. "Parrish Beadle"	100
Thomas Warrett	"Hog Neck"	100
Joseph Dalhorn	"Mades Delight"	78
John Welch	pt. "Cortanys Neck"	68
39:1753:10 ...		
Dennis Tippett	pt. "Suttle Range"	60
	pt. "St. Barberys Addition"	120
George Vawdery	"Underwood" a/s "Wood Land" now called "Woods Pleasure"	344
Margertt Alvey	~~"Conveniency"~~	100
Benn. Spalding	"Harts Delight"	200
	1 lot in Leonard Town	1
James Bailey	"Slipe"	69
	pt. "Baileys Fortune"	168
Ignatious Mattingly	pt. "Mattinglys Hope"	130
	pt. "St. Johns"	50
	"Cleaver"	155
Jesse Wharton	"Notley Hall"	400
	"Neighbourhood"	146
Thomas Vaughon	pt. "Beckworth Ledge" a/s "James Chance"	100
William Daft	pt. "Rocky Point" a/s "Curry Glase"	100
Stephen Greenwell	"Cole Brooke Levell"	129
Mary Taylor (cnp)	"White House"	63

	"Neglect"	53
	"Williams Addition"	22
	pt. "Wastham"	100
39:1753:11 ...		
Isab. Cook	"Jones Fortune"	112
William Boarman	"St. Dorothye"	263
Thomas Reader	"Thomas & Henry"	113
	pt. "Hawns Kirk"	165
	"Chance"	50
	"Rose Land with Addition"	133
	"Boguis Increse"	273
	pt. "St. Johns"	595
	"Workinton Parke"	1539
	"Middle Ground"	102
	"Burrs Gift"	150
	"Madens Lott"	236
	~~"Addition to Rose Land"~~	~~83~~
	pt. "Hope"	36
	pt. "Wastham"	87
	pt. "Denbury Hills"	100
	pt. "Trumans Lodge"	105
	"Inclosure"	14
	pt. "Hawnshirk"	87
	pt. "Parrish Beadle"	100
	"Youngmans Venture"	130
	"Forth Addition"	83
	pt. "Grate St. Thomas"	100
	"Hanworth"	100
	pt. "Dynard"	50
	pt. "Bottom"	50
Edward Hibb	"Little Recovery of Burch Rig."	13
	"Corbett"	100
39:1753:12 ...		
William Hibb, Jr.	"White Cleiff"	50
Thomas Sanner	"Salusbury Plains"	100
Samuel Ashcom (cnp)	"No Name"	881

	"Ashcoms Marsh"	32
Thomas Reswick	pt. 2 tracks of enclosed land	64
	pt. "White Aker"	50
Robert Lydell	"Cynetts Chance"	56
Charles Dylion	"Charles Chance"	75
Marke Stevens	"Netherform Beginning"	50
John Maning	"Bacon Point"	100
	pt. "Revetts"	151
	"Fortune"	50
	"Taunton Dean"	40
	"Crooked Billett"	38
George Dafforn	"White Marsh"	93
	"T.B."	119
James Roach	pt. "Medley"	100
	"Huckelbury Lane"	10
Elinor & Ann Graves	"Hopewell"	131
	"Hardshift"	50
	"Hardshift Addition"	186
39:1753:13 ...		
John Olever	pt. "Cornalius"	39
	"Fourtune"	50
	"Pearth"	62
	"Fortune Outlett"	16
Elizabeth Nelson	pt. "Doe Park"	75
	"Doe Park"	50
George Gravetts	"Gravle Swamp"	108
Thomas Sandage	pt. "Doe Parke"	21
	"North Addition to Doe Parke"	147
Samuel Wood	"Cannough Neck"	100
Anthony Sims	"Wickohandick"	350
John Burruss	pt. "Trent Fort"	129
	pt. "Remainder Charles Lott"	116½
William Cartwright	pt. "Remainder Charles Lott"	166½
	"Ridge"	50
John Cartwright (cnp)	pt. "Longlookd for Come at Last"	75
	"Cartwright Pastor"	20

	pt. "Burruss Guift"	40
George Burruss	pt. "Longlooked for Come at Last"	100
George Dent	pt. "Freestone Point"	174
John Buckman	pt. "Freestone Point"	50
39:1753:14 ...		
John Dent	pt. "Freestone Point"	100
James Crook	"Ludgate"	50
Richard Southon	"Southons Desire"	125
Samuel Southon	"Trumons Lott"	40
	"Little Worth"	25
Thomas Tauny	"Green Meadows"	200
Thomas Norris	pt. "Lewgors Plains"	130
Free School	pt. "Hopton Parke"	100
Stephen Lynch	"Granes Content"	100
	"Plum Point"	162
Rev. Mr. Livers	"Little Britton"	750
	pt. "Brittons Out Lett"	43
Rev. Mr. Ashby	"St. Innegoes Mannor" & "St. George's Island"	3000
	"Chomple Freehold"	25
Robert Chesley	Lott in Leonard Town	2
	pt. "Porke Hall"	50
Henry Reley	"Saturdays Worke"	100
	"Addition to Saturdays Worke"	30
Peter Mills	pt. "St. Johns"	230
39:1753:15 ...		
Winifred Rowson	"Maindens Lott"	100
	"Barwescoate"	50
	"Winnfreds Chance"	36
William Hemmersly	"Beverly"	380
	"Batchellors Hope" a/s "Bashford Mannor"	300
Thomas Alston	"Readers Adventure"	350
	pt. "St. Clements Mannor"	200
William Mills	pt. "Popler Neck"	115
	"Anstnether"	30
Margaret Mills	"Coles Adventure"	150
John Johnson	"St. Peters Wills"	100

Peter Cartwright	pt. "Weston"	100
John Spalding	"Batchellors Rest"	100
Margaret Yates	pt. "Turvey"	93
Edward Ployden	pt. "Tavern"	100
	"Farme"	500
	"Ploydens Discovery"	66
Isaac Shamwell	pt. "Devonsher"	50
	pt. "Trumanica"	50
	"Darbyshire"	130
Thomas Spalding	pt. "St. Thomas"	200
39:1753:16 ...		
Thomas Spalding, Jr.	pt. "Cragburns Purchase"	100
	"Spaldings Addition"	42
	pt. "St. Giles"	35
	"Spaldings Adventure"	207
	"Rich Neck"	150
Benjamin Branson	"Trayton"	57
	"Hillfield"	96½
	"Keatch & Price's Rest"	122
	pt. "Best Land"	10
George Thompson	pt. "Hazard"	100
William Hall	pt. "Graden"	100
William Watson	"Popler Point"	100
James Peake	"Forrist of Dean"	100
George Leigh	"Innis Choice"	100
	"Galloway" or "Bettys Folly"	50
	"Innis Reserve"	25
	"Parriss"	150
	"Inclosure"	170
Marke Bailey	pt. "Bottom"	50
Ath. Ford	pt. "Strand"	91
William Thomas	"Wailes"	200
	"Wailes Addition"	91
	pt. "Boston"	50
39:1753:17 ...		
George Waring (cnp)	pt. "St. Johns"	68

	pt. "Burch Hanger"	75
Luke Mattingly	"Choice Part Hazard"	100
Mary Smith	pt. "Hazard"	57
John Higgs	"Wednesday Project"	95
	"Higgs Purchass"	49
John Harbert	"Harberts Invention"	189
	"Good Yealding"	86
Francis Ratcliff	pt. "Doe Park"	50
William Jenkins	pt. "Truth & Trust"	173
	"Salem"	215
	"Croyden"	100
	"St. Thomas"	200
	"Addition"	103
	"Foxes Range"	70
Thomas Watts	pt. "Truth & Trust"	100
	pt. "St. Thomas"	100
	pt. "Smoot"	50
William Martin	pt. "Hopewell"	74
	"Cracksons Rest"	50
	"Redmons Hardship"	50
	pt. "Hope"	11
Thomas Hall	pt. "Long Looked for Come at Last"	112
39:1753:18 ...		
Charles Beach	"Gosslings Addition"	30
	pt. "Parting Parth"	26
	"Miles Chance"	25
widow Gossling	pt. "Parting Parth"	274
	"Gardin Spott"	80
John Johnson Surthon	pt. "Brotherhood"	140
	"Surthons Hills"	50
	pt. "Wastham"	100
Mathew Guibert	pt. "Dynard"	81
Thiod. Jordon	pt. "Dynard"	50
	pt. "St. Clement Mannor"	100
Thomas Kirkly	"Honest Folks Inheritance"	150
Richard Fenwick (cnp)	"Mayheard Comfort"	100

	"Ganeth Purchass" a/s "Blacks West Discovery"	48½
Thomas Tippett	pt. "Suttle Range"	213
William Lock	"Good Penyworth"	50
	"Locks Venture"	49
Horne Roberts	pt. "Fresh Pond Neck"	203
Thomas Morton	pt. "St. Johns"	100
Peter Brown	pt. "White Aker"	50
39:1753:19 ...		
Mrs. Forbes	"Orppens Guift"	400
	"Holbridge Town"	130
	"Dryden"	483
Charles Righill	pt. "Inclosure"	30
John Ford, Jr.	pt. "Farthing Guift" a/s "Ministerdam"	10
	"Dounham"	100
	"Longindispence"	73
Marke Thompson	pt. "Hatfeilds Hills"	23
Joseph Woodward	pt. "Scotland"	151
John Sissell	pt. "Scotland"	150
Luke Sissell	pt. "Scotland"	50
James Sissell	"Sissells Venture"	88
~~John Thompson~~	~~pt. "Davis's Forrest"~~	~~50~~
Sarah Sissell	pt. "Baileys Rest"	150
James Brown	"Drydocking Addition"	100
James Boyde	pt. "Hopton Parke"	160
Alexander Forguson	pt. "Small Hope"	9
	"Small Hopes Addition"	42
	pt. "Black Creek"	99
39:1753:20 ...		
Thomas Redman	pt."Small Hopes Addition"	100
Marke Taylor	"Branch"	30
Clement Spink	pt. "Guilmotts Hills"	180
	"All That Left"	31¼
	pt. "Guilmotts Hills"	<unr>
John Tennyson	pt. "Out Lett"	50
John Mattingly	"Thames"	150
	"Mattingly Addition"	30

h/o George Craghill	pt. "Out Lett"	119
	"Fish Pond"	243
	"Mitcham Meadows"	100
	pt. "Hamstid"	100
	pt. "Blake Creek"	30
Sarah Greenwell	"Holy Tree"	148
John Smith	pt. "Nuns Oake"	75
William Howard	pt. "Pomfret Feilds"	100
Enock Greenwell	"Hickory Hollows"	119
	"Farthings Adventure"	78
	pt. "Wheatlys Content" a/s "Back Land"	35
Thomas Thompson	"Adjoyner" a/s "St. Johns Addition"	23
	pt. "Dynard"	13
	pt. "Chance"	89
39:1753:21 ...		
John Cartwright (Chop)	pt. "Weston"	100
Mathew Cartwright	pt. "Weston Addition"	100
George Thompson	pt. "Rockey Point"	50
Charles Pane	pt. "Strife"	50
Walter Davis	pt. "Williams Harmeittage"	118
Leonard Paine	pt. "Strife"	50
Clement Newton	"Newtons Rest"	60
	"Newtons Rest with Addition"	37
Samuel Johnson	pt. "Hopewell"	36
	"Pianas Groves"	19
Elizabeth Hayden	"Roachis Discovery"	157
	"Haydens Risque"	81
William Edley	pt. "Haydens Fair"	100
William Hayden	pt. "Haydens Fair"	100
Michael Wilman	pt. "Styles Chance"	100
Mary Watts	pt. "Jesbury Plains"	100
Joseph Lawrance	pt. "Frog Marsh"	100
William Edgerton	pt. "Pountneys Marsh"	100
39:1753:22 ...		
Richard Farthing	pt. "Pountneys Marsh"	100
John Greenwell	pt. "Rochester"	100

Margaret Plummer	"Osbustons Oake"	50
	"Hopsons Choice"	30
William Doxe	"Smith Rest"	100
William Cavanough	pt. "Massom"	250
	"Eyre"	328
Thomas Vowles	"Vowles Purchass"	445
h/o Richard Vowles	pt. "Vowles Purchass"	120
	pt. "Brittons Oute Lett"	1
Robert Hemmett	"Hemmetts Begining"	34
	pt. "Burch Spring"	75
	pt. "Forrest of Harvey"	100
	"Wild Cat Neck"	104½
	"Hickory Flat Hall"	17½
	"Hemmett Chance"	69
h/o Petter Muggs	pt. "Vowles Addition"	80
	"St. Williams"	50
	pt. "Vowles Purchass"	57
	pt. "Rockey Point"	50
James Greenwell s/o William	"Wheatlys Content"	75
Elizabeth King	pt. "Burch Spring"	50
39:1753:23 ...		
Joshua Millard	"Neales Nott"	209½
	pt. "Little St. Thomas"	16
	pt. "St. Johns"	134
Luke Norris	pt. "Wheatleys Content"	69
Ignatious Thompson	"Fibny"	100
Thomas Medley	"Barron Doe"	95
John Mills	"Yealding Bury"	129
	pt. "Hopton Parke"	80
Robert Drury	pt. "Honncards Mount"	40
Richard Cooper (cnp)	pt. "Clarken"	100
	"Frightfull"	180
	"Clarken Addition"	94
	"Dynard"	100
	pt. "Hopewell"	65
	"Expence"	67

	pt. "Cragburns Purchass"	100
Joseph Watson	pt. "Partnership"	65
Richard Burruss	"Holefast"	76
	pt. "Longlooked for Come at Last"	75
John Wilson	"Indiangiant Sepulchre"	203
Abraham Hall	pt. "Gardeners Grove"	50
39:1753:24 ...		
Thomas Hays	pt. "Gardeners Grove"	197
	"Addition to Gardeners Grove"	42
Edward McHune	"Piles Discovery"	112
John Parsons	"Addition"	50
	pt. "Longlooked for Come at Last"	112½
James Watson	"Hedge Barren"	79
James Swann	pt. "Swanns Adventure"	63½
Stephen Cawood	pt. "Williamsons Purchass"	100
	pt. "Wastham"	200
	"Cawoods Expence"	157
Edward Barber	pt. "Swans Forrist"	56
	pt. "Wastham"	250
	pt. "Luckland"	130
John Shanks	pt. "St. Otwell"	100
Joshua Greenwell	"Last Shift"	100
John Wisman Greenwell	"This or None"	50
	"John Wisman Greenwell Parke"	49
Elinor Bisco	pt. "Swans Adventure"	92
h/o Benjamin Gaugh	pt. "St. Margretts"	100
39:1753:25 ...		
Charles Jarbo	pt. "St. Peters Hills"	112
John Evens	pt. "Ishmaells Right"	165
John Smith, Jr.	"Haphazard"	304
John Wheatly	"Hickory Thickett"	48
	pt. "Hannover Addition"	45
John Hoper	"Ashcombs Greenfeild"	100
John Knott	"Strap"	44
Peter Pane	pt. "Howards Mount"	75
Tho. Spalding s/o Tho. (cnp)	pt. "Grate St. Thomas"	100

	pt. "Little St. Thomas"	100
Richard Gardener	"Popler Hill"	200
Dr. McWilliams	pt. "Batchellors Rest"	264
	pt. "St. Clement Mannor"	100
Edward Feild	pt. "Batchellors Rest"	36
William Peake	pt. "Hannouer"	140
	pt. "Hannouer Addition"	60
Henry Neale	pt. "Hilly Lee" a/s "Hilly Till"	250
	pt. "St. Clemment Mannor"	400
Thomas Hulston	"Buckland Plain"	75
39:1753:26 ...		
Phillip Key, Esq.	"Buckwood Lodge"	411
	"Jame's Addition"	158
	pt. "St. Johns"	50
	"Addition to Peters Wells"	104
	pt. "Burch Hanger"	230
	"Creshold Hauen" & timber land	77
	pt. "Wems"	430
	"Woods Pleasure" & pt. "Chessam"	95
	pt. "Meadon Bower" in pt."St.Clement Mannor"	100
	pt. "Finckly"	102
	"Boston"	98
	pt. "Wastham"	87
	"Peach Blosom"	55
	"Luckland" a/s "Covent Garden"	200
	pt. "Dynard"	119
	pt. "Shourance" & "Yealding Bury"	75
	pt. "Yealding Bury"	88
	pt. "Milton Hope"	150
	pt. "Little Yealding"	35
	"Rooms Convenience"	26
	pt. "Notleys Addition"	175
	"Gardeners Landing"	100
	"Parks Addition"	110
Thomas Graves (cnp)	pt. "Graves Chance"	120
	pt. "Baptist Hope"	106

	"Hopewell"	250
	"Joshua Plains"	16¾
	pt. "Hardshift"	10
	"Price William New Casell"	50
	pt. "Grave's Chance"	10
39:1753:27 ...		
Ignatious Greenwell	pt. "Wheatleys Meadows"	123
Mary Wheatly	pt. "Wheatlys Meadows"	153
Charles Daft	pt. "Medley"	200
Peter Peake, Jr.	pt. "Hannover Addition"	50
John Milton	pt. "Burch Hanger"	94
Guilbert Ireland	"Edingbrough 10 Addition"	121½
	pt. "St. Williams Hermitage"	73
	pt. "Hopton Parke"	140
	pt. "Baptist Hope"	153
	pt. "Yealding Bury" a/s "Little Yealding"	17
	"Evens Lott" a/s "Baptist Hope"	50
John Guyther	pt. "Croft"	147
	"Saturdays Venture"	2½
	"Cornelius Swamp"	100
Ignatious Whealor	pt. "Hopton Parke"	50
Capt. Richard Key	"Wolfe Hole"	262
	"Addition to Guiberts Chance"	37
William Rogers	"Rogers Venture"	50
widow Gardener	pt. "St. Johns"	500
widow Ward	"Wards Defence"	100
39:1753:28 ...		
Anthony Brown	"Clarks Rest"	300
Samuel Able	pt. "Kirbys Choice"	118
	pt. "Squable"	25
	"Scrubby Thickett"	25
	pt. "Wheatlys Chance"	41
James Howard	"Mattinglys Hope"	70
	pt. "Cole Parke" a/s "Clarks West Discovery"	122
Peter Oneale	pt. "Cragburns ~~Purchass~~"	60
Kenet Boult	pt. "Collscome"	25

Col. George Clarke	pt. "Massom"	200
	"Cadcocks Measure"	150
	"Court Freehold" or "Hash Hall"	200
	"Fox Hill"	30
	"Adjoyner"	50
	"Grauely Hill"	50
	"Oyster Shell Neck"	50
	"Newgent Venture"	50
	"Blumbury"	100
	"Dunbar"	92
	"Butchers Slipe" a/s pt. "Long Neck"	42
	"Popler Point"	101
Barton Smoot	"Clarkes Range"	393
William Feild	pt. "Batchellors Rest"	100
Samuel Love	pt. "Partnership"	100
39:1753:29 ...		
Thomas Mooney	pt. "Edwards"	115
	"Tradesman Lott"	200
	pt. "Linstied"	18
	pt. "Valentins Grove"	96
Daniel Harris	"Kinston"	50
	"Wheatlys Hill"	32
John Hynes	"Bite the Fox"	19
	"Hunters Hills"	150
James Anderson	pt. "Backers Fancy"	78
	pt. "Cornelius"	39
	"Addition to Charles Parke"	20
Charles Flower	pt. "St. George's Point"	50
Benjamin Williams	"Walnutt Point"	55
	"Esquires Purchase"	37
	pt. "Muggs Adventure"	200
	"Fox Denn"	89
	"Bakers Fancy"	25
	"New Fancy"	25
John Tear	"Hollyday"	142
Enock Fenwick	pt. "Fenwick Mannor"	150

Ignatious Heard	pt. "Well Found"	106
Sab. Truman Grinfeild	"Amricafalix"	152
39:1753:30 ...		
Thomas Newton	"Underwood" a/s "Newtons Property"	124
	"Greenwell Marsh"	14
Ann Grinfeild	"Grinfeild Discovery"	90
	"Trent Neck"	835
	"Stockbardolph"	75
James Truman Grinfeild	"Canada" a/s "Keechs Folly"	133
	"Lamly"	100
	"Punk Neck"	60
	"Holbrige Town"	130
	pt. "Hopton Parke"	100
Nathaniel Grinfeild	"Fork"	60
	"Addition"	78
	"White Haven"	164
	pt. "Indian Creek & Addition"	491
	"Nightwood"/ "Knightwood"	50
	"Bashford"	104
	"Thimbllbe"	109
	"Fishing Place"	50
	pt. "Brough"	75
James Warrick	pt. "St. Johns"	150
John Dunbar	"Chance"	240
Edward Castor	pt. "Redmans Hardship"	50
Peter Jarbo	pt. "Hannouer"	60
	pt. "St. Peters Hill"	113
Ignatious Jarbo	"Hickory Hills"	100
39:1753:31 ...		
John Michael Thomas Tawny	pt. "Fenwick Mannor"	450
Josep Clarke	pt. "St. Johns"	300
Sarah Carter	"Mear Chance"	113
Mary Hammersly	"Carburys Discovery"	190
John Dant	"Hopewell"	100
	pt. "Yoake by Chance"	20
John McKey (cnp)	pt. "McKeys Neck"	153

	pt. "St. Richard Mannor"	50
	pt. "Massom"	100
John Jones	"Poverty"	64
Thomas Yates	pt. "St. Peters Hills"	100
	pt. "Small Hopes"	30
Enock Combs	pt. "Porke Hall"	300
	"Grappell" 2BC	200
	"Wilderpoole" 3Do	300
John Warritt	pt. "Watts Lodge"	90
Thomas Cook, Jr.	pt. "Brough"	68
John Cole (St. George's)	"Jone's Wood"	100
	"Addition to Jone's Wood"	89½
Joseph Harding	"Backys Rest"	100
39:1753:32 ...		
Samuel Belwood	"Ishamels Right"	165
	"Belwoods Grove"	128
	pt. "Stiles Chance"	16
Fairfax Comton	pt. "Honnard Mount"	75
John Read	pt. "Wellclose"	100
	"Brothers Dred"	135
John Norris	"Gaughs Levells"	42
	"Gaughs Conveniency"	48
	"Britton Bay"	150
William Roach	pt. "St. Johns Landing"	117
	pt. "St. Johns Addition"	167
William Guither	"Maids Right"	100
	pt. "Smoot"	100
Thomas Baker	"Chelsey"	100
William Taylor	"Poplar Hill"	63
John Baker	"Drapers Neck"	500
Francis Wheatly	pt. "Wheatlys Content"	66
	pt. "Buck Land Plain"	50
Leonard Greenwell	pt. "Hannouer Addition"	87
Forgus Heath	"Readers Addition"	79
39:1753:33 ...		
Clement Norris (cnp)	"Tants Marsh"	168

	"Norris Frolick"	3½
Thomas Howard	pt. "Guilmotts Hills"	75
Joseph Stevens	pt. "Devonshear"	50
	pt. "Trumania"	50
	"Joseph Venture"	54
Samuel Lee	"Wellilase"	82
	pt. "St. Clemment Manor"	100
John Brady	pt. "Baileys Rest"	100
	"Bradeys Lott"	25
Peter Ford	pt. "St. Giles"	81
	"Mount Pleasant"	100
	"May Pole"	96
	pt. "Strand"	91
Thomas Wheatly	pt. ~~"Wheatlys Content" a/s "Backland <unr>"~~	~~32~~
	"Addition to Wheatlys Content & Addition"	360
John Chisley	pt. "Crackburn"	300
	"Cragburns Island"	13
	"Cragburns Marsh"	17½
	pt. "Indian Creek"	36
Thomas Grinfeild	pt. "Indian Creek"	843
	pt. "Good Luck"	275
Joseph Alvey	"Knotting"	100
39:1753:34 ...		
Thomas Milton	"Burch Hanger"	95
Rev. Mr. Urquhart	pt. "Fawskirk"	250
	"Spring Blosom"	221
	pt. "Keth Price's Rest"	60
Benjamin Grifty	"Venture"	30
Burch Swann	pt. "Swanns Forrist"	40
	pt. "Hopewell"	146½
Thomas Clarke	pt. "Moffitts Will"	69
Thomas Braden	pt. "Moffitts Will"	69
John Bisco	"Barren Woods"	46
Henry Wimsett	"Harberts Griff"	44
	pt. "Nuns Oake"	20
James Dickson	"Dicksons Venture" a/s "Haydens Fair"	115½

h/o Edward Pye	"Underwood"	300
	"New Design"	350
James Adams	pt. "Small Hope Addition"	50
John Graves	pt. "Graves Chance"	94
James Thompson (Hd Chap)	pt. "St. Johns"	50
	"Harberts Swamp"	21
39:1753:35 ...		
Ignatious Greenwell	"St. Ignatious"	100
	"Addition"	23
Phillip Fenwick	pt. "Fenwick Mannor"	200
Daniel Watts	"Watts Lodge"	160
John Plummer	pt. "Elisabeth Mannor"	300
Richard Shirly	"Shirlys Adventure"	150
Thomas Keen	"Keens Rest"	49
Thomas Mathyis	pt. "Frends Conjunction"	72
Edward Aprice	pt. "St. Barberres"	100
John Anderson	"Sourthons Desire"	100
	pt. "Fox Race"	52
Benjamin Been	pt. "Frends Conjunction"	72
John Sykes	pt. "Frends Conjunction"	106
John Thompson	pt. "Mitcham Meadows"	100
George Weld	pt. "Hannouer"	103
h/o Marke Thomas	"Penamsez"	100
	"Brown Woodhouse"	50
	"Lukes Hardship"	7
	"Marks Adventure"	36
39:1753:36 ...		
John Thomas	"Hamton"	100
Thomas Manley	"Chance Conclusion"	97
	"Addition to Chance Conclusion"	26
Henry How	"White Land"	225
John Bisco	pt. "Harrissons Rest"	80
	pt. "Williams Fourtune"	32
Dr. Mury	"Indian Creek"	563
James Smith (cnp)	"Triple Defence"	206
	"Puntneys Over Sight with Addition"	219

	"Addition to Tripple Defence"	87
	"Pine Land"	355
	pt. "Turvey"	201
	"Trinity", "St. Gabrall" & "St. Michael Manor"	3000
Darby Morris	"Bury Berry"	65
	3 lotts in Leonard Town	3
Peter Peak	pt. "Frends Good Will"	100
Benjamin Fenwick	pt. "Fenwicks Mannor"	200
Robert Henley	pt. "Massom"	150
	"Johns Content"	93½
	"Keens Rest"	50
Robert Newgent	"Markeing Place"	100
	"Fox Canted"	11
39:1753:37 ...		
Cornelius Wildman	"Brook Chance"	81
	"Tylers Disapointment"	103
	"Wildmans Venture"	54
	"Golden Grove"	103
	"Wildmans Levetts"	168½
Enock Able	"Saturdays Conclusion"	35
	pt. "Wheatlys Chance"	50
	"Hobson Choice"	23½
John Medley Thompson	pt. "Scotland"	50
Thomas Barber	pt. "Burch Hanger"	20
Charles Greenwell	pt. "Farthings Adventure"	65½
Thomas Jordon	pt. "Collacome"	25
John Clark	"Evans Quarter"	100
Michael Gouldsmith	pt. "St. Clement Mannor"	86
	pt. "Baskford Mannor"	100
William Aud	pt. "Hannouer"	30
John Shircliff	"Shircliff"	250
	"St. Williams"	90
	"Q Name"	100
	pt. "Linstid"	78
	pt. "Linstid Addition"	100
James Chizam	pt. "Bakers Fancy"	100

39:1753:38 ...		
Richard Millard	"Little St. Thomas"	54
	pt. "St. Johns"	50
	"Turners Plains"	16
Thomas Pearce	pt. "Cortany Fancy"	50
K. Truman Grinfeild	pt. "Trent Neck"	1519
William Deacon, Esq.	"Peters"	150
	pt. "Chancellors Point"	112
	"St. Marys Freehold"	255
	"Govennors Feilde"	100
John Lowes	"Warnell"	240
Henry Jarbo	pt. "St. Peters Hills"	126
Henry Bryon	"Williams Indeavours"	50
	pt. "Farthings Adventure"	37
William Leake	pt. "Hatfeilds Hills"	7u5
John Mills	"Wast Feild"	140
	"Summersett"	195
Robert Ford	pt. "Revertts Backside"	172
	pt. "Revertts"	151
	pt. "Chancellors Point"	112
Edward Parsons	pt. "Guiberts Chance"	50
	"Small Addition"	19½
39:1753:39 ...		
Sab. Thompson	"Thompsons Expence"	208
Joseph Jenkins	pt. "Truth & Trust"	400
William Heard	pt. "Wellfound"	106
	pt. "Fenwick Mannor"	175
Hon. George Plator, Esq.	pt. "St. Joseph Mannor"	819
	"Boules Preservation"	890
	pt. "Fenwick Mannor"	400
	"Steuarts"	125
	"Resurrection Manor"	4000
Richard Raper	"Maynards Comfort"	100
	pt. "Baileys Fortune"	45
	pt. "St. Clement Mannor"	50
	pt. "Baptist Hope"	100

Joseph Greenwell	pt. "Kirbys Choice"	67
Thomas Doxe	pt. "Harrissons Rest"	70
Richard Brook	"Dallabrook Mannor"	2000
	"2 Brothers"	235
	"Back Land"	400
Thomas Hobson	pt. "Wems"	100
Elizabeth Hulse	pt. "Wast Ham"	150
Charles King	"Dedford"	300
	pt. "St. Joseph Manor"	200
39:1753:40 ...		
William Williams	"Drydocking"	100
	pt. "Shocks Parke"	26
	pt. "Roberts Neck"	95
	"Harberts Griff"	60
	pt. "Roberts Freedhold" a/s "Medley"	75
Robert Fenwick	pt. "Joseph Mannor"	126
John Marman	pt. "Hopton Parke"	197
Samuel Sgunifer	pt. "Joseph Mannor"	30
Leonard Green	pt. "Fenwick Mannor"	100
Thomas Jane	pt. "Elizabeth Mannor"	100
Ashton Smoote	pt. "Mackeys Neck"	50
	"Toles Last Shift"	100
	"Woodstock"	127
	pt. "Elizabeth Mannor"	247
	pt. "Cross Mannor"	500
Sturton Edward	"St. Thomas"	190
	"Doe Parke"	69
	pt. "Hanouer"	100
Thomas Broom	pt. "No Name"	250
John Lancastor	pt. "Hilly Lee"	250
	pt. "St. Clement Mannor"	400
Peter Gaugh	pt. "Lewgroes Plains"	100
39:1753:41 ...		
James Talton	pt. "Beverdam"	59
	"Elizabeth"	34
James Hager	pt. "Beverdam"	59

John Jarbo	pt. "Hannouer"	16
John Jarbo, Jr.	pt. "Hannouer"	18
	pt. "Heards Security"	24
John Able	pt. "Wheatlys Chance"	31
	pt. "Kirbys Choice"	88
	pt. "St. Joseph Mannor"	56
Cutbert Able	"Wisemans Chance"	100
Benjamin Redman	"Small Hope"	50
Dennis Burn	pt. "Beckworth Lodge"	81½
Joseph Waker	pt. "Guilmotts Hills"	100
	pt. "Addition to Farthings Fortune"	140
John Bailey	pt. "Little Yealding"	107
William Jones	"Saltors Hall"	83
	"Addition to Saltors Hall"	34
	"Jones Convenency"	35½
	pt. "Beeworth Lodge"	81½
	"Jone's Laine"	1¾
	"Muggs Adventure"	52
39:1753:42 ...		
Ruth. Jones	pt. "Davids Forrist Ruts"	50
John Price	"Grove"	50
Henry Spalding	pt. "Josent"	152½
	pt. "Two Brothers"	165
	pt. "New Castle"	50
	pt. "Rich Neck"	98
h/o John Abbington	pt. "St. Richards Mannor"	500
Thomas Duvall	pt. "Partnership"	200
John Watson	pt. "Partnership"	65
George Maxwell	pt. "Indian Creek with Addition"	461
Maj. Abra. Barnes	"Americafilioe Secundus"	956
	pt. "Rangelfeild"	40
	pt. "Forres Harvey"	100
	"Wesbury Mannor"	1250
	pt. "Harris Lodge"	100
Thomas Aprice	pt. "St. Barberry"	200
Edward Bowling	pt. "Collacome"	25

William Doxe	pt. "Patricks Hill"	50
	pt. "Jone's Fourtune"	36
John Morris	pt. "Collacome"	25
39:1753:43 ...		
George Boules	"Steplition Fortune"	200
	"Hazard"	234½
John Tippett	"Tippitts Purchass"	46
William Spalding	pt. "Rich Neck"	152
Marke Norris	pt. "Wheatlys Content"	118
	pt. "Buckland Plains"	70
Ignatious Fenwick	"Hebton Hole"	350
	pt. "Hebton Hole"	70
John Holt	pt. "St. Clement Mannor"	167
Ignatious Whealor	pt. "St. Clement Mannor"	250
John Lee	pt. "St. Clemment Mannor"	200
John Hoskens	pt. "St. Clement Mannor"	100
Bap. Greenwell	pt. "Regester"	100
John Bould	pt. "Cadle"	150
	"Addition to White Aker"	25
John Winsett	pt. "Hatfeild Hills"	27
John Buluck	pt. "St. Clement Mannor"	100
Benn. Neale	pt. "St. Clement Mannor"	200
39:1753:44 ...		
John Bohannon	"Fox Grape Barron"	106
Daniel Downee	"Demby"	250
Thomas Jenking	"Edingbrough"	100
Benjamin Molton	pt. "Bashford Mannor"	200
John Peake	"Forney Branch"	50
Clement Medley	pt. "Medley"	200
William Medley	pt. "Medley"	100
Basiel Peake	pt. "Medley"	100
George Greenwell	pt. "Medley"	50
John Lleweling	pt. "St. Clement Mannor"	400
	pt. "Basford Mannor"	75
John Holland	pt. "Hamstid"	100
John Fenwick	pt. "Crofts"	100

John Taylor	pt. "Frog Marsh"	100
	"Milmans Adventure"	123
Thomas Crane	"Dally"	100
Thomas Waring	"Warners Lott"	148
39:1753:45 ...		
Joseph Ingles	"St. Peters Key"	30
	"Fishing Creek Neck"	44
Richard Milburn	pt. "Halfhead Folly"	100
	"Milburns Chance"	178
	pt. "Cortneys Neck"	82
John Smith	pt. "Mattapony"	289
Clement Spalding	pt. "Jauen"	100
	pt. "Burchhanger"	180
John Eden	pt. "Bashford Mannor"	400
John Bond	pt. "St. Clement Mannor"	650
	pt. "Hopton Parke"	250
	pt. "St. Johns"	438
	"Gardeners Chance"	155
Richard Edgling	"Trumans Hunting Quarter"	200
	pt. "Hope"	64
Justinan Jordan	pt. "St. Clement Mannor"	200
John Boult	pt. "St. Clement Mannor"	100
George Slye	pt. "St. Clement Manor"	1000
Edward Turnner	pt. "Bashford Mannor"	200
George Backstor	"Batchellors Comford"	190
39:1753:46 ...		
Charles Sewall	pt. "Little Elton Head Mannor" a/s "Rich Neck"	50
	"French Discovery"	187
John Blackston	pt. "St. Clement Mannor"	530
John Mason	pt. "St. Clement Mannor"	430
Mary Tennerson	pt. "St. Clement Mannor"	100
Ken. Chaseldine	pt. "St. Clement Mannor"	725
Cyranius Chaseldine	pt. "St. Clement Mannor"	25
John Madock	pt. "Basford Mannor"	125
Charles Carroll, Esq. (cnp)	pt. "St. Clement Mannor"	2474
	<page torn>	209

	pt. "St. Barberrys Addition"	250
	"Lough Brough"	150
	"Addition"	41
	"Temple Bare"	100
John Reswick	pt. 2 tracks of Exch. Land	47
Edward Welch	"Oldfeild"	72
John Atterway Clake	pt. "Pony Point"	750
	"Popler Hill"	200
	"Blake Creek"	50
	"Tower Hill"	25
Robert Hager	pt. "Truth & Trust"	100
39:1753:47 ...		
Col. Nicholas Sewall	"Mattapony Sewall"	911
	"Sewall Discovery"	108
	"Fishing Point"	13
Leonard Davis	pt. "Disart"	62½
	"Mornes Venture"	103
James Wheatly	"Kington" a/s "Nintsquight"	187
	pt. "Wheatlys Addition"	21
John Smith	pt. "Bashford Mannor"	200
Mary McWilliams	pt. "St. Clement Mannor"	300
Sturton Edward, Jr.	"Taunton Den"	164
James Smith (Rock Creek)	pt. "Massom"	100
	"Clark's Parke"	130
Thomas Soot	pt. "Wells"	179
	pt. "Trent Fort"	84
	pt. "Horse Range"	100
James Mills	pt. "Bashford Mannor"	100
Leonard Mattingly	"Audley End"	190
Notley Gouldsmith	pt. "Bashford Mannor"	100
Roger Smith	pt. "Notleys Addition"	275
Dent Soot	pt. "Horse Range"	100
39:1753:48 ...		
Thomas Soot, Jr.	pt. "Wells"	100
Joseph Edwards (cnp)	pt. "Wells"	52
	pt. "Trent Fort"	5

Thomas Win Taylor	"Righting"	100
Clement Medley, Sr.	"No Name"	100
John Somerville	pt. "St. Richard Mannor"	100
	"Rally" a/s "Clarke's Last Discovery"	99
	"St. Jeroms Mannor"	200
John Mich. Waughop	"Waughops Chance"	138
John Coad	pt. "St. Clement Mannor"	300
Anthony Roberts	"Twitenham"	200
Benjamin Burruss	pt. "Trent Fort"	129
Peter Ford, Jr.	pt. "Nons Oake"	75
John Corbett	"Willinbrough"	70
h/o James Heath	"St. Jeroms Mannor"	3300
James Henebrick	"Henebricks Lane"	80
Auston Macy	"Plum Point"	338
39:1753:49 ...		
William Morgan	"Friends Conjunction"	50
William Jordon	pt. "St. Clement Mannor"	135
Mary Jordon	pt. "St. Clement Mannor"	<t>
Jeremiah Jordon	pt. "St. Clement Mannor"	<t>
John Ford (Court House)	pt. "Hannover"	<t>
	pt. "Green Hill"	<t>
	pt. "Lamston Pleasure"	150
	"Rangel"	78
	pt. "St. Peters Hills"	50
	pt. "Heards Security"	39
Francis Thompson	"Hard Fourtune"	100
William Mattingly	"Suttles Range"	80
Thomas Mattingly (carried to Tho. M. in p. 7.)	pt. "St. Johns" a/s "Mattingly Lane"	25
John Ford (weaver)	"Pomifretfeild"	50
	"Minnistordam"	50
Charles Carroll, Esq. (omitted on p. 47.)	"St. Clements Manor"	600
	"Oxford"	<n/g>
	"Hanover"	34
	"Loughborbo"	<n/g>
	"Hannover"	64

39:1754:1 ...		**Acres**
Daniel Clocker	"Clockers Freehold"	50
	"Lewis Neck"	30
Elizabeth Clocker	pt. "St. Anna Freehold"	70½
	"Clockers Fancy"	56
Thomas P. Waughop	"Hunting Quarter"	150
	"Poney Point"	750
	"Smoot Hollow"	150
Nicholas Sawall	pt. "Little Eltonhead Mannor"	1590
Edward Digges	pt. "Little Eltonhead Mannor"	300
William Price	"Brick Hill"	217
	"Parks Addition"	110
Edward Horne	pt. "Halfhead Folly"	100
Ignatius Taylor	pt. "Little Eltonhead Mannor"	60
James Dafforen	"Cole Harbor"	150
Gorge Asquith	"Stinmore"	100
	"Inclosure"	30
	"Thomas & George in Company"	4½
John Rodes	pt. "Jesbury Plains"	330
Isaac Pavett	"Cow Ridge"	50
	"Cross Manner"	150
Robert Pearce	"Cortany Fancy"	<torn>
	"Prices Chance"	<torn>
39:1754:2 ...		
Thomas Thorpe	"Strife"	50
Fargus Keough	"Fargusons Folley"	50
	"Wills Swamp"	50
	"Readers Addition"	79
James Stiles	pt. "Styles Chance"	59
	pt. "What Care I"	28
	pt. "Chance"	6
	pt. "Elizabeth Mannor"	43
John Price	"Gore"	50
	"Farnhans"	83
Robert Greenwell (cnp)	pt. "Backland"	70
	pt. "Lamptons Pleasure"	117

	pt. "Greenwells Marsh"	49
Samuel Debutts	pt. "Massom"	200
	pt. "Hopewell"	100
	"Strife"	100
	"Stinchoms Freehold"	340
	"Clockers Marsh"	100
	"Dunbar"	100
	"Lordships Favour"	100
~~John Stevens~~	~~"Well Close"~~	~~200~~
James White	pt. "Freshpond Neck"	150
William Morgan	"Hazzard"	73
	"Addition to White Burch Freehold"	53
	pt. "Partrick Hills"	15
	"White Burch Freehold"	100
John Bap. Carberry	pt. "Hopton Park"	797
39:1754:3 ...		
Richard Barnhouse	pt. "Cross Manner"	1000
	pt. "Elizabeth Manner"	1000
John Cole	pt. "Riberts Backside"	50
	"Nobles Victor"	50
	"Harberts Grift"	43
	pt. "Shock Park"	24
John Mitchell	"Mitchells Choyce"	47
Cornelius Barber	pt. "Luck Land"	470
	"Nicholas's Hope"	135
Bap. Barber	pt. "Wastham"	250
	pt. "Luck Land"	200
	"Leigh"	100
Elizabeth Donalson	pt. "Mitcham Hills"	280
Philip Key, Jr.	pt. "Mitcham Hills"	100
George Leatham	pt. "Mitcham Meadows"	100
Luke Russell	pt. "Brough"	50
James Gough (cnp)	"St. Barnerds"	100
	"St. Margarets"	200
	"Bacon Neck"	200
	"Proprieties Gift"	50

	"Q Name"	50
	"St. Teratia"	100
39:1754:4 ...		
William Sissell	pt. "Caydle"	50
Thomas Sissell	pt. "White Aker"	50
	pt. "Addition to White Aker"	18
John Thompson	pt. "Davis's Forest"	50
George Bouth	pt. "Hopton Park"	56
Mary Greenwell	pt. "Green Hill"	221
Anthony Nottingham	"Knevetts St. Ann"	100
Clement Stranford	"Leing"	100
Thomas Hatton Combs	"Hattons Rest"	250
	"Addition to Hearts Delight"	152
John Heard	pt. "St. Lawrences Freehold"	193
	pt. "Heards Security"	43
	pt. "Hanover"	350
Peter Howard	"Switham"	100
Mark Jarbo	pt. "Heard Security"	40
John Norris	"Shircliff"	300
	pt. "Wheatleys Content"	93
	pt. "Heard Choyce"	57
39:1754:5 ...		
Mathew Heard	"Pole"	120
	"William Heards Purchase"	115
	"Ashcoms Freehold"	150
	pt. "Hanover Addition"	123
	"Heards Choyce"	100
	pt. "Heard Security"	260
Mark Heard	"Thirds"	425
James Taylor (St. Mary's)	pt. "Snow Hill"	100
Mathew Hebb	"Small Hopes"	56
John French	pt. "Hopton Park"	160
Arthur Thompson	"Thompsons Expence"	125
John Hammond	pt. "Lewgroes Plains"	200
William Watts	"Bushels Rest"	150
	"Timber Swamp"	160

William Hebb	"Gardeners Purchase"	100
	"St. Williams"	114
	"Freehold"	75
	"Cousen"	50
	pt. "Georges"	50
	"No Name"	50
	"Hibtons Hole"	280
	"Hunting Corbutt"	100
	"Mackeys Point"	50
	"Cross Manner"	170
	"Wickahandick"	225
	"Flood Quarter"	50
39:1754:6 ...		
James Thompson	"Small Hope"	100
	pt. "Swamp & Island"	120
	"Farthing Fortune & Addition"	60
	"Mills Meadows"	150
	pt. "Hounslow"	50
	"Prattlewell"	100
	"Small Hopes Addition"	78
	"Davids Hills"	51
Richard Brewer	pt. "Hounslow"	50
Nicholas Mills	"Strife"	200
	"Strifes Addition"	109
	pt. "Wheatleys Chance"	150
	pt. "Squable"	50
	pt. "Medley"	300
h/o James Blomfield	"Coles Addition"	50
	"Roberts Freehold"	90½
John Sanders Power	pt. "St. Barberys"	200
h/o James Neale	pt. "St. Winefreets Freehold"	30
h/o Oswell Neale	pt. "St. Winefreets Freehold"	220
	"Surplist"	452
Robert Cole	"Coles Purchase"	209
Philip Tippett	pt. "Suttles Range" a/s "Rest"	154
Edward Mattingly	pt. "St. Winefreets Freehold"	250

39:1754:7 ...		
William Ward	"Quainton"	100
Thomas Mattingly	"Mount Missery"	100
	pt. "St. Thomas"	150
	pt. "St. Johns" a/s "Mattingly Lane"	25
Vincent Taylor	pt. "St. Teratia"	100
	"Plains"	150
	"Ensgelath"	300
	"Ensgelath Addition"	140
Jos. Guibert	pt. "Dynard"	100
Aben Simmons	"Stratford"	100
	"Tropley"	100
James Wood	"Desertt"	125
	"Arabice"	76
William Mackin	"Beards Choyce"	50
	"St. Margarets Fields"	100
	"St. Margarets Forest"	100
	"Speedwell"	100
John Thompson	pt. "Susquehanna Point"	200
	"Smiths Discovery"	258
	"Q Name"	195
John Suttle	pt. "Suttle Range" a/s "Rest"	136
Andrew Mills	"Woolverhampton"	150
Joseph Edlin	pt. "New Design"	175
39:1754:8 ...		
Charles Tuall	pt. "St. Margerets"	66
John Hilton	pt. "Hopewell"	146
John Edwards	"Price Lott"	100
	"Plains Jerecho"	93
	"Buck Park"	100
Thomas Asquith	pt. "St. Richard Manner"	350
	pt. "Hampstead"	100
	"Hunting Creek"	200
	"Hiccory Hills"	100
Cornelius Mannyng (cnp)	"Neales Nott"	209½
	"Broad Neck"	83

	"Rednor"	404
	pt. "Nuns Oak"	53
Elizabeth Wiseman	"Batchellors Hopewell"	374
	"Force Put"	100
	"Hopewells Delight"	200
	"Back Akers"	100
William Stone	pt. "Graden"	100
Cuthbert Fenwick	pt. "Fenwick Manner"	175
Joseph Hopewell	pt. "Massom"	300
	"Asqueath's Defence"	122
	"Gardners Neck"	200
	"Hogpen Neck"	150
~~Robert Thompson~~	~~pt. "Rockey Point~~"	~~139~~
39:1754:9 ...		
John Price Williams	pt. "Keth & Prices Rest"	190
James Heard	pt. "St. Clement Manner"	150
	pt. "Fenwick Manner"	175
	pt. "Hardship"	147
	"Kennevets Beginning"	100
	"Two Friends"	131
	"Heards Addition"	58
John Sannor	pt. "Fresh Pond Neck"	150
Thomas Rablin	"Best Land"	50
John Thorne	pt. "Desart"	62½
	pt. "Jesham"	50
James Keech	pt. "Keech & Prices Rest"	200
	"Town Neck"	200
	"Satisfaction"	580
	"Remainder"	19
Absolem Tennyson	"Phipes Fort"	100
	"Johns Fortune"	61
	"Guiberts Folly"	36
	pt. "Patrick Hills"	13
	"Inclosure"	62
Meverell Lock (cnp)	"Hulston"	100
	pt. "Trumans Lodge"	150

	pt. "Keech & Prices Rest"	58
Mary Clarke	"Addition"	100
George Mills	purchace from James & Ann Jorden pt. "St. Clements Manor"	150
39:1754:10 ...		
Hugh Hopewell	"Hopewells Adventure"	95
	"Addition to Hopewells Adventure"	52
	pt. "St. Richards Manner"	500
John Arthurs	pt. "Underwood Choyce"	100
Anthony Smith	pt. "Underwood"	100
John Wilkinson	"Industry"	153
William Harrison	pt. "St. Margarets"	100
	"Wards Addition"	36
h/o Charles Gannot	"Gannots Lot"	50
	pt. "Yoke by Chance"	41
Mary Edwards	"Damonds Adventure"	110
	"Edwards Back Land"	52
Thomas Shanks, Jr.	"Shanks Adventure"	101
	pt. "Clarker"	100
	pt. "St. Oswell"	100
	pt. "Cole Parks" a/s "Clark West Discovery"	50
	"Shanks Risque"	102
John Morgan	pt. "Parish Beadle"	100
Thomas Wherett	"Hog Neck"	100
Joseph Dafforen	"Maids Delight"	78
John Welch	pt. "Cortanys Neck"	68
39:1754:11 ...		
Dennis Tippett	pt. "Suttle Range"	60
	pt. "St. Barberys Addition"	120
George Vawdery	"Underwood" a/s "Woodland" now called "Woods Pleasure"	344
Bennedict Spalding	"Hearts Delight"	200
	1 lot in Leonard Town	1
James Bailey	"Slipe"	69
	pt. "Baileys Fortune"	168
William Mattingly	"Clever"	155

James Mattingly	pt. "Mattinglys Hope"	130
	pt. "St. Johns"	50
Jesse Wharton	"Notley Hall" pt. "St. Clement Manner"	400
	"Neighbourhood"	146
Thomas Vaughan	pt. "Beckworths Lodge" a/s "James Chance"	100
William Daft	pt. "Rockey Point" a/s "Curry Glase"	100
Stephen Greenwell	"Colebrook Levell"	129
Mary Taylor	"White House"	63
John Taylor	pt. "Frog Marsh"	100
	"Milmots Adventure"	123
	"Neglect"	53
	"Williams Addition"	22
39:1754:12 ...		
James Somerhill	pt. "Wastham"	100
Isabella Cooke	"Jones Fortune"	112
William Boarman	pt. "Dorothy"	263
William Morgan	pt. "Friends Conjunction"	50
Mary Jorden	pt. "St. Clements Manner"	211
Jeremiah Jorden	pt. "St. Clements Manner"	88
William Jorden	pt. "St. Clements Manner"	135
Thomas Reader (cnp)	"Workington Park"	1539
	"Thomas & Henry"	113
	pt. "Fawnskirk"	165
	"Chance"	50
	"Roseland"	50
	"Bogens Increase"	173
	pt. "St. Johns"	595
	"Middle Ground"	102
	pt. "Burruss Gift"	60
	"Modens Lott"	236
	"Addition to Roseland"	83
	pt. "Hope"	36
	pt. "Wastham"	87
	pt. "Denbury Hills"	100
	pt. "Trumans Lodge"	105
	"Inclosure"	14

	pt. "Fawns Kirk"	87
	pt. "Parish Beadle"	100
	"Youngs Man Venture"	130
	"Fourth Addition"	83
	pt. "Great St. Thomas"	100
	"Kepworth"	100
	pt. "Dynard"	100
	pt. "Bottom"	100
	"Wildmans Levels"	168
	"Rooms Convenancy"	100
	pt. "Hopewell"	151
	pt. "Wandsworth" pt. "St. Clement Manner"	150
39:1754:13 ...		
William Hebb, Jr.	pt. "White Clifts"	50
Thomas Sanner	"Salsbuiry Plains"	100
Samuel Ashcom	"No Name"	881
	"Ashcoms Marsh"	32
Thomas Reswick	pt. 2 tracts of escheate land	64
	pt. "White Aker"	50
Robert Lydell	"Cynetts Chance"	56
Charles Dylion	"Charles Chance"	75
Mark Stevans	"Richards Fancy"	38
	"Natharbets Begining"	50
Thomas James	"Bacon Point"	100
	pt. "Rivetts"	151
	pt. "Fortune"	50
	"Taunton"	40
	"Crooked Billett"	38
William Asquith	"White Marsh"	93
Thomas Swan	"T.B."	119
James Roach	pt. "Medley"	100
	"Hucklebary Lane"	10
Elenor & Anne Graves	"Hopewell"	131
	"Hardshift"	50
	"Hardshift Addition"	186
39:1754:14 ...		

John Oliver	pt. "Cornelius"	39
	"Fortune"	50
	"Pearth"	62
	"Fortune Outlett"	16
	"Archies Hills"	65
Elizabeth Nelson	pt. "Doe Park"	75
	pt. "Addition to Doe Park"	50
George Graves	"Graves Swamp"	108
Thomas Standage	pt. "Doe Park"	21
	"North Addition to Doe Park"	147
Samuel Wood	"Cannoe Neck"	100
Anthony Sims	"Wickohandick"	125
John Burruss	pt. "Trent Fort"	129
	pt. "Remainder Charles Lot"	166½
William Cartwright	pt. "Remainder Charles Lot"	166½
	"Ridge"	50
John Cartwright	pt. "Long Look'd for Come at Last"	75
	"Cartwright Pasture"	20
	pt. "Burruss Gift"	40
George Burruss	pt. "Long Look'd for Come at Last"	100
George Dent	pt. "Freestone Point"	174
John Buckman	pt. "Freestone Point"	50
39:1754:15 ...		
John Dent	pt. "Freestone Point"	100
James Crook	"Ludgate"	50
Richard Sourthon	"Sourthons Desire"	125
Samuel Sourthon	"Trumans Lot"	40
	"Littleworth"	25
Thomas Tauny	"Green Meadows"	200
Thomas Norris	pt. "Lewgors Plains"	130
Free School	pt. "Hopton Park"	100
John Lynch	"Granes Content"	100
	"Plumb Point"	162
Rev. Mr. Arnold Livers	"Little Britain"	750
	pt. "Britains Outlet"	43
Robert Chesley (cnp)	2 lots in Leonard Town	2

	"Vineyard"	343
	pt. "Pork Hall"	50
	"Charles's Park"	130
	"Tobys Last Shift"	100
	"Woodstock"	127
Henry Reiley	"Saturdays Work"	100
	"Addition to Saturdays Work"	30
Peter Mills	pt. "St. Johns"	230
Thomas Bisco	pt. "Mackey's Neck"	50
39:1754:16 ...		
Winifred Rowson	"Maidens Lot"	100
	"Bare Waistcoat"	50
	"Winfreds Chance"	30
William Hemmersly	"Beverly"	380
	"Batchellors Hope"	300
Thomas Alston	"Readers Adventure"	350
	pt. "St. Clement Manner"	200
William Mills	pt. "Poplar Neck"	115
	"Ansterday"	30
John Johnson	pt. "Peters Wills"	100
Peter Cartwright	pt. "Waston"	100
John Spalding	"Batchellors Rest"	100
Margaret Yates	pt. "Survey"	93
Edward Ployden	pt. "Tarvern"	100
	"Farme"	500
	"Ploydens Discovery"	66
Isaac Shamwell	pt. "Devonshire"	50
	pt. "Trumanica"	50
	"Derbyshire"	130
Thomas Spalding	pt. "Great St. Thomas"	200
39:1754:17 ...		
Thomas Spalding (Leonard Town)	pt. "Cragburns Purchase"	100
	"Spaldings Addition"	42
	pt. "St. Giles"	35
	"Spaldings Adventure"	207
	"Rich Neck"	150

Benjamin Branson	"Drayton"	57
	"Kenady" a/s "Keildfield"	96½
	"Keech & Prices Rest"	122
	"Best Land"	10
George Thompson	pt. "Hazzard"	100
William Hall	pt. "Graden"	100
William Watson	"Poplar Point"	100
James Pike	"Forest Denn"	100
George Leigh	"Innis Chance"	100
	"Gallowith"	50
	"Innis's Reserve"	25
	"Paris"	150
	"Inclosure"	170
Peter Dray	pt. "Bottom"	50
Arthur Ford	pt. "Strand"	91
William Thomas	"Wails"	200
	"Wails Addition"	91
	pt. "Boston"	50
39:1754:18 ...		
George Waring	pt. "St. Johns"	66
	pt. "Burch Hanger"	75
Luke Mattingly	"Choice part of Hazzard"	100
Mary Smith	pt. "Hazzard"	57
John Higgs	"Wednesday Project"	98
	"Higgs Purchase"	49
John Harbert	"Harberts Invention"	109
	"Good Yielding"	86
	pt. "Good Yielding" or reservey	67
Francis Redcliff	pt. "Doe Park"	50
William Jenkins	pt. "Truth & Trust"	273
	"Salem"	215
	"Croydon"	100
	"St. Thomas"	300
	"Addition"	103
	"Fox Range"	70
Thomas Watts	"Smoot"	50

William Martin	pt. "Hopewell"	74
	"Cracksons Rest"	50
	"Redmans Hardship"	50
	pt. "Hopeless"	11
Thomas Hall	pt. "Long Look'd for Come at Last"	112
Peter Brown	pt. "White Aker"	222
39:1754:19 ...		
Rev. James Ashby	"St. Innegoes Manner" & "St. Georges Island"	3000
	"Chappel Freehold"	25
Charles Beach	"Gosslings Addition"	30
	pt. "Parting Path"	26
	"Stiles Chance"	25
widow Gossling	pt. "Parting Path"	274
	"Garden Spot"	80
John Johnson Sourthon	pt. "Brotherhood"	140
	"Sourthons Hills"	50
	pt. "Wastham"	100
Mathew Guibert	pt. "Dynard"	81
Thiod. Jorden	pt. "St. Clement Manner"	100
Philip Greenwell	"Honest Jones Inheritance"	150
Richard Fenwick, Jr.	"Mayheard Comforde"	100
	"Janeth Purchase" a/s pt. "Charles West Discovery"	40½
Thomas Tippet	pt. "Suttle Range"	213
William Lock	"Good Pennyworth"	50
	"Fairfield"	50
	"Locks Venture"	49
Horne Roberts	pt. "Fresh Pond Neck"	203
Thomas Morton	pt. "St. Johns"	100
39:1754:20 ...		
Mrs. Forbes	"Orppens Gift"	400
	"Holbridge Town"	130
	"Draydon"	483
Charles Righill	"Joynter"	50
John Ford, Sr.	pt. "Farthing Gift" a/s "Minsterdam"	10
	pt. "Durham"	100
	pt. "Long in Dispence"	75

Mark Thompson	pt. "Hatfields Hills"	25
Henry Cooper	pt. "Scotland"	150
John Sissell	pt. "Scotland"	150
~~Luke Sissell~~	~~pt. "Scotland"~~	<unr>
James Sissell	"Sissells Venture"	88
Sarah Sissell	pt. "Baileys Rest"	150
James Brown	"Drydocking Addition"	100
~~James Boyde~~	~~pt. "Hopton Park"~~	<unr>
Alexander Forguson	pt. "Small Hope"	9
	"Small Hopes Addition"	42
	pt. "Black Creek"	99
Thomas Redman	pt. "Small Hopes Addition"	100
39:1754:21 ...		
Mark Taylor	"Branch"	50
Clement Spink	pt. "Guelmotts Hills"	180
	"All Thats Left"	31¼
	pt. "Guelmotts Hills"	150
John Tennyson	pt. "Outlet"	50
John Mattingly	"Thames"	150
	"Mattingly Addition"	50
Sarah Greenwell	"Holly Tree"	148
John Smith (New Town)	pt. "Nuns Oak"	142
James Smith (Rock Creek)	pt. "Out Let"	119
	"Fresh Pond"	243
	"Mitcham Meadows"	100
	pt. "Hampstead"	100
	pt. "Black Creek"	30
William Howard	"Pomphrey Fields"	100
Enoch Greenwell	"Hiccory Hollows"	119
	"Farthing Adventure"	78
	pt. "Wheatleys Content" a/s "Back Land"	55
Thomas Thompson	"Adjoinder" a/s "St. Johns Addition"	23
	pt. "Dynard"	13
	pt. "Chance"	89
John Cartwright (chpt)	pt. "Weston"	100
39:1754:22 ...		

John Morrell	pt. "Weston Addition"	100
George Thompson	pt. "Rockey Point"	50
Walter Davis	pt. "Twitenham Hermitage"	110
Richard Paine	pt. "Strife"	50
Clement Newton	"Newtons Rest"	63
	"Addition"	37
Samuel Johnson	pt. "Hopewell"	36
	"Addition"	19
Elizabeth Hayden	"Noaches Discovery"	157
	"Haydens Risque"	81
William Edley	pt. "Haydens Fair"	100
William Hayden	pt. "Haydens Fair"	100
Michel Wilman	pt. "Styles Chance"	100
Mary Watts	pt. "Jesbury Plains"	100
John Goss. Lawrence	"Frog Marsh"	100
William Edgerton	pt. "Punkleys Marsh"	100
39:1754:23 ...		
Jus. Greenwell	"Rochester"	100
Margaret Plummer	"Orbustons Oak"	50
William Doxe	"Smith Rest"	100
William Cavanough	pt. "Massom"	250
	"Eyre"	328
h/o Richard Vowell	pt. "Vowells Purchase"	120
	pt. "Brittons Out Let"	1
Robert Hemmet	"Hemmets Beginning"	34
	pt. "Burch Spring"	75
	pt. "Forrest Harvey"	100
	"Wild Cat Neck"	104½
	"Hiccory Plat"	17½
	"Hemmet & Chance"	69
Clement Mattingly	pt. "Vowells Purchase"	239
h/o Peter Muggs	pt. "Vowels Addition"	80
	pt. "Williams"	50
	pt. "Vowells Purchase"	57
	pt. "Rockey Point"	50
James Greenwell s/o William	"Wheatleys Content"	75

Elizabeth King	pt. "Burch Spring"	50
James Brisco	pt. "Hog Neck"	100
39:1754:24 ...		
Joshua Millard	"Neals Lot"	209½
	pt. "Little St. Thomas"	16
	pt. "St. Johns"	134
Luke Norris	pt. "Wheatleys Content"	69
Ignatius Thompson	"Fibney"	100
Thomas Medley	"Barren Doe"	95
John Mills	"Yielding Bury"	99
	pt. "Hopton Park"	80
Robert Drury	"Honnards Mount"	40
Richard Cooper	pt. "Clarker"	100
	"Brightful"	180
	"Coopers Addition"	94
	"Dynard"	100
	"Hopewell"	65
	"Expence"	67
	pt. "Cragburns Purchase"	100
John Waller	pt. "Partnership"	65
Richard Burruss	"Holdfast"	76
	pt. "Long Look'd for Come at Last"	75
John Wilson	"Indian Giant Sgather"	203
Abraham Hall	pt. "Gardeners Grove"	50
39:1754:25 ...		
Thomas Hays	pt. "Gardeners Grove"	197
	"Addition to Gardeners Grove"	82
Edward Mchune	"Piles Discovery"	112
John Parsons	"Addition"	50
	pt. "Long Look'd for Come at Last"	112½
James Watson	"Hedge Barron"	79
James Swan	pt. "Retirement"	63½
Stephen Cawood	pt. "Williamsons Purchase"	100
	pt. "Wastham"	200
	"Cawoods Expence"	157
Edward Barber (cnp)	pt. "Swans Forest"	56

	pt. "Wastham"	250
	pt. "Luckland"	130
John Shanks	pt. "St. Oswell"	100
Jos. Greenwell	"Last Shift"	100
John Wiseman Greenwell	"This or None"	50
	"John Wiseman Greenwells Park"	49
	"Piles Woodlane"	200
Elenor Bisco	pt. "Retirement"	92
h/o Benjamin Gough	pt. "St. Margarets"	100
39:1754:26 ...		
Charles Jarbo	pt. "St. Peters Hills"	112
John Evens	pt. "Eshmels Right"	165
John Smith, Jr.	"Haphazzard"	304
John Wheatley	"Hiccory Thicket"	48
	pt. "Hanover Addition"	45
John Hoper	"Ashcoms Green Field"	100
John Knott	"Sharp"	44
Peter Paine	pt. "Honnard Mount"	75
Thomas Spalding s/o Thomas	pt. "Great St. Thomas"	100
	pt. "Little St. Thomas"	100
Richard Gardener	"Poplar Hill"	200
	"Middle Ground"	50
William McWilliams	pt. "Batchellors Rest"	300
	pt. "St. Clement Manner"	100
William Pike	pt. "Hanover"	140
	pt. "Hanover Addition"	60
Henry Neale	pt. "Hilly Lee"	250
	pt. "St. Clement Manner"	400
Thomas Hulston	"Buck Land"	75
39:1754:27 ...		
Philip Key, Esq. (cnp)	"Bushwood Lodge"	411
	"James Addition"	158
	pt. "St. Johns"	50
	"Addition to Peters Wills"	104
	pt. "Burch Hanger"	230
	"Cuccold Haven" & timber land	77

	pt. "Wems"	430
	"Woods Pleasure" & pt. "Chessam"	95
	pt. "Maiden Bower" (St. Clement)	100
	pt. "Finchly"	102
	"Boston"	98
	pt. "Waston"	87
	pt. "Boston" & "Peach Blossom"	55
	"Luckland"	200
	pt. "Dynard"	119
	pt. "Shourance & Yielding Bury"	75
	pt. "Yielding Bury"	88
	pt. "Milton Hope"	130
	pt. "Little Yielding"	35
	"Rooms Convenience"	26
	"Gardeners Landing"	100
	"Penryne" pt. "St. Clement Manner"	192
Thomas Graves	pt. "Graves Chance"	120
	pt. "Baptis Hope"	106
	"Hopewell"	99
	"Josias Plains"	16¾
	"Hardshift"	10
	"Prince William Newcastle"	50
	pt. "Graves Chance"	10
John Ford (Court house)	pt. "Hanover"	31
	pt. "Green Hill"	29
	pt. "Lamston Pleasure"	150
	"Rangel"	78
	pt. "St. Peters Hills"	50
	pt. "Heard Security"	39
Richard Fenwick	"Chance Conclusion"	97
	"Addition to Chance Conclusion"	26
Mary Bright	pt. "Cold Wells"	65
39:1754:28 ...		
Ignatius Greenwell	pt. "Wheatleys Meadows"	123
Mary Wheatley	pt. "Wheatleys Meadows"	153
Charles Daft	pt. "Medly"	200

Peter Pike, Jr.	pt. "Hanover Addition"	50
John Milton	pt. "Burch Hanger"	94
Guilbert Ireland	"Edinborough 10th Addition"	121½
	pt. "Hermitage"	73
	pt. "Hopton Park"	140
	pt. "Baptis Hope"	153
	pt. "Yielding Bury"	17
	"Evens's Lot" a/s "Hampstead"	50
John Guither	pt. "Croft"	147
	"Saturdays Venture"	2½
	"Cornelius Swam"	100
Ignatius Whealor	pt. "Hopton Park"	50
Capt. Richard Key	"Wolf Hole"	262
	"Addition to Guiberts Chance"	37
William Rogers	"Rogers Venture"	50
Elenor Gardener	pt. "St. Johns"	500
widow Ward	"Wards Defence"	100
39:1754:29 ...		
Anthony Brown	"Clarks Rest"	300
Samuel Able	pt. "Kirby Choyce"	118
	pt. "Squable"	25
	"Scrubby Thicket"	25
	pt. "Wheatleys Chance"	41
Peter O'Neall	pt. "Cragburns Purchase"	60
Kenet Boult	pt. "Calingwood"	25
Col. George Clarke (cnp)	pt. "Massom"	200
	"Cadocks Measure"	150
	"Court Freehold" or "Hearts Hall"	200
	"Fox Hill"	30
	"Adjoinder"	50
	"Gravelly Hill"	50
	"Oyster Shell Neck"	50
	"Newgent Venture"	50
	"Blumbury"	100
	"Dunbar"	92
	"Butchers Slipe"	42

	"Poplar Point"	101
Barton Smoot	"Clarkes Range"	393
William Field	pt. "Batchellors Rest"	50
William Love	pt. "Partnership"	100
Enoch Fenwick, Jr.	pt. "St. Peters Hills"	150
	pt. "Colebrook Level"	35
	pt. "Spinks's Rest"	65
39:1754:30 ...		
Thomas Money	pt. "St. Edwards"	115
	"Tradesman Lot"	200
	pt. "Linsteed"	18
	pt. "Valentines Grove"	96
Daniel Harris	"Kingston"	50
	"Wheatleys"	38
John Hynes	"Bite the Fox"	19
	"Hunters Hills"	150
James Anderson	pt. "Bakers Fancy"	78
	pt. "Cornelius"	39
	"Addition to Charles's Park"	20
Charles Flower	pt. "St. Georges"	50
Benjamin Williams	"Warner Point"	55
	"Esquires Purchase"	37
	pt. "Muggs Adventure"	200
	"Fox Den"	89
	"Bakers Fancy"	25
	"New Fancy"	25
	pt. "Punkleys Marsh"	100
John Lear	"Holyday"	142
Enoch Fenwick	pt. "Fenwick Manner"	175
Ignatius Heard	pt. "Well Found"	106
Sub. Truman Grinfield	"American Fælix"	152
39:1754:31 ...		
Thomas Newton	"Underwood" a/s "Newton's Property"	124
	"Greenwells Marsh"	14
Ann Grinfield (cnp)	"Grinfields Discovery"	90
	"Trent Neck"	835

	"Stockbardolph"	75
James Truman Grinfield	"Keech's Folly"	133
	"Lamb"	100
	"Punk Neck"	60
	"Holbridge Town"	130
	pt. "Hopton Park"	120
Nathanel Greenfield	"Fork"	60
	"Addition"	78
	"White Haven"	164
	"Indian Creek & Addition"	491
	"Nightwood & Bashford"	154
	"Thimblebe"	109
	"Fishing Place"	50
	"Broughland"	75
James Warrick	pt. "St. Johns"	150
John Dunbar	"Chance"	240
Edward Castor	"Redmans Hardship"	50
Peter Jarbo	pt. "St. Peters Hills"	113
John Cole (St. Georges)	"Jones Wood"	100
	"Addition to Jones Wood"	59½
39:1754:32 ...		
John Michael Thomas Tawny	pt. "Fenwick Manner"	450
Joseph Clarke	pt. "St. Johns"	300
	"Mattinglys Hope"	70
	pt. "Cole Park" a/s "Clarks Discovery"	122
Sarah Carter	"Mere Chance"	113
Mary Hemmersly	"Carburys Discovery"	190
John Dant	"Hopewell"	100
	pt. "Yoke by Chance"	20
John McKey	pt. "McKeys Neck"	153
	pt. "St. Richard Manner"	50
	pt. "Massom"	100
John Jones	"Poverty"	64
Thomas Yates (cnp)	pt. "St. Peters Hills"	100
	pt. "Small Hopes"	30
	pt. "Hanover"	60

	pt. "Heards Security"	70
Enoch Combs	pt. "Pork Hall"	300
	"Grape Hill"	200
	"Wilderpole"	300
John Wherrett	pt. "Watts Lodge"	90
Thomas Cook, Jr.	pt. "Brough"	68
Joseph Harding	"Baileys Rest"	100
39:1754:33 ...		
Samuel Belwood	"Ishmaels Right"	165
	"Belwoods Grove"	128
	pt. "Styles Chance"	16
Fairfax Compton	pt. "Honnard Mount"	75
George Rogers	pt. "Well Close"	100
	"Brothers Dread"	135
John Norris	"Goughs Levels"	42
	"Goughs Conveniency"	48
	"Britain Bay"	150
William Roach	pt. "St. Johns Landing"	117
	pt. "St. Johns Addition"	167
William Guither	"Maids Delight"	100
	pt. "Smoot"	100
Cuthbert Clark	"Chelsey"	100
William Taylor	"Poplar Hill"	63
John Baker (Bay Side)	pt. "Drapers Neck"	285
Francis Wheatley	pt. "Wheatleys Content"	66
	pt. "Buckland"	50
Leonard Greenwell	pt. "Hanover Addition"	87
39:1754:34 ...		
Clement Norris	"Tants Marsh"	168
	"Norris's Frolick"	3½
Thomas Howard	pt. "Guilmots Hills"	75
Joseph Stevens	pt. "Devonshire"	50
	"Trumania"	50
	"Josephs Venture"	54
Samuel Lee	"Wellclose"	82
	pt. "St. Clement Manner"	100

John Brady	pt. "Baileys Rest"	100
	"Bracys Lot"	25
Peter Ford	pt. "St. Giles's"	81
	"Mount Pleasant"	100
	"May Pole"	96
	pt. "Strand"	91
Thomas Wheatley	"Addition to Wheatleys Content & Addition"	380
John Chesley	pt. "Clagburn"	300
	"Clagburns Island"	13
	"Clagburns Swamp"	17½
	pt. "Indian Creek"	36
Thomas Grinfield	pt. "Indian Creek"	843
	pt. "Good Luck"	275
Thomas Bond	"Knotting"	100
39:1754:35 ...		
Thomas Milton	"Burch Hanger"	95
Rev. John Urquhart	pt. "Fawnskirk"	250
	"Spring Blossom"	221
	pt. "Keech & Prices Rest"	60
	"Hopewells Chance"	170
Benjamin Gristy	"Venture"	50
Burch Swan	pt. "Hopewell" charged to James Lattimore	57
Thomas Clark	pt. "Moffets Will"	69
Thomas Braden	pt. "Moffets Will"	69
John Bisco	"Barren Wood"	46
Henry Wimset	"Herberts Griff"	44
	pt. "Nuns Oak"	20
James Dickson	"Dicksons Venture" a/s "Haydens Fair"	115½
h/o Edward Pye	"Underwood"	300
	pt. "New Designe"	175
James Adams	pt. "Small Hope Addition"	50
John Graves	pt. "Graves Chance"	94
James Thompson (Hd. Chap.)	pt. "St. Johns"	50
	"Harberts Swamp"	21
39:1754:36 ...		

Ignatius Greenwell s/o Ignatius	"Ignatius's Dread"	100
	"Addition"	25
Wo. Mary Fenwick	pt. "Fenwick Manner"	200
Daniel Wats	"Wats Lodge"	160
John Plummer	pt. "Elizabeth Manner"	300
Richard Shirly	"Shirlys Adventure"	150
Thomas Keen	"Keens Rest"	49
Thomas Mathews	pt. "Friends Conjunction"	72
Edward Aprice	pt. "St. Barberys"	100
John Anderson	"Sourthons Desire"	100
	pt. "Fox Race"	52
Benjamin Bean	pt. "Friends Conjunction"	72
John Sykes	pt. "Friends Conjunction"	106
John Thompson	"Mitcham Meadows"	100
George Wold	pt. "Hanover"	103
John Thomas	"Hampton"	100
39:1754:37 ...		
h/o Mark Thomas	"Penancy"	100
	"Brewers Woodpouse"	50
	"Lukes Hardship"	7
	"Marks Adventure"	36
Henry How	"White Land"	225
John Bisco	pt. "Harrisons Rest"	80
	pt. "Williams Fortune"	32
Dr. Murray	"Indian Creek"	563
James Smith	"Tripple Defence"	206
	"Puntneys Oversight"	219
	"Addition to Tripple Defence"	87
	"Pine Land"	388
	pt. "Turvey"	201
	"Trinity", "St. Gabriel", & "St. Michaels Manner"	3000
Peter Pike	pt. "Friends Goodwill"	100
Benjamin Fenwick	"Fenwick Manner"	200
Robert Henly	pt. "Massom"	150
	"Johns Content"	93½
	"Keens Rest"	50

Robert Newgent	"Marking Place"	100
	"Fox Catched"	11
Lydian Bright	pt. "Cold Wells"	65
39:1754:38 ...		
Cornelius Wildman	"Brook Chance"	81
	"Dylons Disappointment"	103
	"Williams Venture"	54
	"Goulding Grove"	153
	"Tavern"	100
Enoch Able	"Saturdays Conclusion"	55
	pt. "Wheatleys Chance"	50
	"Hopsons Choyce"	23½
John Medley Thompson	pt. "Scotland"	50
Thomas Barber	pt. "Burch Hanger"	20
Charles Greenwell	"Farther Adventure"	65½
Thomas Jorden	pt. "Callingwood"	25
John Clark	"Evans's Quarter"	100
Michael Goldsmith	pt. "St. Clement Manner"	86
	pt. "Bashford Manner"	100
William Aud	pt. "Hanover"	30
John Shircliff	"Shircliff"	250
	"St. Williams"	90
	"Q Name"	100
	pt. "Linstid"	78
	pt. "Linstid Addition"	100
	"Coles Adventure"	150
James Chizzam	pt. "Bakers Fancy"	100
39:1754:39 ...		
Richard Millard	"Little St. Thomas"	84
	pt. "St. Johns"	50
	"Turners Plains"	16
Thomas Pearce	pt. "Cortany Fancy"	50
K. Truman Grinfield	pt. "Trent Neck"	1519
John Lowes	"Warnett"	240
Henry Jarbo	pt. "St. Peters Hills"	126
Henry Bryan (cnp)	"Williams Endeavours"	50

	pt. "Farther Adventure"	37
	"Greens Plot"	44
William Deacon, Esq.	"Peters"	150
	pt. "Chancellers Point"	112
	"St. Marys Freehold"	255
	"Governors Fields"	100
William Leake	pt. "Hatfields Hills"	75
John Mills	"Wastfield"	140
	"Sommersett"	195
Edward Parsons	pt. "Guiberts Chance"	50
	"Small Addition"	19½
Benn. Neale	pt. "St. Clement Manner"	200
39:1754:40 ...		
Sab. Thompson	"Thompsons Expence"	208
Joseph Jenkins	pt. "Truth & Trust"	400
William Heard	pt. "Well Found"	106
	pt. "Fenwick Manner"	175
Hon. George Plator, Esq.	pt. "St. Joseph Manner"	819
	"Bouls Preservation"	890
	pt. "Fenwick Manner"	400
	"Stafford Hope"	125
	"Resurrection Manner"	4000
Richard Raper	"Maynard Comfort"	100
	pt. "Baileys Fortune"	45
	pt. "St. Clement Manner"	50
	pt. "Baptist Hope"	100
Joseph Greenwell	pt. "Kirbys Choyce"	67
Thomas Doxe	pt. "Harrisons Rest"	70
Richard Brook	"Dallabrook Manner"	2000
	"Two Brothers"	235
	"Back Land"	400
Thomas Hobson	pt. "Wems"	100
Elizabeth Wems	"Wastham"	150
Charles King	"Deptford"	300
	pt. "St. Joseph Manner"	200
39:1754:41 ...		

William Williams	"Drydocking"	100
	pt. "Shock Park"	76
	pt. "Roberts Neck" a/s "Medley"	95
	"Harberts Griff"	60
	pt. "Roberts Freehold"	75
Robert Fenwick	pt. "Joseph Manner"	126
John Marman	pt. "Hopton Park"	197
	"Vowells Purchase"	206
Samuel Gunifer	pt. "Joseph Manner"	50
Leonard Green	pt. "Fenwick Manner"	50
Thomas Manley	pt. "Elizabeth Manner"	100
Ashton Smoot	pt. "Elizabeth Manner"	247
	pt. "Cross Manner"	500
Sturton Edwards	"St. Thomas"	190
	"Doe Park"	69
	pt. "Hanover"	100
Thomas Brome	pt. "No Name"	250
John Lancaster	pt. "Hilly Lee"	250
	pt. "St. Clement Manner"	400
Peter Gough	pt. "Lewgroes Plains"	100
39:1754:42 ...		
James Talton	pt. "Beaverdam"	59
	"Elizabeth"	34
James Hager	pt. "Beaver Dam"	59
John Jarbo	pt. "Hanover"	16
John Jarbo, Jr.	pt. "Hanover"	13½
	pt. "Heards Security"	24
John Able	pt. "Wheatleys Chance"	31
	pt. "Kirbys Choyce"	88
	pt. "St. Joseph Manner"	56
Cuthbert Able	"Wiseman Chance"	100
Benjamin Redman	"Small Hope"	50
Dennis Burn	pt. "Beckworths Lodge"	81½
Joseph Walker	pt. "Guilmots Hills"	100
	pt. "Addition to Farthing Fortune"	140
Ignatius Bailey	pt. "Little Yielding"	117

William Jones	"Salters Hall"	83
	"Addition to Salters Hall"	34
	"Jones's Conveniency"	35½
	pt. "Beckworths Lodge"	81½
	"Jones's Lane"	1¾
	"Muggs Adventure"	52
39:1754:43 ...		
Ruth. Jones	pt. "Davie's Forest"	50
John Price	"Grove"	50
Henry Spalding	pt. "Joseph"	152½
	pt. "Two Brothers"	165
	pt. "Newcastle"	50
	pt. "Rich Neck"	98
Thomas Duvall	pt. "Partnership"	200
John Watson	pt. "Partnership"	65
George Maxwell	pt. "Indian Creek with Addition"	461
Maj. Abr. Barnes	"America Fælix Secundus"	956
	pt. "Rangel Field"	40
	pt. "Forest Harvey"	100
	"Westbury Manner"	1250
	pt. "Harrys Lodge"	100
	pt. "Drapers Neck"	215
	"Wallnut Point"	55
Zachariah Bond	pt. "St. Barberry"	200
Edward Bowling	pt. "Callingwood"	25
William Doxe, Jr.	pt. "Patrick Hills"	50
John Morris	pt. "Callingwood"	25
39:1754:44 ...		
George Bowles	"Steplition Fortune"	200
	"Hazzard"	234½
John Tippet	"Tippets Purchase"	46
William Spalding	pt. "Rich Neck"	152
Mark Norris	pt. "Wheatleys Content"	118
	pt. "Buck Plains"	70
Ignatius Fenwick	"Hepton Hole"	350
John Holt	pt. "St. Clement Manner"	167

Ignatius Whealer	pt. "St. Clement Manner"	250
John Lee	pt. "St. Clement Manner"	200
John Hoskens	pt. "St. Clement Manner"	100
Bapt. Greenwell	pt. "Rochester"	100
John Bould	pt. "Cadle"	150
	"Addition to White Aker"	25
John Winser	pt. "Hatfield Hills"	27
John Bulluck	pt. "St. Clement Manner"	100
39:1754:45 ...		
John Bohannon	"Fox Grape Barren"	106
David Downie	"Towns Support"	81
	"Bary"	65
	3 lots in Leonard Town	3
James Jarbo	"Denby"	250
Thomas Jenking	"Eadinborough"	100
Benjamin Molton	pt. "Bashbord Manner"	200
John Pike	"Forney Branch"	50
Clement Medley	pt. "Medley"	200
William Medley	pt. "Medley"	100
Basil Pike	pt. "Medley"	100
George Greenwell	pt. "Medley"	50
John Leweling	pt. "St. Clement Manner"	400
John Holland	pt. "Hampstead Rang"	100
John Fenwick	pt. "Croft"	100
	pt. "Riverts Backside"	172
	pt. "Riverts"	151
	pt. "Chancellors Point"	112
Thomas Crane	"Dally"	100
Thomas Waring	"Warings Lot"	148
39:1754:46 ...		
Joseph Thomas Ingles	pt. "Peters Quay"	50
	"Fishing Creek Neck"	44
Richard Milburn	pt. "Halfhead Folly"	100
	"Milburns Chance"	178
	pt. "Cortanys Neck"	82
John Smith	pt. "Matapany"	289

Clement Spalding	"Spaldings Adventure"	729
	pt. "Tavern" tbc Cornel. Wildman	0
John Eden	pt. "Bashford Manner"	400
John Bond	pt. "St. Clement Manner"	605
	pt. "Hopton Park"	400
	pt. "St. Johns"	438
	"Gardeners Chance"	155
Richard Edgling	"Trumans Hunting Quarter"	200
	pt. "Hope"	64
Justinian Jorden	pt. "St. Clement Manner"	200
John Boult	pt. "St. Clement Manner"	100
George Slye	pt. "St. Clement Manner"	1000
Edward Turner	pt. "Bashford Manner"	200
George Backstor	"Batchellors Comfort"	190
39:1754:47 ...		
Charles Sewall	pt. "Little Eltonhead Manner"	50
	"Sewalls Discovery"	117
John Blackston	pt. "St. Clement Manner"	550
John Mason	pt. "St. Clement Manner"	450
Mary Tennyson	pt. "St. Clement Manner"	100
Ken. Chaseldine	pt. "St. Clement Manner"	725
Cyrenius Chaseldine	pt. "St. Clement Manner"	25
Charles Carrol, Esq.	pt. "St. Clement Manner"	2474
	"Oxford"	209
	pt. "Barberrys Addition"	250
	pt. "Loughbrough"	150
	"Addition"	41
	"Temple Bar"	100
John Madock	pt. "Bashford Manner"	150
John Reswick	pt. 2 tracts of ench. Land	47
Edward Welch	"Ossfield"	72
John Attaway Clark	pt. "Poney Point"	750
	pt. "James Johnsons Neck"	200
	"Blake Creek"	50
	"Tower Hill"	25
Robert Hager	pt. "Truth & Trust"	100

39:1754:48 ...		
Nicholas Lewis Sewall	pt. "Mattapany"	911
	"Sewalls Discovery"	108
	"Fishing Point"	13
Leonard Davis	pt. "Desart"	62½
	"Thornes Venture"	103
James Wheatley	"Kington" a/s "Newtonquit"	117
	pt. "Wheatleys Addition"	21
John Smith	pt. "Bashford Manner"	200
Mary McWilliams	pt. "St. Clement Manner"	300
Sturton Edwards	"Taunton Den"	164
Thomas Suit	pt. "Trent Fort"	84
	pt. "Horse Range"	100
James Mills	pt. "Bashford Manner"	100
Leonard Mattingly	"Audley End"	190
Notley Goldsmith	pt. "Bashford Manner"	100
Roger Smith	pt. "Notleys Addition"	275
Dent Soot	pt. "Horse Range"	100
39:1754:49 ...		
Thomas Soot, Jr.	pt. "Wells"	100
Joseph Edwards	pt. "Wells"	52
	pt. "Trent Fort"	8
Thomas Win Taylor	"Righting"	100
Clement Medley, Sr.	"No Name"	100
John Summerhill	pt. "St. Richard Manner"	100
	"Reileys" a/s "Clarks Discovery"	99
	pt. "St. Jeroms Manner"	200
John Michael Waughop	"Waughops Chance"	138
John Coad	pt. "St. Clements Manner"	300
Anthony Roberts	"Twitenham"	200
Benjamin Burruss	pt. "Trent Fort"	129
Peter Ford, Jr.	pt. "Nun Oak"	75
John Corlett	"Willinborough"	70
h/o James Heath	pt. "St. Jeroms Manner"	5500
James Kendrick	"Kendricks Lane"	80
Auston Macy	pt. "Plumb Point"	338

Elizabeth Lock	pt. "Cold Wells"	65
39:1754:50 ...		
Francs. Thompson	"Hard Fortune"	100
William Mattingley	pt. "Suttle" a/s "Rest"	80
John Ford (wever)	"Pomphreyfield"	50
	"Ministerdam"	54
Henry Taylor	pt. "Taylors Plains"	50½
John Reeves	pt. "Bashford Manner"	100
John Keeley	"Kelleys Luck"	138
Samuel Swan	pt. "Swans Forrest"	45
James Lattimore	pt. "Hopewell"	146
Leonard Paine	"Fox"	100
Ignatius Thompson	"Tebery"	100
William Biggs	pt. "Snow Hill" "St. Clement Manner"	100

39:1755:1 ...		**Acres**
Daniel Clocker	"Clockers Freehold"	50
	"Lewis Neck"	30
Elizabeth Clocker	"St. Anns Freehold"	70½
	"Clockers Fancy"	56
Thomas P. Waughop	"Hunting Quarter"	150
	"Poney Point"	750
	"Smoot Hollow"	150
Nicholas Sewell	pt. "Little Eltonhead Manner"	1590
Edward Digges	pt. "Little Eltonhead Manner"	300
William Price	"Brick Hill"	217
	"Parkes Addition"	110
Edward Horne	pt. "Halfhead Folly"	100
Ignatius Taylor	pt. "Little Eltonhead Manner" a/s "Govers Gift"	60
James Dafforen	"Cole Harber"	150
George Asquith	"Stinmore"	100
	"Inclosure"	30
	"Thomas & George in Company"	4½
John Roades	pt. "Jesbury Plains"	330
Isaac Prevatt	"Cow Ridge"	50
	pt. "Cross Manner"	150
Robert Pearce	pt. "Cortany Fancy"	50
	pt. "Prices Chance"	25
39:1755:2 ...		
Thomas Thorpe	"Strife"	50
Fargus Keough	"Fargesons Folley"	50
	"Wills Swamp"	50
	"Readers Addition"	79
James Stiles	pt. "Stiles Chance"	59
	pt. "What Care I"	28
	pt. "Chance"	6
	pt. "Elizabeth Manner"	43
John Price	"Grove"	50
	"Farnhans"	83
Robert Greenwell (cnp)	pt. "Backland"	70
	pt. "Lamptons Pleasure"	117

	pt. "Greenwells Marsh"	49
Rev. Mr. Moses Tabbs	"~~Stincheoms~~ Freehold"	340
Robert Vaulx	pt. "Massom"	100
Barnaby Egan	pt. "Massom"	100
	pt. "Hopewell"	100
	"Stife"	100
	"Harberts Beginning"	50
	"Clockers Marsh"	100
	"Dunbar"	100
	"Lordships Favour"	100
James White	pt. "Fresh Pond Neck"	150
39:1755:3 ...		
Richard Barnhouse	pt. "Cross Manner"	1000
	pt. "Elizabeth Manner"	1000
John Cole	pt. "Riberts Backside"	50
	"Nobles Victor"	50
	"Harberts Grift"	48
	pt. "Shock Park"	24
John Mitchell	"Mitchells Choyce"	47
Cornelius Barber	pt. "Luckland"	470
	"Nicholas Hope"	135
Bap. Barber	pt. "Wastham"	250
	pt. "Luckland"	200
	"Leighe"	100
Elizabeth Donaldson	pt. "Mitcham Hills"	200
Phillip Key, Jr.	pt. "Mitcham Hills"	100
George Leatham	pt. "Mitcham Meadows"	100
Luke Russell	pt. "Brough"	50
James Gough	"St. Barnerds"	100
	"St. Margarets"	200
	"Bacon Neck"	200
	"Proprities Gift"	50
	"Q Name"	50
	"St. Teratia"	100
William Morgan (cnp)	"Hazzard"	73
	"Addition to White Burch Freehold"	53

	pt. "Patrick Hills"	15
	"White Burch Freehold"	100
39:1755:4 ...		
William Sisell	pt. "Caydle"	50
Thomas Sissell	pt. "White Acre"	50
	pt. "Addition to White Aker"	18
John Thompson	pt. "Davis's Forrest"	50
George Bouth, Jr.	pt. "Hopton Park"	56
Mary Greenwell	pt. "Green Hill"	221
Anthony Nottingham	"Knevets St. Ann"	100
Clement Stranford	"Leing"	100
Thomas Hatton Combs	"Hattons Rest"	250
	"Addition to Hearts Delight"	152
John Heard	pt. "St. Lawrence Freehold"	193
	pt. "Heards Security"	43
	pt. "Hanover"	350
Peter Howard	"Twitenham"	100
Mark Jarbo	pt. "Heard Security"	40
	pt. "Hanover"	20
John Norris	"Shircliff"	300
John Bap. Carberry	pt. "Hopton Park"	797
Hillard Hebb	"Little Recovery of Birth Right"	13
William Mattingley	pt. "Suttles Rest"	80
39:1755:5 ...		
Mathew Heard	"Pole"	120
	"William Heards Purchase"	115
	"Ashcoms Freehold"	150
	pt. "Hanover Addition"	123
	"Heards Choyce"	100
	pt. "Heard Security"	169
Mark Heard	"Thirds"	425
James Taylor (St. Mary's)	pt. "Snow Hill"	100
Mathew Hebb	"Small Hopes"	56
John French	pt. "Hopton Park"	160
Arthur Thompson	"Thompsons Expence"	125
John Hammond	pt. "Lewgroes Plains"	200

William Watts	"Bushells Rest"	150
John Gardner (St. Georges)	"Timber Swamp"	160
William Hebb	"Gardners Purchase"	100
	"St. Williams"	114
	"Freehold"	75
	"Cousen"	50
	"No Name"	50
	"Hibtons Hile"	280
	"Hunting Corbut"	100
	"Mackeys Point"	50
	"Cross Manner"	170
	"Wickahandick"	225
39:1755:6 ...		
James Thompson	"Small Hope"	100
	pt. "Swamp & Island"	120
	"Farthing Fortune & Addition"	60
	"Mills Meadows"	150
	pt. "Hounslow"	50
	"Prattlewell"	100
	"Small Hopes Addition"	78
	"Davids Hills"	51
	pt. "Hatfields Hills" for William Leake	75
Richard Brewer	pt. "Hounslow"	50
Nicholas Mills	"Strife"	200
	"Strifes Addition"	109
	pt. "Wheatlys Chance"	150
	pt. "Squable"	50
	pt. "Medley"	300
h/o James Blomfield	"Coals Addition"	50
	"Roberts Freehold"	90½
John Sanders Power	pt. "St. Barberys"	200
h/o James Neale	pt. "St. Winefrets Freehold"	30
h/o Oswell Neale	pt. "St. Winefrets Freehold"	220
	"Surplist"	452
Robert Cole	"Coles Purchase"	209
Edward Mattingly	pt. "St. Winefrets Freehold"	250

Philip Tippett	pt. "Suttles Range" a/s "Rest"	74
William Mattingly	pt. "Suttles Range" a/s "Rest"	80
39:1755:7 ...		
William Ward	"Quainton"	100
Thomas Mattingly	"Mount Misery"	100
	pt. "St. Thomas"	150
	pt. "St. Johns" a/s "Mattingly Land"	25
Vincent Taylor	pt. "St. Teratia"	100
	"Plains"	150
	"Ensgelath"	300
	"Ensgelath Addition"	140
Jos. Guibert	pt. "Dynard"	100
Aben Simmons	"Stradford"	100
	"Trepley"	100
James Wood	"Desart"	125
	"Arabice"	76
William Mackin	"Beards Choyce"	50
	"St. Margarets Fields"	100
	"St. Margarets Forest"	100
	"Speedwell"	100
John Thompson	pt. "Susquehanna Point"	100
	"Smiths Discovery"	258
	"Q Name"	195
John Suttle	pt. "Suttle Range" a/s "Rest"	136
Andrew Mills	"Woolverhampton"	150
Joseph Edelin	pt. "New Designe"	350
39:1755:8 ...		
John Hilton	pt. "Hopewell"	146
John Edwards	"Price Lot"	100
	"Plains Jerecho"	98
	"Buck Park"	100
Thomas Asquith	pt. "St. Richards Manner"	350
	pt. "Hampstead"	180
	"Hunting Creek"	200
	"Hiccory Hills"	100
Cornelius Mannyng (cnp)	"Neales Lot"	209½

	"Broad Neck"	83
	"Rednor"	404
	pt. "Nuns Oak"	63
Elizabeth Wiseman	"Batchellors Hopewell"	374
	"Force Put"	100
	"Hopewells Delight"	200
	"Back Akers"	100
William Stone	pt. "Graden"	100
Cuthbert Fenwick	pt. "Fenwick Manner"	175
Joseph Hopewell	pt. "Massom"	300
	"Asqueaths Defence"	122
	"Gardners Neck"	200
	"Hogpen Neck"	150
Robert Thompson	pt. "Rockey Point"	100
39:1755:9 ...		
John Price Williams	pt. "Keech & Prices Rest"	190
James Heard	pt. "St. Clement Manner"	150
	pt. "Fenwick Manner"	175
	pt. "Hardship"	147
	"Kennevets Beginning"	100
	"Two Friends"	131
	"Heards Addition"	58
John Sannor	pt. "Fresh Pond Neck"	150
Thomas Rablin	"Best Land"	50
John Thorne	pt. "Desart"	62½
	pt. "Jesham"	50
James Keech	pt. "Keech & Prices Rest"	200
	"Town Neck"	200
	"Satisfaction"	580
	"Remainder"	19
Absal. Thompson	"Phipes Fort"	100
	"Johns Fortune"	61
	"Guiberts Folley"	36
	pt. "Patrick Hills"	13
	"Inclosure"	62
Meverell Lock (cnp)	"Hulston"	100

	pt. "Trumans Lodge"	150
	pt. "Keech & Prices Rest"	58
Mary Clarke	"Addition"	100
George Mills	pt. "St. Clements Manner"	150
39:1755:10 ...		
Hugh Hopewell	"Hopewells Adventure"	95
	"Addition to Hopewells Adventure"	52
	pt. "St. Richards Manner"	500
John Arthurs	pt. "Underwoods Choyce"	100
Anthony Smith	pt. "Underwood"	100
John Wilkinson	"Industry"	153
William Harrison	pt. "St. Margarets"	166
	"Wards Addition"	36
h/o Charles Gannot	"Gannets Lot"	50
	pt. "Yoke by Chance"	41
Mary Edwards	"Damonds Adventure"	110
	"Edwards Back Land"	52
Thomas Shanks, Jr.	"Shanks Adventure"	101
	pt. "Clarker"	100
	pt. "St. Oswell"	100
	pt. "Cole Park" a/s "Clark West Discovery"	50
Clement Hayden	"Shanks Risque"	102
John Morgan	pt. "Parish Beadle"	100
Joseph Dafforen	"Maids Delight"	78
John Welch	pt. "Cortanys Neck"	68
39:1755:11 ...		
Dennis Tippet	pt. "Suttle Range"	60
	pt. "St. Barberry's Addition"	120
George Vawdery	"Underwood" a/s "Woodland" now called "Woods Pleasure"	344
Bennedict Spalding	"Hearts Delight"	200
	1 lot in Leonard Town	1
Clement Stratford	"Slipe"	69
	pt. "Baileys Fortune"	168
Ignatius Mattingly	"Clever"	155
James Mattingly (cnp)	pt. "Mattinglys Hope"	135

	pt. "St. Johns"	50
Jesse Wharton	"Notley Hall" or "St. Clement Manner"	400
	"Neighbourhood" or "St. Clement Manner"	146
Thomas Vaughan	pt. "Beckworths Lodge" a/s "James Chance"	100
William Daft	pt. "Rockey Point" a/s "Curry Glase"	100
Stephen Greenwell	"Colebrook Level"	129
John Taylor	pt. "Frog Marsh"	100
	"Millmots Adventure"	123
	"Neglect"	53
	"Williams Addition"	22
	"Whitehouse"	63
	pt. "Chancellors Point"	64
39:1755:12 ...		
James Summerhill	pt. "Wastham"	100
Issabella Cook	"Jones Fortune"	112
William Boarman	"St. Dorothy"	263
William Morgan	pt. "Friends Conjunction"	50
Mary Jorden	pt. "St. Clement Manner"	211
Jeremiah Jorden	pt. "St. Clement Manner"	35
William Jorden	pt. "St. Clement Manner"	135
Thomas Reader (cnp)	"Thomas & Henry"	113
	pt. "Fawnskirk"	165
	"Chance"	50
	"Roseland"	50
	"Bozens Increase"	273
	pt. "St. Johns"	595
	"Workington Park"	932
	"Middle Ground"	102
	pt. "Burrus Gift"	60
	"Modens Lot"	236
	"Addition to Roseland"	83
	pt. "Hope"	36
	pt. "Wastham"	87
	pt. "Denbury Hills"	100
	pt. "Trumans Lodge"	105
	"Inclosure"	14

	pt. "Fawnskirk"	87
	pt. "Parish Beadle"	100
	"Young Mans Venture"	130
	"Fourth Addition"	83
	pt. "Great St. Thomas"	100
	"Hipworth"	100
	pt. "Dynard"	100
	pt. "Bottom"	50
	"Wildmans Levels"	188½
	"Rooms Conveniency"	100
	pt. "Hopewell"	151
	pt. "St. Clement Manner"	150
39:1755:13 ...		
William Hebb, Jr.	"White Cliff"	50
Thomas Sannor	"Salisbury Plains"	100
Samuel Ashcom	"No Name"	881
	"Ashcoms Marsh"	32
Thomas Reswick	pt. of 2 tracts of exch. Land	64
	pt. "White Aker"	50
Robert Lydell	"Cynets Chance"	56
Charles Dylion	"Charles Chance"	75
Mark Stevens	"Richards Fancy"	38
Dr. Thomas James	"Bacon Point"	100
	pt. "Rivets"	151
	pt. "Fortune"	50
	"Taunton"	40
	"Crooked Billet"	38
William Asquith	"White Marsh"	93
Thomas Swan	"T.B."	119
James Roach	pt. "Medley"	100
	"Huckleberry Lane"	10
Eleanor & Ann Graves	"Hopewell"	131
	"Hardshift"	50
	"Hardshift Addition"	186
39:1755:14 ...		
John Oliver (cnp)	pt. "Cornelius"	39

	"Fortune"	50
	"Pearth"	62
	"Fortune Outlet"	16
	"Archies Hills"	65
Elizabeth Nelson	pt. "Doe Park"	75
	pt. "Addition to Doe Park"	50
George Graves	"Graves Swamp"	108
Thomas Standage	pt. "Doe Park"	21
	"North Addition to Doe Park"	147
Samuel Wood	"Cannoe Neck"	100
Anthony Sims	"Wickehandick"	125
John Burruss	pt. "Trent Fort"	129
	pt. "Remainder Charles Lot"	166½
William Cartwright	pt. "Remainder Charles Lot"	166½
	"Ridge"	50
John Cartwright	pt. "Long Look'd for Come at Last"	75
	"Cartwright Pasture"	20
	pt. "Burruss Gift"	40
George Burruss	pt. "Long Look'd for Come at Last"	100
George Dent	pt. "Freestone Point"	174
John Buckman	pt. "Freestone Point"	50
39:1755:15 ...		
John Dent	pt. "Freestone Point"	100
James Crook	"Ludgate"	50
Richard Southon	"Southons Desire"	125
Samuel Southon	"Trumans Lott"	40
	"Little Worth"	25
	"Southerns Supply"	21
Thomas Tauney	"Green Meadows"	200
Thomas Norris	pt. "Lewgers Plains"	130
	pt. "Wheatly's Content"	95
	pt. "Heards Choyce"	57
Free School	pt. "Hopton Park"	100
John Lynch	"Granes Content"	100
	"Plumb Point"	152
Robert Chesley (cnp)	2 lots in Leonard Town	2

	"Vineyard"	343
	pt. "Pork Hall"	50
	"Charles's Park"	130
	"Toby's Last Shift"	100
	"Woodstock"	127
Henry Reiley	"Saturdays Work"	100
	"Addition to Saturdays Work" tbc Nicholas Mills	30
Peter Mills	pt. "St. Johns"	230
Thomas Bisco	pt. "Mackeys Neck"	50
39:1755:16 ...		
Winefred Rowson	"Maidens Lot"	100
	"Bare Waistcoat"	50
	"Winifreds Chance"	36
William Hemmersly	"Beverly"	380
	"Batchellors Hope"	300
Thomas Alston	"Readers Adventure"	350
	pt. "St. Clement Manner"	200
William Mills	pt. "Poplar Neck"	115
	"Ansterday"	30
John Johnson	pt. "Peters Wills"	100
Peter Cartwright	pt. "Waston"	100
John Spalding	"Batchellors Rest"	100
Margaret Yates	pt. "Turvey"	93
Edward Ployden	pt. "Tarvern"	100
	"Farme"	500
	"Ploydens Discovery"	66
Isaac Shamwell	pt. "Devonshire"	50
	pt. "Trumanica"	50
	"Derbyshire"	130
Thomas Spalding	pt. "Great St. Thomas"	200
39:1755:17 ...		
Thomas Spalding (Leonard Town)	pt. "Cragburns Purchase"	100
	"Spaldings Addition"	42
	pt. "St. Giles's"	35
	"Spaldings Adventure"	207
	"Rich Neck"	150

Benjamin Branson	"Drayton"	57
	"Kenady" a/s "Kuldfield"	96½
	"Keech & Prices Rest"	122
	pt. "Best Land"	100
George Thompson	pt. "Hazzard"	100
William Hall	pt. "Graden"	100
William Watson	"Edinborough"	100
James Pike	"Forest Den"	100
George Leigh	"Innis Chance"	100
	"Gallowith"	50
	"Innis's Reserve"	25
	"Paris"	150
	"Inclosure"	170
Peter Dray	pt. "Bottom"	50
Arthur Ford	pt. "Strand"	91
William Thomas	"Wails"	200
	"Wails Addition"	91
	pt. "Boston"	50
39:1755:18 ...		
George Waring	pt. "St. Johns"	68
	pt. "Burch Hanger"	75
Luke Mattingly	"Choice part Hazzard"	100
John Higgs	"Wednesday Project"	98
	"Higgs Purchase"	49
John Harbert	"Harberts Invention"	109
	"Good Yielding"	86
	pt. "Good Yielding" or reservey	87
Fran. Redcliff	pt. "Doe Park"	50
William Jenkins	pt. "Truth & Trust"	273
	"Salem"	215
	"Croyden"	100
	"St. Thomas"	300
	"Addition"	103
	"Fox Range"	70
Thomas Watts	"Smoot"	50
William Martin (cnp)	pt. "Hopewell"	74

	"Cracksons Rest"	50
	"Redmans Hardship"	50
	pt. "Hopeless"	11
Thomas Hall	pt. "Long Look'd for Come at Last"	112
Peter Brown	pt. "White Aker"	222
39:1755:19 ...		
Rev. James Ashby	"St. Innegoes Manner" & "St. Georges Island"	3000
	pt. "Britains Outlet"	f. 50
Charles Beach	"Gosslings Addition"	30
	pt. "Parting Path"	26
	"Stiles Chance"	25
widow Gosling	pt. "Parting Path"	274
	"Garden Spot"	80
John Johnson Sourthon	pt. "Brotherhood"	140
	"Sourthons Hills"	50
	pt. "Wastham"	100
Mathew Guibert	pt. "Dynard"	81
Thiod. Jorden	pt. "St. Clement Manner"	130
Philip Greenwell	"Honest Jones Inheritance"	150
Richard Fenwick, Jr.	"Mayheard Comforde"	100
	"Ganeths Purchase" a/s pt. "Charles West Discovery"	40½
	"Fenwicks Gain"	55
Thomas Tippet	pt. "Suttle Range"	213
William Lock	"Good Pennyworth"	50
	"Fair Field"	50
	"Locks Venture"	49
Horne Roberts	pt. "Fresh Pond Neck"	203
Thomas Morton	pt. "St. Johns"	100
39:1755:20 ...		
Mrs. Forbes	"Orpens Gift"	400
	"Holeridge Town"	130
	"Draydon"	488
Charles Righill	"Jointer"	50
John Ford, Sr. (cnp)	pt. "Farthing Gift" a/s "Minsterdam"	10
	pt. "Durham"	100

	pt. "Long in Dispence"	75
Mark Thompson	pt. "Hatfields Hills"	25
Henry Cooper	pt. "Scotland"	150
John Sissell	pt. "Scotland"	150
Luke Sissell	pt. "Scotland"	50
James Sissell	"Sissells Venture"	88
Sarah Sissell	pt. "Baileys Rest"	150
James Brown	"Drydocking Addition"	100
James Boyde	pt. "Hopton Park"	150
Alexander Forguson	pt. "Small Hope"	9
	"Small Hopes Addition"	42
	pt. "Black Creek"	99
Thomas Redman	pt. "Small Hopes Addition"	100
39:1755:21 ...		
Mark Taylor	"Branch"	50
Clement Spink	pt. "Guellmots Hills"	180
	"All Thats Left"	31¼
	pt. "Guellmots Hills"	150
John Tennyson	pt. "Outlet"	50
John Mattingly	"Thames"	150
	"Mattingly Addition"	50
Sarah Greenwell	"Holly Tree"	148
John Smith (New Town)	pt. "Nuns Oake"	142
William Howard	"Pomphrey Fields"	100
Enoch Greenwell	"Hiccory Hollows"	119
	"Farthing Adventure"	78
	pt. "Wheatleys Content" a/s "Back Land"	55
Thomas Thompson	"Adjoinder" a/s "St. Johns Addition"	23
	pt. "Dynard"	13
	pt. "Chance"	89
John Key	pt. "Weston"	100
	pt. "Knotleys Addition"	175
	"Gardners Landing"	100
James Smith (Rock Creek) (cnp)	pt. "Outlet"	119
	"Fresh Pond"	243
	"Mitcham Meadows"	100

	pt. "Hampstead"	100
	pt. "Black Creek"	30
39:1755:22 ...		
John Horrell	pt. "Weston Addition"	100
George Thompson	pt. "Rockey Point"	50
Walter Davis	pt. "Twitenham Hermitage"	110
Richard Paine	pt. "Strife"	50
Clement Newton	"Newtons Rest"	63
	"Addition"	37
Samuel Johnson	pt. "Hopewell"	36
	"Addition"	19
Elizabeth Hayden	"Roaches Discovery"	251
	"Haydens Risque"	81
William Edley	pt. "Hayden Fair"	100
William Hayden	pt. "Hayden Fair"	100
Michael Wilman	pt. "Styles Chance"	100
Mary Watts	pt. "Jesbury Plains"	100
John Goss Lawrence	"Frog Marsh"	100
William Edgerton	pt. "Punkleys Marsh"	100
William Bigges	pt. "St. Clement Manner"	100
Francis Thompson	"Hard Fortune"	100
39:1755:23 ...		
Ju. Greenwell	"Rochester"	100
Margaret Plummer	"Orbustons Oak"	50
	"Hobsons Choice"	30
William Doxe	"Smith Rest"	100
William Cavannough	pt. "Massom"	250
	"Eyre"	328
h/o Richard Vowel	pt. "Vowels Purchase"	120
	pt. "Britains Outlet"	1
h/o Richard Vowel for Thomas Vowell	"Vowells Purchase"	58
Robert Hemmet (cnp)	"Hemmets Beginning"	34
	pt. "Burch Spring"	75
	pt. "Forest Harvey"	100
	"Wild Cat Neck"	104½

	"Hiccory Plat"	17½
	"Hemmet & Chance"	69
h/o Peter Muggs	pt. "Vowells Addition"	80
	"St. Williams"	50
	pt. "Vowells Purchase"	57
	pt. "Rockey Point"	50
James Greenwell s/o William	"Wheatleys Content"	75
Elizabeth King	pt. "Burch Spring"	50
James Bisco, Jr.	pt. "Hog Neck"	100
39:1755:24 ...		
Joshua Millard	"Neals Lot"	209½
	pt. "Little St. Thomas"	16
	pt. "St. Johns"	134
Luke Norris	pt. "Wheatleys Content"	69
Jana. Thompson	"Fibny"	100
Thomas Medley	"Barren Doe"	95
John Mills	"Yielding Bury"	99
	pt. "Hopton Park"	80
Robert Drury	"Honnards Mount"	40
Richard Cooper	pt. "Clarker"	100
	"Frightfull"	180
	"Coopers Addition"	94
	"Dynard"	100
	"Hopewell"	65
	"Expence"	67
	pt. "Cragburns Purchase"	100
John Waller	pt. "Partnership"	65
Richard Burruss	"Holdfast"	76
	pt. "Long Look'd for Come at Last"	75
John Wilson	"Indian Giant Syuther"	203
Abraham Hall	pt. "Gardners Grove"	50
39:1755:25 ...		
Thomas Hays	pt. "Gardeners Grove"	197
	"Addition to Gardeners Grove"	82
Edward Mchune	"Piles Discovery"	112
John Parsons (cnp)	"Addition"	50

	pt. "Long Look'd for Come at Last"	112½
James Watson	"Hedge Barren"	79
James Swan (should be John Swan)	pt. "Retirement"	63½
Stephen Cawood	pt. "Williamsons Purchase"	100
	pt. "Wastham"	200
	"Cawoods Expence"	157
Edward Barber	pt. "Swans Forest"	56
	pt. "Wastham"	250
	pt. "Luckland"	130
John Shanks	pt. "St. Oswell"	100
Jos. Greenwell	"Last Shipt"	100
John Wiseman Greenwell	"This or None"	50
	"John Wiseman Greenwell Park"	49
	"Piles Wood Lane"	200
Hezekiah Bisco	pt. "Retirement"	92
h/o Benjamin Gough	pt. "St. Margarets"	100
39:1755:26 ...		
Charles Jarbo	pt. "St. Peters Hills"	112
John Evens	pt. "Ishmaels Right"	165
John Smith, Jr.	"Haphazzard"	304
John Wheatley	"Hiccory Thicket"	48
	pt. "Hanover Addition"	45
John Hoper	"Ashcoms Greenfield"	100
John Knott	"Sharp"	44
Peter Paine	pt. "Honnard Mount"	75
Thomas Spalding s/o Thomas	pt. "Great St. Thomas"	100
	pt. "Little St. Thomas"	100
William McWilliams	pt. "Batchellors Rest"	300
	pt. "St. Clement Manner"	100
	"Josias Plains"	16¾
William Pike	pt. "Hanover"	140
	pt. "Hanover Addition"	60
	pt. "Heards Security"	91
Henry Neale	pt. "Hilly Lee"	250
	pt. "St. Clement Manner"	400

Thomas Hulston	"Back Land"	75
Richard Gardener	"Poplar Hill"	200
	"Middle Ground"	50
	"Floods Quarter"	50
39:1755:27 ...		
Thomas Graves	pt. "Graves Chance"	120
	pt. "Baptis Hope"	106
	"Hopewell"	99
	"Hardshift"	10
	"Prince William Newcastle"	50
	pt. "Graves Chance"	10
John Ford (Court House)	pt. "Hanover"	80
	pt. "Green Hill"	89
	pt. "Lamston Pleasure"	150
	"Rangel"	80
	pt. "St. Peters Hills"	50
	pt. "Heard Security"	39
	"Fords Inclosure"	255
Richard Fenwick	"Chance Conclusion"	97
	"Addition to Chance Conclusion"	26
Mary Bright	pt. "Cold Wells"	65
Philip Key, Esq. (cnp)	"Bushwood Lodge"	411
	pt. "Thames"	40
	"James Addition"	158
	pt. "St. Johns"	50
	"Addition to Peters Wills"	104
	pt. "Burch Hanger"	230
	"Cuccold Haven" & timber land	77
	pt. "Wems"	430
	"Woods Pleasure" & pt. "Chesham"	95
	pt. "Maiden Bower"	100
	pt. "Finchly"	102
	"Boston"	98
	pt. "Waston"	87
	pt. "Boston" & "Peach Blossom"	55
	"Luck Land"	200

	pt. "Dynard"	182
	pt. "Shourance" & "Yielding Bury"	75
	pt. "Milton Hope"	150
	pt. "Little Yielding"	35
	"Penryn" or "St. Clement Manner"	192
John Key	pt. "Notleys Addition"	175
	"Gardners Landing" (f. 21)	100
39:1755:28 ...		
Jan. Greenwell	pt. "Wheatleys Meadows"	123
Mary Wheatley	pt. "Wheatleys Meadows"	153
Charles Daft	pt. "Medly"	200
Peter Pike, Jr.	pt. "Hanover Addition"	50
John Milton	pt. "Burch Hanger"	94
Guilbert Ireland	"Edinborough 10th Addition"	121½
	pt. "Hermitage"	73
	pt. "Hopton Park"	140
	pt. "Baptis Hope"	153
	pt. "Yielding Bury"	17
	"Evens Lot" a/s "Hampstead"	50
John Guyther	pt. "Croft"	147
	"Saturdays Venture"	2½
	"Cornelius Swamp"	100
Ignatius Wheller	pt. "Hopton Park"	50
Capt. Richard Key	"Wolf Hole"	262
	"Addition to Guiberts Chance"	37
William Rogers	"Rogers Venture"	50
Eleanor Gardener	pt. "St. Johns"	500
Leah Ward	"Wards Defence"	100
39:1755:29 ...		
Anthony Brown	"Clarks Rest"	300
Samuel Able	pt. "Kirbys Choyce"	118
	pt. "Squable"	25
	"Scrubby Thicket"	25
	pt. "Wheatleys Chance"	41
Peter O'Neale	pt. "Cragburns Purchase"	60
Kenet Boult	pt. "Calingwood"	25

John Black	pt. "Massom"	200
	"Cadocks Measure"	150
	"Court Freehold" or "Harts Hall"	200
	"Fox Hill"	30
	"Adjoinder"	50
	"Gravelly Hill"	50
	"Oyster Hill Neck"	50
	"Newgent Venture"	50
	"Blumbury"	100
	"Dunbar"	92
	"Butchers Slipe"	42
	"Poplar Point"	101
Barton Smoot	"Clarks Range"	393
William Field	pt. "Batchellors Rest"	50
William Love	pt. "Partnership"	100
Enoch Fenwick, Jr.	pt. "St. Peters Hills"	150
	pt. "Colebrook Levell"	35
	pt. "Spinks's Rest"	65
39:1755:30 ...		
Thomas Moony	pt. "St. Edwards"	115
	"Tradesman Lot"	200
	pt. "Linsteed"	18
	pt. "Valentines Grove"	96
Daniel Harris	"Kingstone"	50
	"Wheatleys"	38
John Hynes	"Bite the Fox"	19
	"Hunters Hills"	150
James Anderson	pt. "Bakers Fancy"	78
	pt. "Cornelius"	39
	"Addition to Charles's Park"	20
Charles Flower	pt. "St. Georges"	50
Benjamin Williams (cnp)	"Esquires Purchase"	37
	pt. "Muggs Adventure"	200
	"Fox Den"	87
	"Bakers Fancy"	25
	"New Fancy"	25

	pt. "Punkleys Marsh"	100
John Tear	"Holy Day"	142
Enoch Fenwick	pt. "Fenwick Manner"	175
Ignatius Heard	pt. "Well Found"	106
Sab. Truman Grinfield	"America Felix"	152
39:1755:31 ...		
Thomas Newton	"Underwood" a/s "Newtons Propriety"	124
	"Greenwells Marsh"	14
Ann Grinfield	"Grinfields Discovery"	90
	"Trent Neck"	835
	"Stockbardolph"	75
James Truman Grinfield	"Keeches Folly"	133
	"Lamly"	100
	"Punk Neck"	60
	"Holbridge Town"	130
	pt. "Hopton Park"	120
Nathaniel Grinfield	"Fork"	60
	"Addition"	78
	"Whitehaven"	164
	"Indian Creek & Addition"	491
	"Nightwood & Bashford"	154
	"Thimblebe"	109
	"Fishing Place"	50
	"Brough Land"	75
James Warrick	pt. "St. Johns"	150
John Dunbar	"Chance"	240
Edward Castor	"Redmans Hardship"	50
Ignatius Chamberlin	pt. "St. Peters Hills"	118
John Cole (St. Georges)	"Jones Wood"	100
	"Addition to Jones Wood"	59½
Lydian Bright	pt. "Cold Wells"	65
39:1755:32 ...		
John Michael Thomas Tauny	pt. "Fenwick Manner"	450
Joseph Clarke	pt. "St. Johns"	300
	"Mattinglys Hope"	70
	"Cole Park" a/s "Charles Discovery"	122

Sarah Carter	"Meer Chance"	113
Mary Hemmersly	"Carbury's Discovery"	190
John Dant	"Hopewell"	100
	pt. "Yoke by Chance"	20
John Jones	"Poverty"	64
Thomas Yates	pt. "St. Peters Hills"	100
	pt. "Small Hopes"	30
	pt. "Hanover"	60
	pt. "Heards Security"	70
Enoch Combs	pt. "Pork Hall"	300
	"Grape Hill"	200
	"Wilderpole"	300
John Wherret	pt. "Watts Lodge"	90
Thomas Cook, Jr.	pt. "Brough"	68
Joseph Harding	"Baileys Rest"	100
John McKey	pt. "McKeys Neck"	153
	pt. "St. Richard Manner"	50
	pt. "Massom"	100
39:1755:33 ...		
Samuel Bellwood	"Ishmaels Right"	155
	"Bellwoods Grove"	128
	pt. "Styles Chance"	16
Fairfax Compton	pt. "Honnard Mount"	75
George Rogers	pt. "Well Close"	100
	"Brothers Dread"	135
John Norris	"Goughs Levels"	42
	"Goughs Conveniency"	48
	"Britain Bay"	150
William Roach	pt. "St. Johns Landing"	117
	pt. "Johns Addition"	167
William Guither	"Maids Delight"	100
	pt. "Smoot"	100
Cuthbert Clark	"Chelsey"	100
William Taylor	"Poplar Hill"	63
	"Taylors Lot"	22
John Baker (Bay Side)	pt. "Drapers Neck"	285

Fra. Wheatley	pt. "Wheatleys Content"	66
	pt. "Buck Land"	50
Leonard Greenwell	pt. "Hanover Addition"	87
George Would	pt. "Hanover"	108
John Thomas	"Hampton"	100
39:1755:34 ...		
Clement Norris	"Tants Mark"	168
	"Norris's Frolick"	3½
Thomas Howard	pt. "Guilberts Hills"	75
Jos. Stevens	pt. "Devonshire"	50
	"Trumanica"	50
	"Josephs Venture"	54
Samuel Lee	"Well Close"	82
	pt. "St. Clement Manner"	105
John Brady	pt. "Baileys Rest"	100
	"Bracys Lot"	25
Peter Ford	pt. "St. Giles"	81
	"Mount Pleasant"	100
	"May Pole"	96
	pt. "Strand"	91
Thomas Wheatley	"Addition to Wheatleys Content & Addition"	380
John Chesley	pt. "Clagburn"	300
	"Clagburns Island"	43
	"Clagburns Swamp"	17½
	pt. "Indian Creek"	36
Thomas Grinfield	pt. "Indian Creek"	843
	pt. "Goodluck"	275
Thomas Bond	"Knotting"	100
39:1755:35 ...		
Rev. John Urquhart	pt. "Fawns Kirk"	200
	"Spring Blossom"	221
	pt. "Keech & Prices Rest"	60
	"Hopewells Chance"	170
Benjamin Gristy	"Venture"	50
Thomas Clark	pt. "Moffats Will"	69
Thomas Brayden	pt. "Moffats Will"	69

John Bisco	"Barren Wood"	46
Henry Wimsett	"Harbetts Grieff"	44
	pt. "Nuns Oak"	20
James Dickson	"Dicksons Venture" or "Haidens Fair"	115½
h/o Edward Pye	"Underwood"	300
John Adams	"Small Hope with Addition"	50
John Graves	pt. "Graves Chance"	94
James Thompson (head Chaptico)	pt. "St. Johns"	50
	"Harbets Swamp"	21
Joseph Stevens, Jr.	"Stevens Chance"	46
	"Pirnassed"	75
39:1755:36 ...		
Ignatius Greenwell s/o Ignatius	"Ignatius Dread"	100
	"Addition"	20
Mary Fenwick	pt. "Fenwick Manner"	200
Daniel Watts	"Watts Lodge"	160
John Plummer	pt. "Elizabeth Manner"	300
Richard Shirley	"Shirleys Adventure"	150
Thomas Keen	"Keens Rest"	49
Thomas Mathews	"Friends Conjunction"	72
Edward Aprice	pt. "Saint Barbarys"	100
John Anderson	"Southerns Desire"	100
	pt. "Fox Rest"	52
Benjamin Bean	pt. "Friends Conjunction"	72
John Sykes	pt. "Friends Conjunction"	106
John Thompson	"Mitcham Meadows"	100
39:1755:37 ...		
Mark Thomas	"Penancy"	100
	"Brewers Wood House"	50
	"Luke's Hardship"	7
	"Marks Adventure"	36
Henry How	"White Land"	225
	"Howes Fortune"	19
	"Howes Adventure"	42
John Bisco	pt. "Harrisons Rest"	80
	pt. "Williams Fortune"	32

Dr. William Murray	"Indian Creek"	563
Peter Peake	pt. "Friends Goodwill"	100
Benjamin Fenwick	pt. "Fenwick Manner"	200
Robert Henley	pt. "Massom"	158
	"Johns Content"	93½
	"Keens Rest"	50
Robert Newgent	"Marking Place"	105
	"Fox Catched"	11
James Smith	"Trinity", "St. Gabriel" & "St. Michaels Manner"	3000
	"Pountleys Oversight"	198
	"Tripple Defence"	206
	"Addition to Tripple Defence"	87
	"Pine Land"	388
	pt. "Turvey"	201
	"Hazzard"	57
39:1755:38 ...		
Cornelius Wildman	"Brooke Chance"	81
	"Dylons Disappointment"	103
	"Williams Venture"	54
	"Goulding Grove"	153
	"Tavern"	100
Enoch Able	"Saturdays Conclusion"	55
	pt. "Wheatleys Chance"	50
	"Hopsons Choyce"	23½
John Medley Thompson	pt. "Scotland"	50
Thomas Barber	pt. "Burch Hanger"	20
Charles Greenwell	"Farther Adventure"	65½
Thomas Jorden	pt. "Collingwood"	25
John Clark	"Evans's Quarter"	100
Michael Goldsmith	pt. "St. Clement Manner"	86
	pt. "Basford Manner"	100
William Aud	pt. "Hanover"	30
James Chizzam	"Baker's Fancy"	100
John Shircliffe (cnp)	"Shircliff"	250
	"St. Williams"	90
	"Q Name"	100

	pt. "Linsted"	78
	pt. "Linsted Addition"	100
	"Coles Adventure"	150
39:1755:39 ...		
Richard Millard	"Little Saint Thomas"	84
	pt. "Saint Johns"	50
	"Turners Plains"	16
Thomas Pearce	pt. "Cortany Fancy"	50
Kelley Truman Greenfield	pt. "Trent Neck"	1519
Henry Lowes	"Warnett"	240
Henry Jarbo	pt. "St. Peters Hills"	126
Henry Bryan	"Williams Endeavours"	50
	pt. "Farther Adventure"	37
	"Greens Plott"	44
William Deacon, Esq.	pt. "St. Peters"	50
	pt. "Chanlors Point"	112
	pt. "St. Marys Freehold"	248
William Hicks	pt. "Saint Peters"	100
	"Governers Fields"	100
	"Chappell"	25
	pt. "St. Marys Freehold"	7
John Miles	"Wastfield"	140
	"Somersett"	195
Edward Parsons	pt. "Guiberts Chance"	50
	"Small Addition"	19½
39:1755:40 ...		
Arther Thompson	"Thompsons Expence"	200
Joseph Jenkins	pt. "Truth & Trust"	400
William Heard	pt. "Well Found"	106
	pt. "Fenwick Manner"	175
Mr. George Plater	pt. "St. Joseph Manner"	819
	"Bouls Preservation"	890
	pt. "Fenwick Manner"	400
	"Staffords Hope"	125
	"Resurrection Manner"	4000

Richard Raper or Clement Shalford	"Maynards Comford"	100
	pt. "Baileys Fortune"	45
	pt. "Saint Clement Manner"	50
	pt. "Baptiss Hope"	100
Thomas Doxe	pt. "Harrisons Rest"	70
Richard Brooke	"Dalle Brooke Manner"	2000
	"Two Brothers"	235
	pt. "Back Land"	400
Thomas Hobson	pt. "Weems"	100
Elizabeth Hules	"Wastham"	150
Charles King	"Deptford"	300
	pt. "Saint Josephs Manner"	200
Joseph Greenwell	pt. "Kirbys Choyce"	67
39:1755:41 ...		
William Williams	"Drydocking"	100
	pt. "Shock Park"	76
	pt. "Roberts Neck" a/s "Medly"	45
	"Harberts Gift"	60
	pt. "Roberts Freehold"	75
Robert Fenwick	pt. "Joseph Manner"	126
John Mareman	pt. "Hopton Park"	197
	"Vowles Purchace"	156
Samuel Gunifer	pt. "Joseph Manner"	50
Leonard Green	pt. "Fenwick Manner"	100
Thomas Manley	pt. "Elizabeth Manner"	100
Thomas Bladen, Esq.	pt. "Elizabeth Manner"	247
	pt. "Cross Manner"	500
Sturton Edwards	"St. Thomas"	190
	"Doe Park"	69
	pt. "Hanover"	100
Thomas Brome	pt. "No Name"	200
John Lancaster	pt. "Hilley Lee"	250
	pt. "St. Clement Manner"	400
Peter Gough	pt. "Lewgroes Plains"	100
39:1755:42 ...		
James Hager	pt. "Beverdam"	59

John Able	pt. "Wheatleys Chance"	31
	pt. "Kirbys Choyce"	88
	pt. "St. Joseph Manner"	56
Cuthbert Able	"Wisemans Chance"	100
Benjamin Redman	"Small Hope"	50
Dennis Burn	pt. "Beckworth Lodge"	81½
Joseph Walker	pt. "Guilmoth Hills"	100
	"Addition to Farthing Fortune"	140
Ignatius Bailey	pt. "Little Yielding"	117
William Jones	"Salters Hall"	89
	"Addition to Salters Hall"	34
	"Jones Convenancy"	35½
	pt. "Beckworths Lodge"	81½
	"Jones's Lane"	1¾
	"Muggs Adventure"	52
John Jarbo	pt. "Hanover"	17
	pt. "Heards Security"	24
Thomas Warring	"Warring Lott"	148
Mathias Nottingham	"Salmon"	50
39:1755:43 ...		
Ruther Jones	pt. "Davis's Forrest"	50
John Price	"Grove"	50
Henry Spalding	pt. "Joseph"	152½
	"Two Brothers"	165
	pt. "New Castle"	50
	pt. "Rich Neck"	98
Thomas Devaun	pt. "Partnership"	200
John Watson	pt. "Partnership"	65
George Maxwell	pt. "Indian Creek with Addition"	461
Maj. Abraham Barns	"America Felix Secundus"	986
	pt. "Bengefield"	40
	pt. "Forrest Harvey"	100
	"Westbury Manner"	1258
	pt. "Harveys Lodge"	100
	pt. "Drapers Neck"	215
	"Walnutt Point"	55

Zachariah Bond	pt. "St. Barbary"	200
William Doxee	pt. "Patricks Hills"	50
Edward Bowling	pt. "Collingwood"	25
John Morris	pt. "Collingwood"	25
Francis Knott	pt. "Hazzard"	56
Peter Peake	pt. "Wolverhampton"	75
39:1755:44 ...		
George Bowles	"Steplition Fortune"	200
	"Hazzard"	234
John Tippett	"Tippetts Purchace"	46
William Spalding	pt. "Rich Neck"	152
Mark Norris	pt. "Wheatleys Content"	118
	pt. "Burch Plains"	70
Ignatius Fenwick	"Hepton Hole"	350
	pt. "Hepton Hole"	70
John Holt	pt. "St. Clements Manner"	167
Ignatius Whealler	pt. "St. Clement Manner"	250
John Lee	pt. "St. Clement Manner"	200
John Hoskins	pt. "St. Clement Manner"	100
John Baptiss Greenwell	pt. "Rochester"	100
John Bould	pt. "Cadle"	150
	"Addition to White Aker"	24
John Wimsett	pt. "Hatfields Hills"	73
John Bullock	pt. "St. Clements Manner"	100
Thomas Wherrett	"Hogg Neck"	100
39:1755:45 ...		
John Bohannon	"Fox Grape Barren"	106
David Downee	"Town Support"	81
	"Bary"	85
	3 lots in Leonard Town	3
James Jarbo	"Denby"	250
Thomas Jenkins	"Poplar Point"	100
Benjamin Molten	pt. "Bashford Manner"	200
John Pike	"Forney Branch"	50
Clement Medley	pt. "Medley"	200
William Medley	pt. "Medley"	100

Basil Pike	pt. "Medley"	100
George Greenwell	pt. "Medley"	50
John Llewelling	pt. "St. Clements Manner"	400
John Fenwick	pt. "Rivetts Backside"	172
	pt. "Rivetts"	151
	pt. "Chancellors Point"	112
	pt. "Croffs"	100
Bennett Neale	pt. "St. Clements Manner"	200
Austin Macey	pt. "Plumb Point"	338
Elizabeth Lock	pt. "Cold Wells"	65
39:1755:46 ...		
Stephen Chilton	pt. "Peters Quay"	50
	"Fishing Creek Neck"	44
Richard Milburn	pt. "Halfhead Folley"	100
	"Milburns Chance"	178
	pt. "Cortany Neck"	82
John Smith	pt. "Mattapany"	289
Clement Spalding	"Spaldings Adventure"	729
	pt. "Tavern"	0
John Eden	pt. "Bashford Manner"	277
John Bond	pt. "St. Clement Manner"	605
	pt. "Hopton Park"	400
	pt. "Saint Johns"	438
	"Gardners Chance"	155
Richard Edgling	"Trumans Hunting Quarter"	200
	pt. "Hope"	64
Justenian Jorden	pt. "St. Clement Manner"	200
John Boult	pt. "St. Clement Manner"	100
Edward Turner	pt. "Bashford Manner"	200
George Backster	"Batchellors Comfort"	190
George Slye	pt. "St. Clements Manner"	1000
39:1755:47 ...		
Charles Sawall	pt. "Little Eltonhead Manner"	50
	"Sawalls Discovery"	117
John Blackston	pt. "St. Clements Manner"	550
	pt. "St. Clements Island"	100

John Mason	pt. "St. Clements Manner"	450
Mary Tennyson	pt. "St. Clement Manner"	100
Kened. Cheseldine	pt. "St. Clement Manner"	725
Cyrenius Cheseldine	pt. "St. Clement Manner"	25
Charles Carroll, Esq.	pt. "St. Clement Manner"	1650
	"Oxford"	209
	pt. "Barbarys Addition"	250
	pt. "Laughbrough"	150
	"Addition"	41
	"Temple Barr"	100
John Madock	pt. "Basford Manner"	150
John Reswick	pt. 2 tracts escheated land	47
Edward Welch	"Ossfield"	72
John Attaway Clark	pt. "Poney Point"	750
	pt. "James Johnsons Neck"	200
	"Blake Creek"	50
	"Tower Hill"	25
Robert Hager	pt. "Truth & Trust"	100
39:1755:48 ...		
Nicholas Lewis Sawell	pt. "Mattapany"	911
	"Sawalls Discovery"	108
	"Fishing Point"	13
Leonard Davis	pt. "Desart"	62½
	"Thornes Venture"	103
James Wheatley	"Kington" a/s "Neutonquit"	117
	pt. "Wheatleys Addition"	21
John Smith	pt. "Bashford Manner"	200
Mary McWilliams	pt. "St. Clement Manner"	300
Sturton Edwards, Jr.	"Taunton Denn"	154
Thomas Suit	pt. "Trent Fort"	84
	pt. "Horse Range"	100
James Mills	pt. "Basford Manner"	100
Leonard Mattingly	"Audley End"	190
Notley Goldsmith	pt. "Bashford Manner"	100
Roger Smith	pt. "Notleys Addition"	275
Dent Soot	pt. "Horse Range"	100

Thomas Crane	"Dalley"	100
John Forder (wever)	"Pomphrey Field"	50
	"Ministerdam"	54
Henry Taylor	"Taylors Plains"	50½
39:1755:49 ...		
Thomas Soot, Jr.	pt. "Wells"	100
Joseph Edwards	pt. "Wells"	52
	pt. "Trent Fort"	8
Thomas Winnefred Taylor	pt. "Righting"	100
Clement Medley, Sr.	"No Name"	100
John Somervell	pt. "St. Richards Manner"	100
	"Baileys" a/s "Clarks Discovery"	99
	pt. "St. Jeroms Manner"	200
John Michaell Waughop	"Waughops Chance"	138
John Coad	pt. "St. Clement Manner"	300
Anthony Roberts	"Whitenham"	200
Benjamin Burruss	pt. "Trent Fort"	129
Peter Ford, Jr.	"Nuns Oak"	75
John Corlett	"Willingburrough"	70
h/o James Heath	pt. "St. Jeroms Manner"	5500
James Kendrick	"Kendricks Lane"	80
John Reeves	pt. "Bashford Manner"	100
John Kelley	"Kelleys Luck"	138
	"Kelleys Fortune"	182
39:1755:50 ...		
James Tarlton	pt. "Bever Dam"	59
	pt. "Elizabeth"	54
Samuel Swan	pt. "Swans Forrest"	40
James Lattimore	pt. "Hopewell"	89
Leonard Paine	"Fox"	100
Ignatius Thompson	"Tebery" (no such land)	500
Arnold Livers	"Little Britten"	750
	pt. "Brittan's Outlett"	43
James Bailey	pt. "St. Clements Manner"	45
Thomas Yates, Jr.	pt. "St. Clement Manner"	100
John Goldsmith	pt. "Bashford Manner"	100

Samuel Madox	pt. "Bashford Manner"	58
Thomas Vowles	pt. "Vowles Purchace"	50
Thomas Melton	pt. "Burch Hanger"	95

39:1756:1 ...		Acres
Daniel Clocker	"Clockers Freehold"	50
	"Lewis Neck"	30
Elizabeth Clocker	"St. Ann's Freehold"	78½
	"Clocker's Fancy"	56
Thomas Palmer Waughop	"Hunting Quarter"	150
	"Poiney Point"	750
	"Smoots Hollow"	150
Nicholas Sewall	pt. "Little Eltonhead Manner"	1590
Edward Digges	pt. "Little Eltonhead Manner"	300
William Price	"Brick Hill"	217
	"Park's Addition"	110
Edward Horn	pt. "Halfhead Folley"	100
Ignatius Taylor	pt. "Little Eltonhead Manner" a/s "Gover's Gift"	60
James Dafforon	"Cole Harbour"	150
George Aisquith	"Stinmore"	100
	"Inclosure"	30
	"Thomas & George in Company"	4¼
John Roades	pt. "Jesbury Plains"	330
Isaac Pavatt	"Cow Ridge"	50
	pt. "Cross Manner"	150
Robert Pearce	pt. "Cortany's Fancy"	50
	pt. "Price's Chance"	25
39:1756:2 ...		
Thomas Thorp	"Strife"	50
Fargus Keough	"Farguson's Folley"	50
	"Wills Swamp"	50
	"Reeder's Addition"	79
James Stiles	pt. "Stiles Chance"	59
	"What Care I"	28½
	pt. "Chance"	6
	pt. "Elizabeth Manner"	43
John Price	"Grove"	50
	"Farnham"	83
Robert Greenwell (cnp)	pt. "Backland"	70
	pt. "Lampton's Pleasure"	117

	pt. "Greenwells Marsh"	49
Rev. Moses Tabbs	"Itchcombs Freehold"	348
Robert Vaulx	pt. "Massom"	100
Barnaby Egan	pt. "Massom"	100
	pt. "Hopewell"	100
	"Strife"	100
	"Harberts Beginning"	58
	"Clocker's Marsh"	100
	"Dunbar"	100
	"Lordships Favour"	100
James White	pt. "Fresh Pond Neck"	150
39:1756:3 ...		
Richard Barnhouse	pt. "Cross Manner"	1000
	pt. "Elizabeth Manner"	1000
John Cole	pt. "Rivets Backside"	50
	"Nobles Victor"	50
	"Harberts Gift" or "Grief"	43
	pt. "Shock Park"	24
John Mitchell	"Mitchells Choice"	47
Cornelius Barber	pt. "Luckland" or "Eastham"	470
	"Nicholls's Hope"	135
Baptist Barber	pt. "Wastham"	250
	pt. "Luckland" or "Eastham"	200
	"Leighe"	100
Elizabeth Donaldson	pt. "Mitchams Hills"	200
Philip Barton Key	pt. "Mitchams Hill"	100
George Leatham	pt. "Mitcham Meadows"	100
Luke Russell	pt. "Brough"	50
James Gough	"St. Barnards"	100
	"St. Margarets"	200
	"Bacon Neck"	200
	"Proprietors Gift" a/s "Lordships Favour"	50
	"Q Name" a/s "Lordships Favour"	50
	"St. Teresia" a/s "Lordships Favour"	100
William Morgan (cnp)	"Hazzard"	73
	"Addition to White Burch Freehold"	53

	pt. "Patricks Hills"	15
	"White Burch Freehold"	100
39:1756:4 ...		
William Sissell	"Caydle"	50
Thomas Sissell	pt. "White Acre"	50
	"Addition to White Acre"	18
John Thompson	pt. "Davis's Forrest"	50
George Booth, Jr.	pt. "Hopton Park"	56
Mary Greenwell	pt. "Green Hill"	221
Athanasius Nottingham	"Knevet St. Ann"	100
Clement Stratford	"Leeing Leigh"	100
Thomas Hatton Combs	"Hatton's Rest"	250
	"Addition to Harts Delight"	152
John Heard	pt. "St. Laurence Freehold"	193
	pt. "Heards Security"	43
	pt. "Hanover"	350
Peter Howard	"Twittenham"	100
Mark Jarbo	pt. "Heards Security"	40
	pt. "Hanover"	20
John Norris	"Shiercliffe"	300
John Bap. Carbery	pt. "Hopton Park"	797
Edward Hill. Hebb	"Little Recovery of Birth Right"	13
William Mattingly	pt. "Suttles Range"	80
39:1756:5 ...		
Matthew Heard	"Poale"	120
	"William Heards Purchase"	115
	"Ashcom's Freehold"	150
	pt. "Hanover Addition"	123
	"Heards Choice"	100
	pt. "Heards Security"	169
Mark Heard	"Thirds"	425
James Taylor (St. Mary's)	pt. "Snow Hill Manor"	100
Matthew Hebb	"Small Hopes"	56
John French	pt. "Hopton Park"	160
Arthur Thompson	"Thompson's Expence"	125
John Hammond	pt. "Lewgroe's Plains"	200

William Watts	"Bushells Rest"	150
John Gardiner (St. George's)	"Timber Swamp"	160
William Hebb	"Gardiners Purchase"	100
	"St. Williams"	114
	"Freehold"	75
	"Cousin"	50
	"St. Georges Point"	50
	"No Name"	50
	"Hibtons Hole"	280
	"Corbet"	100
	"Mackey's Point" or "Mackey's Neck"	50
	"Cross Mannor"	170
	"Wickahamick"	225
39:1756:6 ...		
James Thompson	"Small Hope"	100
	pt. "Swamp & Island"	120
	"Farthings Fortune"	50
	"Addition to Fortune"	10
	"Mills's Meadows"	150
	pt. "Hounslow"	100
	"Prattlewell"	100
	"Small Hopes Addition"	75
	"Davids Hills"	51
	pt. "Hatfield Hills" for William Lake	75
Richard Brewar	pt. "Hounslow"	50
Nicholas Mills	"Strife"	200
	"Stifes Addition"	109
	pt. "Wheatly's Chance"	150
	pt. "Squabble"	50
	pt. "Medley"	300
h/o James Blomfield	"Coal's Addition"	50
	"Roberts's Freehold"	90½
John Sanders Power	pt. "St. Barbary's"	200
h/o James Neale	pt. "St. Winifreds Freehold"	30
h/o Rosswell Neale	pt. "St. Winifreds Freehold"	220
	"Surplusst" in "Winifreds Freehold"	452

Robert Cole	"Cole's Purchase"	209
Edward Mattingly	pt. "St. Winifreds Freehold"	250
Philip Tippett	pt. "Suttle's Range" a/s "Rest"	74
William Warthen	pt. "Suttle's Range" a/s "Rest"	80
39:1756:7 ...		
William Ward	"Quainton"	100
Thomas Mattingly	"Mount Misery"	100
	pt. "St. Thomas"	150
	pt. "St. John's" a/s "Mattingly's Lane"	25
Vincent Taylor	pt. "St. Teresia"	100
	"Plains"	150
	"Engelath"	300
	"Engelath Addition"	140
Joshua Guibert	pt. "Dynard"	100
Abell Simmons	"Stratford"	100
	"Trophey"	100
James Wood	"Desart"	125
	"Arabia"	76
William Meeken	"Beards Choice"	50
	"St. Margarets Fields"	100
	"St. Margarets Forrest"	100
	"Speedwell" or "Sherwell"	100
John Thompson	pt. "Susquehanna Point"	100
	"Smith's Discovery"	258
	"Susquehannah Point" & "Edloes Addition"	195
John Suttle	pt. "Suttles Range" a/s "Rest"	136
Andrew Mills	"Woolverhampton"	150
Joseph Edelin	pt. "New Design"	350
39:1756:8 ...		
John Hilton	pt. "Hopewell"	146
John Edwards	"Price's Lot"	100
	"Plains Jericho"	93
	"Back Park"	100
Thomas Aisquith (cnp)	pt. "St. Richards Manner"	350
	pt. "Hamstard"	100
	"Hunting Neck"	200

	"Hickory Hills"	100
Cornelius Manning	"Neale's Lot"	209½
	"Broad Neck"	83
	"Rednor"	404
	pt. "Nuns Oak"	63
Elizabeth Wiseman	"Batchellors Hopewell Rectified"	374
	"Force Putt"	100
	"Hopewells Delight"	200
	"Back Acres Beginning"	100
William Stone	pt. "Graden"	100
Cuthbert Fenwick	pt. "Fenwick Manner"	175
Joseph Hopewell	pt. "Massom"	300
	"Aisquith's Defence"	122
	"Gardiner's Neck"	200
	"Hogpen Neck"	150
39:1756:9 ...		
John Price Williams	pt. "Keith & Price's Rest"	198
James Heard	pt. "St. Clements Manner"	155
	pt. "Fenwick Manner"	175
	pt. "Hardship"	147
	"Kennevets Beginning"	100
	"Two Friends"	131
	"Heards Addition"	58
John Sannor	pt. "Freshpond Neck"	150
Thomas Rabling	"Best Land"	50
John Thorn	pt. "Desart"	62½
	pt. "Jesham"	50
James Keech	pt. "Keeth & Prices Rest"	200
	"Town Neck"	200
	"Satisfaction"	580
	"Remainder"	19
Absolom Tennison	"Phipes's Fort"	100
	"John's Fortune"	61
	"Guiberts Folley"	36
	pt. "Patricks Hills"	13
	"Inclosure"	62

Meverell Lock	"Hulston"	100
	pt. "Trumans Lodge"	150
	pt. "Keeth & Prices Rest"	58
Mary Clark	"Addition"	100
George Mills	pt. "St. Clements Manner"	150
39:1756:10 ...		
Hugh Hopewell	"Hopewells Adventure"	95
	"Addition to Hopewells Adventure"	52
	pt. "St. Richards Manner"	500
John Arthurs	pt. "Underwoods Choice"	100
Anthony Smith	pt. "Underwood"	100
John Wilkinson	"Industry"	153
William Harrison	pt. "St. Margarets"	166
	"Ward's Addition"	36
h/o Charles Ganyot	"Ganyot's Lot"	50
	pt. "Yoke by Chance"	41
Mary Edwards	"Damond's Adventure"	110
	"Edwards Backland"	52
Thomas Shanks, Jr.	"Shank's Adventure"	101
	pt. "Clarker"	100
	pt. "St. Oswell"	100
	pt. "Cole Park" a/s "West Discovery"	50
Clement Hayden	"Shank's Risque"	102
John Morgan	pt. "Parish Beedle"	100
Joseph Dafforon	"Maids Delight"	78
John Welch	pt. "Cortany's Neck"	68
39:1756:11 ...		
Dennis Tippett	pt. "Suttles Range"	60
	pt. "St. Barbary's Addition"	120
George Vaudry	"Underwood" a/s "Wood Land" now called "Woods Pleasure"	344
Benedict Spalding	"Hearts Delight"	200
	1 lot in Leonard Town	1
Clement Stratfort	"Slipe"	69
	pt. "Baily's Fortune"	168
Ignatius Mattingly	"Clever"	155

James Mattingly	pt. "Mattingly's Hope"	130
	pt. "St. John's"	50
Jesse Wharton	"Notley Hall" or "St. Clements Manner"	400
	"Neighbourhood" or "St. Clements Manner"	146
Thomas Vaughon	pt. "Beckworths Lodge" a/s "James's Chance"	100
William Daft	pt. "Rockey Point" a/s "Curry Glass"	100
Stephen Greenwell	"Cole Branch Level"	129
John Taylor	pt. "Frog Marsh"	100
	"Millmast's Adventure"	123
	"Neglect"	53
	"Williams' Addition"	22
	"White House"	63
	pt. "Chancellor's Point"	64
39:1756:12 ...		
James Somerhill	pt. "Wastham"	100
Issabella Cooke	"Jones Fortune"	112
William Boarman	"St. Dorothy"	263
Mary Jordan	pt. "St. Clements Manner"	211
William Morgan	pt. "Friends Conjuction"	50
Jeremiah Jordan	pt. "St. Clements Manner"	85
William Jordan	pt. "St. Clements Mannor"	135
Thomas Reeder (cnp)	"Thomas & Henry"	113
	pt. "Faunskirk"	165
	"Chance"	50
	"Rose Land"	50
	"Bagen's Increase"	273
	pt. "St. Johns"	595
	"Workinton Park"	932
	"Middle Ground"	102
	pt. "Burroughes Gift"	60
	"Modens Lot"	236
	"Addition to Rose Land"	83
	pt. "Hope"	36
	pt. "Wastham"	87
	pt. "Denbury Hills"	100
	pt. "Trumans Lodge"	105

	"Inclosure"	14
	pt. "Faunskirk"	87
	pt. "Parish Beedle"	100
	"Young Mans Venture"	130
	"Fourth Addition"	83
	pt. "St. Thomas"	100
	"Hipworth"	100
	pt. "Dynard"	100
	pt. "Bottom"	50
	"Wildman's Levells"	168½
	"Room's Conveniency"	100
	pt. "Hopewell"	151
	pt. "St. Clements Manner"	150
39:1756:13 ...		
William Hebb, Jr.	"White Cliff"	59
Thomas Sanner	"Salisbury Plains"	100
Samuel Ashcom	"No Name"	881
	"Ashcoms Marsh"	32
Thomas Reshwick	pt. 2 tracts escheat land	64
	pt. "White Acre"	50
Robert Lydell	"Synetts Chance"	56
Charles Dylion	"Charles's Chance"	75
Mark Stevens	"Richardson's Fancy"	38
Dr. Thomas James	"Bacon Point" or "Beanes Point"	100
	pt. "Rivets"	151
	pt. "Fortune"	50
	"Taunton"	40
	"Crooked Billet"	38
William Aisquith	"White Marsh"	93
Thomas Swann	"T.B."	119
James Roach	pt. "Medley"	100
	"Huckleberry Lane"	10
Elianor & Ann Greaves	"Hopewell"	131
	"Hard Shift"	50
	"Hard Shift Addition"	186
39:1756:14 ...		

John Olliver	pt. "Cornelius"	39
	"Fortune"	50
	"Pearth"	62
	"Fortune Outlet"	16
	"Archies Hills"	65
Elizabeth Nelson	pt. "Doe Park"	75
	pt. "Addition to Doe Park"	50
George Greaves	"Greaves's Swamp"	108
Thomas Standage	pt. "Doe Park"	21
	"North Addition to Doe Park"	147
Samuel Wood	"Cannoe Neck"	100
Anthony Sims	"Wichehandick"	125
John Burroughes	pt. "Trent Fort"	129
	pt. "Remainder Charles's Lot"	166½
William Cartwright	pt. "Remainder Charles's Lot"	166½
	"Ridge"	50
John Cartwright	pt. "Long Look'd for Come at Last"	75
	"Cartwright's Pasture"	20
	"Burroughes Gift"	40
George Burroughes	pt. "Long Look'd for Come at Last"	100
George Dent	pt. "Free Stone Point"	174
John Buckman	pt. "Freestone Point"	50
39:1756:15 ...		
John Dent	pt. "Freestone Point"	100
James Crooke	"Ludgate"	50
Richard Sothoron	"Sothoron's Desire"	125
Samuel Sothoron	"Truman's Lot"	40
	"Littleworth"	25
	"Sothoron's Supply"	21
Thomas Taney	"Green Meadows"	200
Thomas Norris	pt. "Leugroes Plains"	130
	pt. "Wheatly's Content"	95
	pt. "Heard's Choice"	57
Free School	pt. "Hopton Park"	100
John Lynch	"Granes Content"	100
	"Plumb Point"	162

Robert Chesley	2 lots in Leonard Town	2
	"Vineyard"	343
	pt. "Pork Hall"	50
	"Charles's Park"	130
	"Toby's Last Shift"	100
	"Wood Stock"	127
Henry Reily	"Saturday's Work"	100
	"Addition to Saturday's Work"	30
Peter Mills	pt. "St. Johns"	230
Thomas Biscoe	pt. "McKey's Neck"	50
39:1756:16 ...		
Winefred Rowson	"Maiden's Lot"	100
	"Bare Waiscoat"	50
	"Winefreds Chance"	36
William Hamersly	"Beverly"	380
	"Batchellors Hope"	300
Thomas Allstone	"Reeders Adventure"	350
	pt. "St. Clements Manner"	200
William Mills	pt. "Poplar Neck"	115
	"Ansterday" or "Anstenthem"	30
John Johnson	pt. "Peters Wells"	100
Peter Cartwright	pt. "Waston Addition"	100
John Spalding	"Batchellors Rest"	100
Martin Yates	pt. "Turvey"	93
Edmond Plowden	pt. "Tavern"	100
	"Farme"	500
	"Plowden's Discovery"	66
Isaac Shemwell	pt. "Devonshire"	50
	pt. "Trumania"	50
	"Derbyshire"	130
Thomas Spalding	pt. "~~Great~~ St. Thomas"	200
39:1756:17 ...		
Thomas Spalding (Leonard Town) (cnp)	pt. "Cragburns Purchase"	100
	"Spaldings Addition"	42
	pt. "St. Giles"	35
	"Spaldings Adventure"	207

	"Rich Neck"	150
Benjamin Branson	"Drayton"	57
	"Kenady" a/s "Kieldfield"	96½
	"Keith & Prices Rest"	122
	pt. "Best Land"	10
George Thompson	pt. "Hazard"	100
William Hall	pt. "Graden"	100
William Watson	"Edenborough"	100
James Pike	"Forrest Den"	100
George Leigh	"Innis's Chance"	100
	"Gallowith"	50
	"Innis's Reserve"	25
	"Perth"	150
	"Inclosure"	170
Peter Drury	pt. "Bottom"	50
Athanasius Ford	pt. "Strand"	91
William Thomas	"Wails"	200
	"Wails Addition"	91
	pt. "Boston"	50
	"Bogg's" (additional rent roll)	19
39:1756:18 ...		
George Warring	pt. "St. Johns"	68
	pt. "Burch Hanger"	75
Luke Mattingly	pt. "Hazzard"	100
John Higgs	"Wednesday Project"	98
	"Higgs's Purchase"	49
John Harbert	"Harberts Invention"	109
	"Good Yielding"	86
	pt. "Good Yielding" on resurvey	67
Francis Ratcliff	pt. "Doe Park"	50
William Jenkins	pt. "Truth & Trust"	273
	"Salem"	215
	"Croyden"	100
	"St. Thomas"	300
	"Addition"	103
	"Fox Range"	70

Thomas Watts	"Smoot"	50
William Martin	pt. "Hopewell"	74
	"Crackson's Rest"	50
	"Redmans Hardship"	50
	pt. "Hopeless"	11
Thomas Hall	pt. "Long Look'd for Come at Last"	112
Peter Brown	pt. "White Acre"	222
39:1756:19 ...		
Rev. James Ashby	"St. Innego's Manner" & "St. Georges Island"	3000
Charles Beech	"Goslings Addition"	30
	pt. "Parting Path"	26
	"Stiles Chance"	25
Elizabeth Gosling (widow)	pt. "Parting Path"	274
	"Garden Spot"	80
Henry G. Sothoron	pt. "Brotherhood"	140
	"Sothorons Hills"	50
	pt. "Wastham"	100
Matthew Guibert	pt. "Dynard"	81
Thead. Jordan	pt. "St. Clements Mannor"	130
Philip Greenwell	"Honest Jones Inheritance"	150
Richard Fenwick, Jr.	"Mayheard's Comfort"	100
	"Gareths Purchase" a/s pt. "Charles West Discovery"	40½
	"Fenwicks Gain"	55
Thomas Tippett	pt. "Suttle's Range"	213
William Lock	"Good Pennyworth"	50
	"Fairfield"	50
	"Lock's Venture"	49
Horn Roberts	pt. "Freshpond Neck"	203
Thomas Morton	pt. "St. Johns"	100
39:1756:20 ...		
Mrs. Forbes	"Orphans Gift"	400
	"Holbridge Town"	133
	"Drayden"	483
Charles Ridghill	"Inclosure"	50
John Ford, Sr. (cnp)	pt. "Farthings Gift" a/s "Minsterdam"	10

	pt. "Durham"	100
	pt. "Long in Dispence"	75
Mark Thompson	pt. "Hatsfield Hills"	25
Henry Cooper	pt. "Scotland"	150
John Sissell	pt. "Scotland"	150
Luke Sissell	pt. "Scotland"	50
James Sissell	"Sissell's Venture"	88
Sarah Sissell	pt. "Baily's Rest"	150
James Brown	"Drydocking Addition"	100
James Boyde	pt. "Hopton Park" tbc John Bond	160
Alexander Forgisson	pt. "Small Hope"	9
	"Small Hope Addition"	42
	pt. "Black Creek"	99
Thomas Redman	pt. "Small Hopes Addition"	100
39:1756:21 ...		
Mark Tyler	"Branch"	50
Clement Spink	pt. "Guellmots Hills"	180
	"All Thats Left"	31¼
	pt. "Guellmotts Hills"	150
John Tennison	pt. "Outlet"	50
John Mattingly	"Thames" tbc Mr. Key	110
	"Mattingly's Addition"	50
Sarah Greenwell	"Holly Tree"	148
John Smith (Newtown)	"Nun's Oake"	142
William Howard	"Pomphry Fields"	100
Enoch Greenwell	"Hickory Hollows"	119
	"Farthings Adventure"	78
	pt. "Wheatly's Content" a/s "Back Land"	55
Thomas Thompson	"Adjoinder" a/s "St. John's Addition"	23
	pt. "Dynard"	13
	pt. "Chance"	89
John Key	pt. "Weston"	100
	pt. "Knotleys Addition"	175
	"Gardiner's Landing"	100
James Smith (Rock Creek) (cnp)	pt. "Outlet"	119
	"Fresh Pond"	1243

	"Mitcham Meadows"	100
	pt. "Hampstead"	100
	pt. "Black Creek"	30
39:1756:22 ...		
John Horrill	pt. "Weston Addition"	100
	pt. "Weston Addition"	13
	"Horrills Meadows"	10
George Thompson	pt. "Rockey Point"	50
Walter Davis	pt. "St. Williams Hermitage"	110
Richard Payne	pt. "Strife"	50
Clement Newton	"Newton's Rest"	63
	"Newton's Rest with Addition"	37
Samuel Johnson	pt. "Hopewell"	36
	"Addition" or "Piana's Groves"	19
Elizabeth Hayden	"Roach's Discovery"	251
	"Hayden's Risque"	81
William Edley	pt. "Hayden's Fair"	100
William Hayden	pt. "Hayden's Fair"	100
Michael Wellman	pt. "Style's Chance"	100
Mary Watts	pt. "Jesbury Plains"	100
John Goss Laurence	"Frogg Marsh"	100
William Egerton	pt. "Punkley's Marsh"	100
William Biggs	pt. "St. Clements Mannor"	100
Fran. Thompson	"Hard Fortune"	100
39:1756:23 ...		
Just. Greenwell	pt. "Rochester"	100
Margaret Plummer	"Orbuston's Oake"	50
	"Hobson's Choice"	30
William Doxey	"Smiths Rest"	108
William Cavenough	pt. "Massom"	250
	"Eyre"	328
h/o Richard Vowle	pt. "Vowle's Purchase"	120
	pt. "Brittan's Outlet"	1
Robert Hammett (cnp)	"Hammetts Beginning"	34
	pt. "Burch Spring"	75
	pt. "Forrest Harvey"	100

	"Wild Cat Neck"	104½
	"Hickory Hall"	17½
	"Hammett & Chance"	64
Clement Mattingly	pt. "Vowle's Purchase"	239
h/o Peter Muggs	pt. "Vowle's Addition"	80
	"St. Williams"	50
	pt. "Vowle's Purchase"	57
	pt. "Rockey Point"	50
James Greenwell	"Wheatly's Content"	75
Elizabeth King	pt. "Burch Springs"	50
James Biscoe, Jr.	pt. "Hogg Neck"	100
39:1756:24 ...		
Joshua Millard	"Neale's Lot"	209½
	pt. "Little St. Thomas"	16
	pt. "St. Johns"	134
Luke Norris	pt. "Wheatly's Content"	69
Ignatius Thompson	"Fibny"	100
Thomas Medley	"Barren Doe"	95
John Mills	"Yielding Bury"	99
	pt. "Hopton Park"	80
Robert Drury	"Honnards Mount"	40
Richard Cooper	pt. "Clarker"	100
	"Frightful"	180
	"Clarken Addition"	94
	"Dynard"	100
	"Hopewell"	65
	"Expence"	67
	pt. "Cragburn's Purchase"	100
John Walter	pt. "Partnership"	65
Richard Burroughes	"Hold Fast"	76
	pt. "Long Look'd for Come at Last"	75
John Willson	"Indian Giants Sepulchre"	203
Abraham Hall	"Gardners Grove"	50
39:1756:25 ...		
Thomas Hayes	pt. "Gardiner's Grove"	197
	"Addition to Gardiner's Grove"	82

Edward Mahorny	"Piles's Discovery"	112
John Parsons	"Addition"	50
	pt. "Long Look'd for Come at Last"	112
James Watson	"Hedge Barren"	79
James Swann	pt. "Swann's Adventure"	63½
Stephen Cawood	pt. "Williamson's Chance"	100
	pt. "Wastham"	200
	"Cawoods Expence"	157
Edward Barber	pt. "Swann's Forest"	56
	pt. "Wastham"	250
	pt. "Luckland" or "Eastham"	38
John Shanks	pt. "St. Oswell"	100
Joshua Greenwell	"Last Shift"	100
John Wiseman Greenwell	"This or None"	50
	"John Wiseman Greenwell's Park"	49
	"Piles's Wood Lane"	200
Hezekiah Briscoe	pt. "Retirement"	92
h/o Benjamin Gough	pt. "St. Margarets"	100
39:1756:26 ...		
Charles Jarbeo	pt. "St. Peters Hills"	112
John Evans	"Ishmael's Right"	165
John Smith, Jr.	"Haphazzard"	304
John Wheatly	"Hickory Thickett"	48
	pt. "Hanover Addition"	45
John Knott	"Sharp"	44
Peter Payne	pt. "Honnards Mount"	75
John Hooper	"Ashcoms Greenfield"	100
Thomas Spalding s/o Thomas	pt. "~~Great~~ St. Thomas"	100
	pt. "Little St. Thomas"	100
William McWilliams	pt. "Batchellors Rest"	300
	pt. "St. Clements Mannor"	100
	"Josias Plains"	16¾
William Peake	pt. "Hanover"	140
	pt. "Hanover Addition"	60
	pt. "Heards Security"	91
Henry Neale (cnp)	pt. "Hillelee"	250

	pt. "St. Clements Mannor"	400
Thomas Hulston	"Buck Land Plains" included in "Wheatlys Plains" (Thomas Wheatly)	35
Richard Gardiner	"Poplar Hill"	200
	"Middle Ground"	50
	"Floods Quarter"	50
39:1756:27 ...		
Thomas Greaves	pt. "Greaves's Chance"	120
	pt. "Baptist Hope"	106
	"Hopewell"	99
	"Hardshift"	10
	"Prince William Newcastle"	50
	pt. "Greaves's Chance"	10
John Ford (Courthouse)	pt. "Lampton's Pleasure"	150
	"Ford's Inclosure"	255
Richard Fenwick	"Chance Conclusion"	97
	"Addition to Chance Conclusion"	26
Mary Bright	pt. "Cold Wells"	65
Philip Key, Esq. (cnp)	"Bushwoods Lodge"	411
	pt. "Thames"	40
	"James Addition"	158
	pt. "St. Johns"	50
	"Addition to Peters Wills"	104
	pt. "Burch Hanger"	230
	"Cuckold Haven" & timber land	77
	pt. "Wems"	430
	"Woods Pleasure" & pt. "Chesham"	95
	pt. "Maiden Bower"	100
	pt. "Finchly"	102
	"Boston"	98
	pt. "Westham"	87
	pt. "Boston & Peach Blossom"	55
	"Luck Land" a/s "Covent Garden"	200
	pt. "Dynard"	119
	pt. "Shurance" & "Yieldingberry"	75
	pt. "Milton Hope"	150

	pt. "Yieldingbury"	88
	pt. "Little Yielding"	35
	"Penryn" or "St. Clements Manner"	192
39:1756:28 ...		
Ignatius Greenwell	pt. "Wheatly's Meadows"	123
Mary Wheatly	pt. "Wheatly's Meadows"	153
Charles Daft	pt. "Medley"	200
Peter Peake, Jr.	pt. "Hannover Addition"	50
John Melton	pt. "Burch Hanger"	94
Gilbert Ireland	"Edenborough 10th Addition"	121½
	pt. "St. Williams Hermitage"	73
	pt. "Hopton Park"	140
	pt. "Baptis Hope"	153
	pt. "Yieldingbury"	17
	"Evans's Lot" a/s "Hampstead"	50
John Guither	pt. "Croft Rectified"	147
	"Saturday's Venture"	2½
	"Cornelius Swamp"	100
Ignatius Wheeler	pt. "Hopton Park"	50
Capt. Richard Ward Key	"Wolf Hole"	262
	"Addition to Guiberts Chance"	37
William Rogers	"Roger's Venture"	50
Elianor Gardiner	pt. "St. John's"	500
Leah Ward	"Ward's Defence"	100
39:1756:29 ...		
Anthony Brown	"Clark's Rest"	300
Samuel Abell	pt. "Kirby's Chance"	118
	pt. "Squable"	25
	"Scrubby Thicket"	25
	pt. "Wheatly's Chance"	41
Peter Oneale	pt. "Cragburn's Purchase"	60
Kenelm Boult	pt. "Collingwood"	25
John Black (cnp)	pt. "Massom"	200
	"Cadocks Measure"	150
	"Court Freehold" or "Harts Hall"	200
	"Fox Hill"	30

	"Adjoinder"	50
	"Gravelly Hill"	50
	"Oyster Shell Neck"	50
	"Newgents Venture"	50
	"Blumberry"	100
	"Dunbarr"	92
	"Butchers Slipe"	42
	"Poplar Point"	101
Barton Smoot	"Clark's Range"	393
William Field	pt. "Batchellors Rest"	50
William Love	pt. "Partnership"	100
Enoch Fenwick, Jr.	pt. "St. Peter's Hills"	150
	pt. "Cole Brook Level"	35
	pt. "Spinks Rest"	65
39:1756:30 ...		
Thomas Moony	pt. "St. Edwards"	115
	"Tradesman's Lot"	200
	pt. "Linstead"	18
	pt. "Valentines Grove"	96
Daniel Harris	"Kingston"	50
	"Wheatly's Hill"	38
John Hynes	"Bite the Fox"	19
	"Hunters Hills"	150
James Anderson	pt. "Baker's Fancy"	78
	pt. "Cornelius"	39
	"Addition to Charles Park"	20
Charles Flower	pt. "St. Georges Point"	50
Benjamin Williams	"Esquires Purchase"	37
	pt. "Muggs Adventure"	200
	"Fox's Den"	89
	"Baker's Fancy"	25
	"New Fancy"	25
	pt. "Punkley's Marsh"	100
John Tear	"Hollyday"	142
Enoch Fenwick	pt. "Fenwick Mannor"	175
Ignatius Heard	pt. "Well Found"	106

Sabina Truman Greenfield	"America Felix"	152
39:1756:31 ...		
Thomas Newton	"Underwood" a/s "Newton's Propriety"	124
	"Greenwell's Marsh"	14
Ann Greenfield	"Greenfield's Discovery"	98
	"Trent Neck"	835
	"Stockbardolph"	75
James Truman Greenfield	"Keeche's Folley"	133
	"Lamly"	100
	"Punk Neck"	60
	"Holbridge Town"	130
	pt. "Hopton Park"	120
Nathaniel Truman Greenfield	"Fork"	60
	"Addition"	78
	"Whitehaven"	164
	"Indian Creek & Addition"	491
	"Nighthood" & "Bashford Mannor"	154
	"Thimblebe"	109
	"Fishing Place"	50
	"Brough Land"	75
James Warwick	pt. "St. John's"	150
John Dunbar	"Chance"	240
Edward Caster for h/o (N) Redman	"Redman's Hardship"	50
John Cole (St. George's)	"Jone's Wood"	100
	"Addition to Jones Wood"	59½
Lydia Bright	pt. "Cold Wells"	65
Ignatius Chamberlane	pt. "St. Peter's Hills" tbc Enoch Fenwick Jr. (f. 29)	113
39:1756:32 ...		
John Michaell Thomas Taney	pt. "Fenwick Mannor"	450
Joseph Clarke	"Mattingly's Hope"	70
	pt. "St. Johns"	300
	pt. "Cole Park" a/s "Charles's Discovery"	122
Sarah Carter	"Meer Chance"	113
Mary Hamersly	"Carbury's Discovery"	190
John Dant (cnp)	"Hopewell"	100

	pt. "Yoke by Chance"	20
John Jones	"Poverty"	64
Thomas Yates	pt. "St. Peter's Hills"	100
	pt. "Small Hopes"	30
	pt. "Hanover"	60
	pt. "Heards Security"	70
Enoch Combs	pt. "Pork Hall"	300
	"Grape Hill"	200
	"Wilderpole"	300
John Wherret	pt. "Watts's Lodge"	90
Thomas Cooke, Jr.	pt. "Brough"	68
Joseph Harding	"Baily's Rest"	100
John McKey	pt. "McKey's Neck"	153
	pt. "St. Richard's Mannor"	50
	pt. "Massom"	100
39:1756:33 ...		
Samuel Bellwood	"Ishmael's Right"	65
	"Bellwoods Grove"	128
	pt. "Stiles's Chance"	16
Fairfax Compton	pt. "Honard Mount"	75
George Rogers	pt. "Well Close"	100
	"Brothers Dread"	135
John Norris	"Gough's Levels"	42
	"Gough's Conveniency"	48
	"Brittain Bay"	1
William Roach	pt. "St. John's Landing"	117
	pt. "St. John's Addition"	167
William Guither	"Maids Right"	100
	pt. "Smoot"	100
Cuthbert Clark	"Chesley"	100
William Taylor	"Poplar Hill"	63
	"Taylor's Lot"	22
John Baker (bayside)	pt. "Draper's Neck"	285
Francis Wheatly	pt. "Wheatly's Content"	66
	"Buckland"	50
Leonard Greenwell	pt. "Hanover Addition"	87

George Would	pt. "Hanover"	103
John Thomas	"Hampton"	100
39:1756:34 ...		
Clement Norris	"Tants Mark"	168
	"Norris's Frolick"	3½
Thomas Howard	pt. "Guilmots Hills"	75
Joseph Stevens	pt. "Devonshire"	50
	"Trumania"	50
	"Joseph's Venture"	54
Samuel Lee	"Well Close"	82
	pt. "St. Clements Mannor"	105
John Bready	pt. "Baily's Rest"	100
	"Bready's Lot"	25
Peter Ford	pt. "St. Giles's"	81
	"Mount Pleasant"	100
	"May Pole"	96
	pt. "Strand"	91
Thomas Wheatly	"Wheatly's Plains"	204
John Chesley	pt. "Cragburn"	300
	"Cragburns Island"	13
	"Cragburn's Marsh"	17½
	pt. "Indian Creek"	36
Thomas Greenfield	pt. "Indian Creek"	843
	pt. "Good Luck"	275
Thomas Bond	"Knotting"	100
39:1756:35 ...		
Rev. John Urquhart	pt. "Fawnskirk"	250
	"Spring Blossom"	221
	pt. "Keith & Price's Rest"	60
	"Hopewell's Chance"	170
Benjamin Gristy	"Venture"	50
Thomas Clark	pt. "Moffat's Will"	69
Thomas Breedon	pt. "Moffat's Will"	69
John Biscoe	"Barren Wood"	46
Henry Wimsat	"Harberts Grief"	44
	pt. "Nun's Oake"	20

James Dickson	"Dickson's Venture" or "Hayden's Fair"	115½
h/o Edward Pye	"Underwood"	300
John Adams	"Small Hope with Addition"	50
John Greaves	pt. "Greaves's Chance"	94
James Thompson (head Chaptico)	pt. "St. John's"	50
	"Harberts Swamp"	21
Joseph Stevens, Jr.	"Stevens's Chance"	46
	"Parnasses"	75
39:1756:36 ...		
Ignatius Greenwell	"St. Ignatius's"	100
	"Addition"	25
Mary Fenwick	pt. "Fenwick Mannor"	200
Daniel Watts	"Watts's Lodge"	160
John Plummer	pt. "Elizabeth Mannor"	300
Richard Shirley	"Shirley's Adventure"	150
Thomas Keen	"Keen's Rest"	49
Thomas Matthews	"Friends Conjunction"	72
Edward Aprice	pt. "St. Barbary's"	100
John Anderson	"Sothoron's Desire"	100
	pt. "Fox's Race"	52
Benjamin Beane	pt. "Friends Conjuction"	72
John Sykes	pt. "Friends Conjuction"	106
	"Thompson Lot"	n/g
John Thompson	"Mitcham Meadows"	100
	"Thompson's Lot"	172
39:1756:37 ...		
h/o Mark Thomas	"Penancy"	100
	"Brewer's Woodhouse"	50
	"Lukes Hardship"	7
	"Mark's Adventure"	36
Henry How	"White Land"	225
	"How's Fortune"	14
	"How's Advance"	42
John Biscoe	pt. "Harrison's Rest" a/s "Williams Fortune"	80
	pt. "Williams Fortune"	32
Dr. William Marray	"Indian Creek"	563

Peter Peake	pt. "Friends Goodwill"	100
Benjamin Fenwick	pt. "Fenwick Mannor"	200
Robert Henley	pt. "Massom"	150
	"John's Content"	93½
	"Keen's Rest"	50
Robert Newgent	"Marking Place"	100
	"Fox Catched"	11
James Smith	"Trinity", "St. Gabriel" & "St Michael's Mannor"	3000
	"Pountly's Oversight"	198
	"Tripple Defence"	206
	"Addition to Tripple Defence"	87
	"Pine Land"	388
	pt. "Turvey"	201
	"Hazzard"	57
39:1756:38 ...		
Cornelius Wildman	"Brooke Chance"	81
	"Dyllions Disappointment"	103
	"Williams Venture"	54
	"Goulding Grove"	153
	"Tavern"	100
Enoch Abell	"Saturday's Conclusion"	55
	pt. "Wheatly's Chance"	50
	"Hobson's Choice"	23½
John Medley Thompson	pt. "Scotland"	50
Thomas Barber	pt. "Burch Hanger"	20
Charles Greenwell	"Farther Adventure"	65½
Thomas Jordan	pt. "Collingwood"	25
John Clark	"Evans's Quarter"	100
Michael Goldsmith	pt. "St. Clements Mannor"	86
	pt. "Bashford Mannor"	100
William Aude	pt. "Hanover"	30
James Chizzam	"Baker's Fancy"	100
John Shiercliffe (cnp)	"Shiercliffe"	250
	"St. Williams"	90
	"Q Name"	100
	pt. "Linstead"	78

	pt. "Linstead Addition"	100
	"Coles Adventure"	150
39:1756:39 ...		
Richard Millard	"Little St. Thomas"	84
	"St. John's"	50
	"Turner's Plains"	16
Thomas Pearce	pt. "Cortany's Fancy"	50
Kenelm T. Greenfield	pt. "Trent Neck"	1519
Henry Lowes	"Warnett"	240
Henry Jarbo	pt. "St. Peters Hills"	126
Henry Bryan	"Williams's Endeavour"	50
	pt. "Farther Adventure"	37
	"Green's Plot"	44
William Deacon, Esq.	pt. "St. Peter's"	50
	pt. "Chandler's Point"	112
	pt. "St. Mary's Freehold"	248
William Hicks	pt. "St. Peters"	100
	"Governor's Fieldy"	100
	"Chapple Freehold"	25
	pt. "St. Mary's Freehold"	7
John Miles	"Wastfield"	100
	"Somerset"	195
Edward Parsons	pt. "Guiberts Chance"	50
	"Small Addition"	19½
39:1756:40 ...		
Sabastian Thompson	"Thompson's Expence"	108
Joseph Jenkins	pt. "Truth & Trust"	400
William Heard	pt. "Wellfound"	186
	pt. "Fenwick Mannor"	175
George Plater, Esq.	pt. "St. Joseph's"	819
	"Bowle's Preservation"	898
	pt. "Fenwick Mannor"	400
	"Steuarts Hope"	125
	"Resurrection Mannor"	4000
Richard Raper (cnp)	"Maynard's Comfort"	100
	pt. "Baily's Fortune"	45

	pt. "St. Clements Mannor"	50
	pt. "Baptist's Hope"	100
Thomas Doxey	pt. "Harrison's Rest"	78
Richard Brooke	"DelleBrooke Mannor"	2000
	"Two Brother"	285
	pt. "Back Land"	400
Thomas Hobson	pt. "Weems"	100
Elizabeth Hulse	pt. "Wastham"	150
Charles King	"Deptford"	300
	pt. "St. Joseph's"	200
Just. Greenwell	pt. "Kirby's Choice"	67
39:1756:41 ...		
William Williams	"Dry Docking"	100
	pt. "Shock Park"	76
	pt. "Roberts Neck" a/s "Medley"	95
	"Harberts Grief"	60
	pt. "Roberts Freehold"	75
Robert Fenwick	pt. "St. Joseph's"	126
John Mareman	pt. "Hopton Park"	197
	"Vowles's Purchase"	156
Samuel Genifer	pt. "St. Joseph's"	50
Leonard Green	pt. "Fenwick Mannor"	50
Thomas Manly	pt. "Elizabeth Mannor"	100
Thomas Bladen, Esq.	pt. "Elizabeth Mannor"	247
	pt. "Cross Mannor"	500
Stourton Edwards	"St. Thomas"	190
	"Doe Park"	69
	pt. "Hanover"	100
Thomas Brome	pt. "No Name"	250
John Lancaster	pt. "Hillelee"	250
	pt. "St. Clements Mannor"	400
Peter Gough	pt. "Lewgroess Plains"	100
39:1756:42 ...		
James Hagoe	pt. "Beverdam"	59
John Abell (cnp)	pt. "Wheatly's Chance"	31
	pt. "Kirby's Choice"	88

	pt. "St. Joseph's"	56
Cuthbert Abell	"Wiseman's Chance"	180
Benjamin Redman	"Small Hope with Addition"	50
Dennis Burn	pt. "Beckworths Lodge"	81½
Joseph Walker	pt. "Guillmotts Hills"	100
	"Addition to Fortune"	140
Ignatius Baily	pt. "Little Yielding"	117
William Jones	"Salters Hall"	83
	"Addition to Salters Hall"	34
	"Jones Conveniency"	35½
	pt. "Beckworths Lodge"	81½
	"Jones's Lane"	2¾
	"Mugg's Adventure"	52
John Jarbeo	pt. "Hanover"	17
	pt. "Heards Security"	24
Thomas Warring	"Warren's Lot"	148
Matthias Nottingham	"Salmon"	50
39:1756:43 ...		
Ruth Jones	"Davis's Forrest"	50
Henry Spalding	pt. "Joseph"	152
	"Two Brother"	165
	pt. "New Castle"	50
	pt. "Rich Neck"	98
Thomas Devaun	pt. "Partnership"	200
John Watson	pt. "Partnership"	65
George Maxwell	pt. "Indian Creek with Addition"	461
Col. Abra. Barnes	"America Felix Secundus"	956
	pt. "Ranglefield"	40
	pt. "Forrest Harvey"	100
	"Westbury Mannor"	1250
	pt. "Forest Lodge"	100
	pt. "Draper's Neck"	215
	"Walnut Point"	55
Zachariah Bond	pt. "St. Barbary's"	200
William Doxey, Jr.	pt. "Patricks Hills"	50
Edm. Bowling	pt. "Callicoaw"	25

John Morris	pt. "Callicoaw"	25
Francis Knott	pt. "Hazzard"	56
Peter Peake	pt. "Woolverhampton" tbc Andrew Mills	0
39:1756:44 ...		
George Bowles	"Steplikon Fortune"	20
	"Hazzard"	234½
John Tippet	"Tippets Purchase"	46
William Spalding	pt. "Rich Neck"	152
Mark Norris	pt. "Wheatly's Content"	118
	pt. "Buckland Plains"	70
Ignatius Fenwick	"Hepton Hole"	350
	pt. "Hepton Hole"	70
John Holt	pt. "St. Clements Mannor"	167
Ignatius Wheeler	pt. "St. Clements Mannor"	250
John Lee	pt. "St. Clements Mannor"	200
John Haskins	pt. "St. Clements Mannor"	100
John Bapt. Greenwell	pt. "Rochester"	100
John Bould	pt. "Cadle"	150
	"Addition to White Acre"	25
John Wimsatt	pt. "Hatfield's Hill"	73
John Bullock	pt. "St. Clements Mannor"	100
Thomas Wherrit	"Hogg Neck"	100
39:1756:45 ...		
John Bohannan	"Fox Grape Barren"	106
David Downie	"Town Support"	81
	"Bary"	65
	3 lots in Leonard Town	3
James Jarbeo	"Denby"	250
Thomas Jenkins	"Poplar Point"	100
Benjamin Moulton	pt. "Bashford Mannor"	200
John Pike	"Forny Branch"	50
Clement Medley	pt. "Medley"	200
William Medley	pt. "Medley"	100
Basil Peake	pt. "Medley"	100
George Greenwell	pt. "Medley"	50
John Lewellin	pt. "St. Clements Mannor"	400

John Fenwick	pt. "Rivets Backside"	172
	pt. "Rivets"	151
	pt. "Chancellors Point"	112
	pt. "Crofts Rectified"	100
Bennet Neale	pt. "St. Clements Mannor"	200
Austin Leigh Massey	"Plumb Point"	308
Elizabeth Lock	pt. "Cold Wells"	65½
39:1756:46 ...		
Stephen Chilton	pt. "Peter's Quay"	50
	"Fishing Creek Neck"	44
Richard Milburn	pt. "Halfhead Folley"	100
	"Milburns Chance"	178
	pt. "Cortany's Neck"	82
John Smith	pt. "Mattapany"	289
Clement Spalding	"Spalding's Adventure"	729
John Eden	pt. "Bashford Mannor"	277
John Bond	pt. "St. Clements Mannor"	605
	pt. "Hopton Park"	400
	pt. "St. Johns"	438
	"Gardiners Chance"	155
	pt. "Burlington" or "St. Clements Mannor"	25
Richard Edelen	"Truman's Hunting Quarter"	200
	pt. "Hope"	64
Just. Jordan	pt. "St. Clements Mannor"	200
George Baxter	"Batchellors Comfort"	190
George Slye	pt. "St. Clements Mannor"	1000
	"Wee Bitt"	50
John Boult	pt. "St. Clements Mannor"	100
Edward Turner	pt. "Bashford Mannor"	200
39:1756:47 ...		
Charles Sewall	pt. "Little Eltonhead Mannor"	58
	"Sewalls Discovery"	117
John Blackiston	pt. "St. Clements Mannor"	550
	pt. "St. Clements Island"	100
John Mason	pt. "St. Clements Mannor"	450
Mary Tennison	pt. "St. Clements Mannor"	100

Kenelm Chiseldyne	pt. "St. Clements Mannor"	725
Cyrenius Chiseldyne	pt. "St. Clements Mannor"	25
Charles Carroll, Esq.	pt. "St. Clements Mannor"	1650
	"Orford"	209
	pt. "Barbary's Addition"	250
	pt. "Longbrough"	150
	"Addition"	41
	"Temple Barr"	100
John Maddox	pt. "Bashford Mannor"	150
John Reshwick	pt. 2 tracts escheated land	47
Edward Welsh	"Osfield"	72
John Attaway Clarke	pt. "Poney Point"	750
	pt. "James Johnson's Neck"	200
	"Blake Creek"	50
	"Tower Hill"	25
Robert Hagoe	pt. "Truth & Trust"	100
39:1756:48 ...		
Nicholas Lewis Sewall	pt. "Mattapany Level"	911
	"Sewell's Discovery"	108
	"Fishing Point"	13
	pt. "Jesham"	50
Leonard Davis	pt. "Desart"	62½
	"Thorn's Venture"	103
James Wheatly	"Kington" a/s "Newtonquit"	117
	pt. "Wheatly's Addition"	21
John Smith	pt. "Bashford Mannor"	200
Mary McWilliams	pt. "St. Clements Mannor"	300
Stourton Edwards, Jr.	"Taunton Dean"	164
Thomas Suite	pt. "Trent Fort"	84
	pt. "Horse Range"	100
James Mills	pt. "Bashford Mannor"	100
Leonard Mattingly	"Audly End"	190
Notley Goldsmith	pt. "Bashford Mannor"	100
Roger Smith	pt. "Notley's Addition"	275
Dent Suite	pt. "Horse Range"	100
Thomas Crane	"Dally"	100

John Ford (weaver)	"Pomphry Fields"	50
	"Minsterdam"	54
Henry Taylor	"Taylor's Plains"	50½
39:1756:49 ...		
Thomas Suite, Jr.	pt. "Wells"	100
Joseph Edwards	pt. "Walls"	52
	pt. "Trent Fort"	8
Thomas Wyn Taylor	pt. "Righting"	100
Clement Medley, Sr.	"No Name"	100
John Somervell	pt. "St. Richards Mannor"	100
	"Bayly's" a/s "Clark's Discovery"	99
	pt. "St. Jeroms Mannor"	200
John Michael Waughop	"Waughop's Chance"	138
John Coode	pt. "St. Clements Mannor"	300
Anthony Roberts	"Twittenham"	200
Benjamin Burroughes	pt. "Trent Fort"	129
Peter Ford, Jr.	"Nun's Oake"	75
John Curlett	"Willingborough"	70
h/o James Heath	pt. "St. Jerom's Mannor"	5500
James Kindrick	"Kindricks Lane"	80
John Reeves	pt. "Bashford Mannor"	100
John Kelley	"Kelly's Luck"	138
	"Kelley's Fortune"	182
39:1756:50 ...		
James Tarlton	pt. "Beverdam"	59
	pt. "Elizabeth"	34
Samuel Swann	pt. "Swann's Forrest"	40
	"Swanns Venture"	140
James Latimore	pt. "Hopewell"	89½
Leonard Payne	"Fox"	100
Rev. Arnold Livers	"Little Brittain"	750
	pt. "Brittains Outlet"	43
James Baily	pt. "St. Clements Mannor"	45
Thomas Yates, Jr.	pt. "St. Clements Mannor"	100
John Goldsmith	pt. "Bashford Mannor"	100
Samuel Maddox	pt. "Bashford Mannor"	38

Thomas Vowles	pt. "Vowle's Purchase"	50
Thomas Melton	pt. "Burch Hanger"	95
George Bullock	pt. "Burlington" or "St. Clements Mannor"	75
39:1756:51-3	**...**	
39:1756:54	**entries left out.**	
James Boyd	pt. "Hopton Park" included in John Bond	n/g
John Mattingly	pt. "Thames" included in Mr. Keys	40
Ignatius Chamberlain	pt. "St. Peters Hills" included in Enoch Fenwick, Jr.	113
Peter Peake	pt. "Wolverhampton" included in Andrew Mills	75
Sarah Lee (widow)	"Forest Lodge"	50
John Apprice, Zachariah Bond, & Jos. Peters	pt. "St. Barbaras"	200

39:1757:1 ...		Acres
Daniel Clocker	"Clockers Freehold"	50
	"Lewis's Neck"	30
Elisabeth Clocker	"St. Anne's Freehold"	70¼
	"Clockers Fancy"	56
Thomas Palmer Waughop	"Hunting Quarter"	150
	"Poiney Point"	750
	"Smoots Hallow"	150
Nicholas Sewall	pt. "Little Elton Head Mannor"	1590
Edward Digges	pt. "Little Elton Head Mannor"	300
William Price	"Brick Hall"	217
	"Park's Addition"	100
Ignatius Taylor	pt. "Little Eltonhead Mannor" a/s "Governours Gift"	60
James Dafforon	"Cole Harbour"	150
George Aisquith	"Stinmore"	100
	"Inclosure"	33
	"Thomas & George in Company"	4½
John Roades	pt. "Jesbury Plains"	330
Isaac Pavatt	"Cow Ridge"	50
	pt. "Cross Manner"	150
Robert Pearce	pt. "Cortany's Fancy"	50
	pt. "Prices Chance"	25
39:1757:2 ...		
Thomas Thorp	"Strife"	50
Fargus Keough	"Surgeons Folley"	50
	'Wills Swamp"	150
	"Readers Addition"	79
James Styles	pt. "Styles Chance"	59
	pt. "What Care I"	28½
	pt. "Chance"	6
	pt. "Elizabeth Mannor"	43
John Price	"Grove"	50
	"Farnhans"	83
Robert Greenwell (cnp)	pt. "Backland"	70
	pt. "Lamptons Pleasure"	117

	pt. "Greenwells Marsh"	49
Robert Vaulx	pt. "Massom"	100
Barnaby Egan	pt. "Massom"	100
	pt. "Hopewell"	100
	pt. "Strife"	100
	"Harberts Beginning"	50
	"Clockers Marsh"	100
	"Lordships Favour"	100
	"Dunbar"	100
	"Addition" taken up by Mr. DeButts	20
Rev. Moses Tabbs	"Itchcombs Freehold"	340
James White	pt. "Fresh Pond Neck"	150
39:1757:3 ...		
Richard Barnhouse	pt. "Cross Mannor"	1000
	pt. "Elizabeth Mannor"	1000
John Cole (Newtown)	pt. "Rivits Backside"	50
	"Nobles Victor"	50
	"Harberts Gift"	43
	pt. "Shock Park"	24
John Mitchell	"Mitchells Choice"	47
Cornelius Barber	pt. "Luckland"	470
	"Nicholls's Hope"	135
Baptist Barber	pt. "Wastham"	250
	pt. "Luckland"	200
	"Leighe"	100
Elizabeth Donaldson	pt. "Mitcham Hills"	200
Philip Barton, Esq.	pt. "Mitcham Hills"	100
George Latham	pt. "Mitcham Meadows"	100
Luke Russell	pt. "Brough"	50
James Gough	"St. Barnards"	100
	"St. Margarets"	200
	"Bacon Neck"	200
	"Proprietarys Gift"	50
	"Q Name"	50
	"St. Teresia"	100

William Morgan (St. Michaels)	"Hazzard"	73
	"Addition to White Birch Freehold"	53
	pt. "St. Patricks Hills"	15
	"White Birch Freehold"	100
39:1757:4 ...		
William Sissell	pt. "Caydle"	50
Thomas Sissell	pt. "White Acre"	50
	pt. "Addition to White Acre"	18
John Thompson	pt. "Davis's Forrest"	50
George Booth, Jr.	pt. "Hopton Park"	56
Mary Greenwell	pt. "Green Hill"	221
Athanasius Nottingham	"Nevit's St. Ann"	100
Clement Stratford	"Leeing"	100
Thomas Hatton Combs	"Hattons Rest"	250
	"Addition to Hearts Delight"	152
John Heard	pt. "St. Laurence Freehold"	193
	pt. "Heards Security"	43
	pt. "Hanover"	350
Peter Howard	"Twittenham"	100
Mark Jarbeo	pt. "Heards Security"	40
	pt. "Hanover"	20
John Norris	"Shiercliffe"	300
John Bapt. Carbery	pt. "Hopton Park"	797
Edward Hillard Hebb	"Little Recovery of Birth Right"	13
William Mattingly	pt. "Suttles Rest"	80
39:1757:5 ...		
Matthew Heard	"Pole"	120
	"William Heards Purchase"	115
	"Ashcoms Freehold"	150
	pt. "Hanover Addition"	123
	"Heards Choice"	100
	pt. "Heards Security"	169
Mark Heard	"Thirds"	425
James Taylor (St. Mary's)	pt. "Snow Hill"	100
Matthew Hebb	"Small Hopes"	56
John French	pt. "Hopton Park"	160

Arthur Thompson	"Thompson's Expence"	125
John Hammond	pt. "Lewgroes Plains"	209
William Watts	"Bushel's Rest"	150
John Gardiner (St. Georges)	"Timber Swamp"	100
	"Addition to Timber Swamp"	60
William Hebb	"Gardiners Purchase"	100
	"St. Williams"	114
	"Freehold"	75
	"Cousin"	50
	"St. Georges"	50
	"No Name"	50
	"Hibton's Hole"	280
	"Hunting Corbut" a/s "No Name"	100
	"Mackey's Point"	50
	"Cross Manor"	170
	"Wickahandick"	225
	"Gardiners Gore"	42
James Thompson	"Small Hope"	100
	pt. "Swamp & Island"	120
	"Farthings Fortune & Addition"	60
	"Mills Meadows"	150
	pt. "Hounslow"	50
	"Prattlewell"	100
	"Small Hopes Addition"	78
	"Daviss Hills"	51
	pt. "Hatsfield Hills" for William Lake	75
Richard Brewar	pt. "Hounslow"	50
39:1757:6 ...		
Nicholas Mills	"Strife"	200
	"Strife's Addition"	109
	pt. "Wheatlys Chance"	150
	pt. "Squable"	50
	pt. "Medley"	300
James Bromfield	"Coles Addition"	50
	"Roberts Freehold"	90¾
John Sanders Power	pt. "St. Barbarys"	200

h/o James Neale	pt. "St. Winifreds Freehold"	30
h/o Roswell Neale	pt. "St. Winifreds Freehold"	220
	"Surplust"	452
Robert Cole	"Coles Purchase"	209
Edward Mattingly	pt. "St. Winefreds Freehold"	250
Philip Tippett	pt. "Suttles Range" a/s "Rest"	74
William Warthen	pt. "Suttles Range" a/s "Rest"	80
William Ward	"Quainton"	100
Thomas Mattingly	"Mount Misery"	100
	pt. "St. Thomas"	150
	pt. "St. Johns" a/s "Mattingly's Lane"	25
Vincent Taylor	pt. "St. Teresia"	100
	"Plains"	150
	"Engelath"	300
	"Engelath Addition"	140
Joshua Guibert	pt. "Dynnard"	100
39:1757:7 ...		
John Suttle	pt. "Suttles Range" a/s "Rest"	136
Andrew Mills	"Woolverhampton"	150
Joseph Edelen	pt. "New Design"	350
John Hilton	pt. "Hopewell"	146
John Edwards	"Price's Lott"	100
	"Plains of Jericho"	93
	"Buck Park"	100
	"John Edwards's Discovery"	214
Thomas Aisquith	pt. "St. Richards Mannor"	350
	pt. "Hamstead"	100
	"Hunting Creek"	200
	"Hickory Hills"	100
Cornelius Manning	"Neale's Lot"	209½
	"Broad Neck"	83
	"Rednor"	404
	pt. "Nuns Oake"	63
Elizabeth Wiseman (cnp)	"Batchellors Hopewell"	374
	"Force Putt"	100
	"Hopewell's Delight"	200

	"Back Acres"	100
39:1757:8 ...		
William Stone	pt. "Graden"	100
Cuthbert Fenwick	pt. "Fenwick Mannor"	175
Joseph Hopewell	pt. "Massom"	300
	"Aisquiths Defence"	122
	"Gardners Neck"	200
	"Hogpen Neck"	150
John Price Williams	pt. "Keith & Prices's Rest"	190
James Heard	pt. "St. Clements Mannor"	150
	pt. "Fenwick Mannor"	175
	pt. "Hardship"	147
	"Kennevitts Beginning"	100
	"Two Friends"	131
	"Heards Addition"	58
John Sanner	pt. "Fresh Pond Neck"	150
Thomas Rabling	"Best Land"	50
John Thorn	pt. "Desart"	62½
	pt. "Jesham"	50
James Keech	pt. "Keech & Prices Rest"	200
	"Town Neck"	200
	"Satisfaction"	580
	"Remainder"	19
Absolom Tennison	"Phipes Fort"	100
	"John's Fortune"	61
	"Guiberts Folley"	36
	pt. "Patricks Hills"	13
	"Inclosure"	62
Meverell Lock	"Hulston"	100
	pt. "Trumans Lodge"	150
	pt. "Keith & Price's Rest"	58
Mary Clark	"Addition"	100
39:1757:9 ...		
George Mills	pt. "St. Clements Mannor"	150
Hugh Hopewell (cnp)	"Hopewells Adventure"	95
	"Addition to Hopewells Adventure"	52

	pt. "St. Richards Mannor"	500
John Arthurs	pt. "Underwoods Choice"	100
Anthony Smith	pt. "Underwood"	100
John Wilkinson	"Industry"	153
William Harrison	pt. "St. Margarets"	166
	"Ward's Addition"	36
h/o Charles Ganyot	"Ganyot's Lot"	50
	pt. "Yoke by Chance"	41
Mary Edwards	"Damonds Adventure"	110
	"Edwards's Back Land"	52
Thomas Shanks, Jr.	"Shanks's Adventure"	104
	pt. "Clarker"	100
	pt. "St. Oswell"	100
	pt. "Cole Park" a/s "Clark's West Discovery"	50
Clement Hayden	"Shanks's Risque"	102
John Morgan	pt. "Parish Beedle"	100
Joseph Dafforon	"Maids Delight"	78
John Welsh	pt. "Cortany's Neck"	68
39:1757:10 ...		
Dennis Tippett	pt. "Suttles Range"	60
	pt. "St. Barbary's Addition"	120
George Vaudry	"Underwood" a/s "Wood Land" now called "Wood's Pleasure"	344
Benedict Spalding	"Hearts Delight"	200
	1 lot in Leonard Town	1
Clement Stratford	"Slipe"	69
	pt. "Baily's Fortune"	168
Ignatius Mattingly	"Clever"	185
James Mattingly	pt. "Mattingly's Hope"	130
	pt. "St. Johns"	50
Jesse Wharton	"Notley Hall" or pt. "St. Clements Mannor"	400
	"Neighbourhood" or pt. "St. Clements Mannor"	146
Thomas Vaughan	pt. "Beckworths Lodge" a/s "James Chance"	200
William Daft	pt. "Rockey Point" a/s "Curry Glass"	100
Stephen Greenwell	"Cole Brook Level"	129
John Taylor (cnp)	pt. "Frogg Marsh"	100

	"Millmots Adventure"	123
	"Neglect"	53
	"Williams's Addition"	22
	"White House"	63
	pt. "Chancellors Point"	64
	"Taylor Chance"	53
39:1757:11 ...		
James Somerhill	pt. "Wastham"	100
Issabella Cooke	"Jones Fortune"	112
William Boarman	"St. Dorothy"	263
Mary Jordan	pt. "St. Clements Mannor"	211
William Morgan	pt. "Friends Conjunction"	50
Jeremiah Jordan	pt. "St. Clements Mannor"	85
William Jordan	pt. "St. Clements Mannor"	135
Thomas Reeder (cnp)	"Thomas & Henry"	113
	pt. "Fawns Kirk"	165
	"Chance"	50
	"Rose Land"	50
	pt. "St. Johns"	595
	"Workington Park"	932
	"Middle Ground"	102
	pt. "Burroughes's Gift"	60
	"Maidens Lot"	60
	"Addition to Rose Land"	83
	pt. "Hope"	36
	pt. "Wastham"	87
	pt. "Denbury Hills"	100
	pt. "Trumans Lodge"	105
	"Inclosure"	14
	pt. "Faunkirk"	87
	pt. "Parish Beedle"	100
	"Young Mans Venture"	130
	"Fourth Addition"	209
	pt. "Great St. Thomas"	100
	"Hipworth"	100
	pt. "Dynard"	100

	pt. "Bottom"	50
	"Wildmans Levels"	168½
	"Room's Conveniency"	100
	pt. "Hopewell"	151
	pt. "St. Clements Mannor"	150
39:1757:12 ...		
William Hebb, Jr.	"White Cliff"	50
Thomas Sanner	"Salsbury Plains"	100
Samuel Ashcom	"No Name"	32
Thomas Reshwick	pt. 2 tracts of escheat land	64
	pt. "White Acre"	50
Robert Lydell	"Synetts Chance"	56
Charles Dyllion	"Charles's Chance"	75
Mary Stevens	"Richards Fancy"	38
Dr. Thomas James	"Bacon Point"	100
	pt. "Rivetts"	151
	pt. "Fortune"	50
	"Taunton"	40
	"Crooked Billet"	38
William Aisquith	"White Marsh"	93
Thomas Swann	"T.B."	119
James Roach	pt. "Medley"	100
	"Hucklebury Lane"	10
Elianor & Ann Greaves	"Hopewell"	131
	"Hardshift"	50
	"Hardshift Addition"	186
John Olliver	pt. "Cornelius"	39
	"Fortune"	50
	"Pearth"	62
	"Fortune Outlet"	16
	"Archies Hills"	65
39:1757:13 ...		
Elizabeth Nellson	pt. "Doe Park"	75
	pt. "Addition to Doe Park"	50
George Greaves	"Greaves's Swamp"	108
Thomas Standage (cnp)	pt. "Doe Park"	21

	"North Addition to Doe Park"	147
Samuel Wood	"Cannoe Neck"	100
Anthony Sims	"Wickahandick"	125
John Burroughes	pt. "Trent Fort"	129
	pt. "Remainder Charles's Lot"	166¼
William Cartwright	pt. "Remainder Charles's Lott"	166¼
	"Ridge"	50
John Cartwright	pt. "Long Look'd for Come at Last"	75
	"Cartwrights Pasture"	20
	pt. "Burroughes's Gift"	40
George Burroughes	pt. "Long Look'd for Come at Last"	100
George Dent	pt. "Freestone Point"	174
John Buckman	pt. "Freestone Point"	50
John Dent	pt. "Freestone Point"	100
James Crooke	"Ludgate"	50
Richard Sothoron	"Sothorons Desire"	125
39:1757:14 ...		
Samuel Sothoron	"Trumans Lot"	40
	"Little Worth"	25
	"Sothorons Supply"	21
Thomas Taney	"Green Meadows"	200
Thomas Norris	pt. "Lewgors Plains"	130
	pt. "Wheatly's Content"	95
	pt. "Heards Choice"	57
Free School	pt. "Hopton Park"	300
John Lynch	"Granes Content"	100
	"Plumb Point"	162
Robert Chesley	2 lots in Leonard Town	2
	"Vine Yard"	363
	pt. "Pork Hall"	40
	"Charles's Park"	130
	"Toby's Last Shift"	100
	"Woodstock"	127
Henry Reily	"Saturday's Work"	100
	"Addition to Saturday's Work"	24
Peter Mills	pt. "St. Johns"	230

Thomas Biscoe	pt. "McKey's Neck"	50
Winefred Rowson	"Maidens Lot"	100
	"Bare Waistcoat"	50
	"Winefreds Chance"	36
William Hamersly	"Beverly"	380
	"Batchellors Hope"	300
Thomas Allstone	"Reeder's Adventure"	350
	pt. "St. Clements Mannor"	200
39:1757:15 ...		
William Mills	pt. "Poplar Neck"	115
	"Ansterday"	30
John Johnson	"Peter's Wills"	100
Peter Cartwright	pt. "Weston"	100
John Spalding	"Batchellors Rest"	100
Martin Yates	pt. "Turvey"	93
Edmund Plowden	pt. "Tavern"	100
	"Farme"	500
	"Plowden's Discovery"	66
Isaac Shemwell	pt. "Devonshire"	50
	pt. "Trumania"	50
	"Derbyshire"	130
Thomas Spalding	pt. "Great St. Thomas"	200
Thomas Spalding (L. Town)	pt. "Craggburns Purchase"	100
	"Spaldings Addition"	42
	pt. "St. Giles"	35
	"Spaldings Adventure"	207
	"Rich Neck"	150
Benjamin Branson	"Drayton"	57
	"Kenady" a/s "Kielfield"	96½
	"Keith & Prices Rest"	122
	"Best Land"	10
George Thompson	pt. "Hazzard"	100
William Hall	pt. "Graden"	100
William Watson	"Edenborough"	100
39:1757:16 ...		
James Pike	"Forrest Den"	100

George Leigh	"Innis Chance"	100
	"Gallowith"	50
	"Innis's Reserve"	25
	"Parish"	150
	"Inclosure"	170
Peter Drury	pt. "Bottom"	50
Athanasius Ford	pt. "Strand"	91
William Thomas	"Wails"	200
	"Wails Addition"	91
	pt. "Boston"	100
	"Boggs"	19
George Warren	pt. "St. Johns"	68
	pt. "Burch Hanger"	75
Luke Mattingly	"Choice part of Hazzard"	100
John Higgs	"Wednesday's Project"	98
	"Higgs's Purchase"	49
John Harbert	"Harberts Invention"	109
	"Good Yielding"	86
	"Good Yielding" on resurvey	67
Francis Ratcliff	pt. "Doe Park"	50
William Jenkins	pt. "Truth & Trust"	273
	"Salem"	215
	"Croyden"	100
	"St. Thomas"	300
	"Addition"	103
	"Fox Range"	70
Thomas Watts	"Smoot"	50
	"Watts his Hazzard"	65
39:1757:17 ...		
William Martin	pt. "Hopewell"	74
	"Crackson's Rest"	50
	"Redmans Hardship"	50
	pt. "Hopeless"	11
Thomas Hall	pt. "Long Looked for Come at Last"	112
Peter Brown	pt. "White Acre"	222
Rev. James Ashby	"St. Innigo's Mannor" & "St. Georges Island"	3000

Charles Beech	"Goslings Addition"	30
	pt. "Parting Parth"	26
	"Stiles's Chance"	25
Elizabeth Gosling	pt. "Parting Path"	274
	"Garden Spott"	80
Henry Greenfield Sothoron	pt. "Brotherhood"	140
	"Sothoron's Hills"	50
	pt. "Wastham"	100
Matthew Guibert	pt. "Dynard"	81
Theadorus Jordan	pt. "St. Clements Mannor"	130
Philip Greenwell	"Honest Jones Inheritance"	150
Richard Fenwick, Jr.	"Mayheards Comfort"	100
	"Ganeths Purchase" a/s pt. "Charles's West Discovery"	40½
	"Fenwicks Gain"	55
Thomas Tippett	pt. "Suttles Range"	213
39:1757:18 ...		
William Lock	"Good Pennyworth"	50
	"Fairfield"	50
	"Lock's Venture"	49
Horn Roberts	pt. "Fresh Pond Neck"	203
Thomas Morton	pt. "St. Johns"	100
Mrs. Dryden Forbes	"Orphan's Gift"	400
	"Holbridge Town"	130
	"Drayden"	483
Charles Ridghill	"Joyntar"	50
John Ford, Sr.	pt. "Farthings Gift" a/s "Ministerdam"	10
	pt. "Durham"	100
	pt. "Long in Dispence"	75
Mark Thompson	pt. "Hatsfield Hills"	25
Henry Cooper	pt. "Scotland"	150
John Sissell	pt. "Scotland"	150
Luke Sissell	pt. "Scotland"	50
James Sissell	"Sissells Venture"	85
Sarah Sissell	pt. "Baily's Rest"	150
James Brown	"Drydocking Addition"	100

Alexander Forgisson	pt. "Small Hope"	9
	"Small Hope Addition"	42
	pt. "Black Creek"	99
39:1757:19 ...		
Thomas Redman	pt. "Small Hopes Addition"	100
Mark Taylor	"Branch"	50
Clement Spink	pt. "Guelmots Hills"	180
	"All Thats Left"	31¼
	pt. "Guelmots Hills"	150
John Tennison	pt. "Outlet"	50
John Mattingly	"Thames"	110
	"Mattingly's Addition"	50
Sarah Greenwell	"Holly Tree"	148
John Smith (Newtown)	pt. "Nun's Oake"	142
William Howard	"Phomphry's Fields"	100
Enoch Greenwell	"Hickory Hollows"	119
	"Farthings Adventure"	78
	pt. "Wheatlys Content" a/s "Back Land"	55
Thomas Thompson	"Adjoinder" a/s "St. Johns Addition"	23
	pt. "Dynard"	13
	pt. "Chance"	89
John Key	pt. "Weston"	100
	pt. "Knotley's Addition"	175
	"Gardiners Landing"	100
James Smith (Rock Creek)	pt. "Outlet"	119
	"Fresh Pond"	243
	"Mitcham Meadows"	100
	pt. "Hamstead"	100
	pt. "Black Creek"	30
39:1757:20 ...		
John Horrill	pt. "Weston Addition"	100
	pt. "Weston Addition"	13
	"Horrills Meadows"	10
George Thompson	pt. "Rockey Point"	50
Walter Davis	pt. "St. Williams Hermitage"	110
Richard Payne	pt. "Strife"	50

Clement Newton	"Newton's Rest"	63
	"Newtons Rest with Addition"	37
Samuel Johnson	pt. "Hopewell"	36
	"Addition to Pianas Grove"	19
Elizabeth Hayden	"Roach's Discovery"	251
	"Haydens Risque"	81
William Edley	pt. "Haydens Fair"	100
William Hayden	pt. "Haydens Fair"	100
Michael Wellman	pt. "Styles Chance"	100
Mary Watts	pt. "Jesbury Plains"	100
John Goss Laurence	"Frogg Marsh"	100
William Egerton	pt. "Punkley's Marsh"	100
William Biggs	pt. "St. Clements Mannor"	100
Francis Thompson	"Hard Fortune"	100
39:1757:21 ...		
Justinian Greenwell	pt. "Rochester"	100
Margaret Plummer	"Orbuston's Oake"	50
	"Hobson's Choice"	30
William Doxey	"Smiths Rest"	100
William Cavenough	pt. "Massom"	250
	"Eyre"	328
h/o Richard Vowles	pt. "Vowles's Purchase"	120
	pt. "Brittains Outlet"	1
Richard Hammett	"Hammetts Beginning"	34
	pt. "Burch Spring"	75
	pt. "Forrest Harvey"	100
	"Wildcat Neck"	104½
	"Hickory Flatt"	17½
	"Hammett & Chance"	69
Clement Mattingly	pt. "Vowles's Purchase"	239
h/o Peter Muggs	pt. "Vowles's Addition"	80
	"St. Williams"	50
	pt. "Vowles's Purchase"	57
	pt. "Rockey Point"	50
James Greenwell	"Wheatley's Content"	57
Elizabeth King	pt. "Burch Springs"	50

James Biscoe, Jr.	pt. "Hog Neck"	100
39:1757:22 ...		
Joshua Millard	"Neale's Lot"	209
	pt. "Little St. Thomas"	16
	pt. "St. Johns"	134
Luke Norris	pt. "Wheatly's Content"	69
Ignatius Thompson	"Tibny"	100
Thomas Medley	"Barren Doe"	95
John Mills	"Yieldingbury"	99
	pt. "Hopton Park"	80
Robert Drury	"Honnards Mount"	40
Richard Cooper	pt. "Clarker"	100
	"Frightfull"	180
	"Coopers Addition"	94
	"Dynard"	100
	"Hopewell"	65
	"Expence"	67
	pt. "Cragburn's Purchase"	100
John Walter	pt. "Partnership"	65
Richard Burroughes	"Holdfast"	76
	pt. "Long Look'd for Come at Last"	75
John Willson	"Indian Giant Sepulcher"	203
Abraham Hall	pt. "Gardiner's Grove"	50
Thomas Hayes	pt. "Gardiner's Grove"	147
	"Addition to Gardiner's Grove"	82
39:1757:23 ...		
Edward Mahorny	"Piles's Discovery"	112
John Parsons	"Addition"	50
	pt. "Long Look'd for Come at Last"	112½
James Watson	"Hedge Barron"	79
James Swann	pt. "Retirement"	63½
Stephen Cawood	pt. "Williamsons's Purchase"	100
	"Westham"	200
	"Caywoods Expence"	157
Edward Barber (cnp)	pt. "Swann's Forrest"	56
	pt. "Westham"	250

	pt. "Luckland"	130
John Shanks	pt. "St. Oswell"	100
Joshua Greenwell	"Last Shift"	100
John Wiseman Greenwell	"This or None"	50
	"John Wiseman Greenwell's Park"	49
	"Piles's Wood Lane"	200
Hezekiah Briscoe	pt. "Retirement"	92
h/o Benjamin Gough	pt. "St. Margarets"	100
Charles Jarbeo	pt. "St. Peters Hill"	112
John Evans	pt. "Ishmaels Right"	165
39:1757:24 ...		
John Smith, Jr.	"Haphazzard"	304
John Wheatly	"Hickory Thicket"	48
	pt. "Hanover Addition"	45
John Knott	"Sharp"	44
John Hooper	"Ashcom's Greenfield"	100
Peter Payne	pt. "Howards Mount"	75
Thomas Spalding, Jr.	pt. "Great St. Thomas"	100
	pt. "Little St. Thomas"	100
William McWilliams	pt. "Batchellors Rest"	300
	pt. "St. Clements Manor"	100
	"Josias Plains"	16¾
William Peake	pt. "Hanover"	140
	pt. "Hanover Addition"	60
	pt. "Heards Security"	91
Henry Neale	pt. "Hillalee"	250
	pt. "St. Clements Mannor"	400
Thomas Hulston	pt. "Buck Land"	35
Richard Gardiner	"Poplar Hill"	200
	"Middle Ground"	50
	"Floods Quarter"	50
Thomas Greaves (cnp)	pt. "Greaves Chance"	120
	pt. "Baptist Hope"	106
	"Hopewell"	99
	"Hardshift"	10
	"Prince William New Castle"	50

	pt. "Greaves Chance"	10
39:1757:25 ...		
John Ford (Courthouse)	pt. "Lamptons Pleasure"	150
	"Fords Inclosure"	255
Richard Fenwick	"Chance Conclusion"	97
	"Addition to Chance Conclusion"	26
Mary Bright	pt. "Cold Wells"	65
Philip Key, Esq.	"Bushwoods Lodge"	411
	pt. "Thames"	40
	"James Addition"	158
	pt. "St. Johns"	50
	"Addition to Peters Wills"	104
	pt. "Burch Hanger"	230
	"Cuckhold Haven" & timberland	77
	pt. "Wems"	430
	"Woods Pleasure" & pt. "Chesham"	95
	pt. "Maiden Bower"	100
	pt. "Finchly"	102
	"Boston"	98
	pt. "Westham"	87
	pt. "Boston" & "Peach Blossom"	55
	"Luck Land"	200
	pt. "Dynard"	119
	pt. "Shurance" & "Yieldingbury"	75
	pt. "Milton Hope"	150
	pt. "Little Yielding"	35
	"Penryn" or pt. "St. Clements Mannor"	192
Ignatius Greenwell	pt. "Wheatly's Meadows"	123
Mary Wheatly	pt. "Wheatly's Meadows"	153
Charles Daft	pt. "Medley"	200
39:1757:26 ...		
Peter Peake, Jr.	pt. "Hanover Addition"	50
John Melton	pt. "Burch Hanger"	94
Gilbert Ireland (cnp)	"Edenborough with Addition"	121½
	pt. "Hermitage"	73
	pt. "Hopton Park"	140

	pt. "Baptist Hope"	153
	pt. "Yieldingbury"	17
	"Evans's Lot" a/s "Hampstead" a/s "Baptist Hope"	50
John Guither	pt. "Croft"	147
	"Saturday's Venture"	2½
	"Cornelius's Swamp"	100
Ignatius Wheeler	pt. "Hopton Park"	50
Capt. Richard Ward Key	"Wolf Hole"	262
	"Addition to Guiberts Chance"	37
William Rogers	"Rogers's Venture"	50
Elianor Gardiner	pt. "St. Johns"	500
Leah Ward	"Wards Defence"	100
Anthony Brown	"Clark's Rest"	300
Samuel Abell	pt. "Kirby's Choice"	118
	pt. "Squable"	25
	"Scrubby Thickett"	25
	pt. "Wheatly's Chance"	41
39:1757:27 ...		
Peter Oneale	pt. "Cragburn's Purchase"	60
Kenelm Boult	pt. "Colingwood"	25
John Black	pt. "Massom"	200
	"Cadock Measure"	150
	"Court Freehold" or "Hearts Delight"	230
	"Fox Hall"	30
	"Ajoinder"	50
	"Gravelly Hill"	50
	"Oystershell Neck"	50
	"Newgent's Venture"	50
	"Blumberry"	100
	"Dunbar"	92
	"Butchers Slipe" or "Long Neck"	42
	"Poplar Point"	101
Barton Smoot	"Clarke's Range"	393
William Field	pt. "Batchellors Rest"	188
William Love	pt. "Partnership"	100
Enoch Fenwick, Jr. (cnp)	pt. "St. Peters Hills"	150

	"Cole Brooke Levell"	35
	"Spinks Rest"	65
Thomas Moony	pt. "St. Edward"	115
	"Tradesmans Lott"	200
	pt. "Linstead"	18
	pt. "Valentines Grove"	96
Daniel Harris	"Kingston"	50
	"Wheatlys"	38
39:1757:28 ...		
John Hynes	"Bite the Fox"	19
	"Hunters Hills"	150
James Anderson	pt. "Baker's Fancy"	78
	pt. "Cornelius"	39
	"Addition to Charles's Park"	20
Charles Flower	pt. "St. Georges"	50
Benjamin Williams	"Esquire's Purchase"	37
	pt. "Mugg's Adventure"	200
	"Fox Den"	89
	"Bakers Fancy"	25
	"New Fancy"	25
	pt. "Punkly's Marsh"	100
John Tear	"Hollyday"	142
Enoch Fenwick	pt. "Fenwick Mannor"	175
Ignatius Heard	pt. "Wellfound"	106
Sabina Truman Greenfield	"America Felix"	152
Thomas Newton	"Underwood" a/s "Newtons Property"	124
	pt. "Greenwells Marsh"	19
Ann Greenfield	"Greenfield's Discovery"	90
	"Trent Neck"	835
	"Stockbardolph"	75
39:1757:29 ...		
James Truman Greenfield	"Keech's Folley"	133
	"Lamby"	100
	"Punch Neck"	60
	"Holbridge Town"	130
	pt. "Hopton Park"	120

Nathaniel Truman Greenfield	"Fork"	60
	"Addition"	78
	"White Haven"	164
	"Indian Creek & Addition"	491
	"Nighthood" & "Bashford"	154
	"Thimblebee"	109
	"Fishing Place"	50
	"Brough Land"	75
James Warwick	pt. "St. Johns"	150
John Dunbar	"Chance"	240
Edward Caster for h/o (N) Redman	"Redman's Hardship"	50
John Cole	"Jones Wood"	100
	"Addition to Jones Wood"	59½
Lydia Bright	pt. "Cold Wells"	65
John Michael Thomas Taney	pt. "Fenwick Mannor"	450
Joseph Clarke	"Mattingly's Hope"	70
	pt. "St. Johns"	300
	pt. "Charles West Discovery"	122
Sarah Carter	"Meer Chance"	113
39:1757:30 ...		
Mary Hamersly	"Carberry's Discovery"	190
John Dant	"Hopewell"	100
	pt. "Yoke by Chance"	20
John Jones	"Poverty"	64
Thomas Yates	pt. "St. Peters Hills"	100
	pt. "Small Hopes"	30
	pt. "Hanover"	60
	pt. "Heards Security"	70
Enoch Combs	pt. "Pork Hall"	300
	"Grane Hill"	200
	"Wilderpole"	300
John Wherrett	pt. "Watts' Lodge"	90
Thomas Cooke, Jr.	pt. "Brough"	68
Joseph Harding	"Baily's Rest"	100
John McKey (cnp)	pt. "McKey's Neck"	153

	pt. "St. Richards Mannor"	50
	pt. "Massom"	100
Samuel Bellwood	"Ishmaels Right"	165
	"Bellwood's Grove"	128
	pt. "Styles Chance"	16
Fairfax Compton	pt. "Honnard Mount"	75
39:1757:31 ...		
George Rogers	pt. "Well Close"	100
	"Brothers Dread"	135
John Norris	"Gough's Levells"	42
	"Goughs Conveniency"	48
	"Brittains Bay"	150
William Roach	pt. "St. John's Landing"	217
	pt. "John's Addition"	167
William Guither	"Maids Delight"	100
	pt. "Smoot"	100
Cuthbert Clarke	"Chesley"	100
William Taylor	"Poplar Hill"	63
	"Taylor's Lot"	22
John Baker (Bayside)	pt. "Drapers Neck"	285
Francis Wheatly	pt. "Wheatly's Content"	66
	pt. "Buck Land"	50
Leonard Greenwell	pt. "Hanover Addition"	87
George Would	pt. "Hanover"	103
John Thomas	"Hampton"	100
39:1757:32 ...		
Clement Norris	"Tant's Mark"	168
	"Norris's Frolick"	3¼
Thomas Howard	pt. "Gillmots Hills"	75
Joseph Stevens	pt. "Devonshire"	50
	"Trumania"	50
	"Josephs Venture"	54
Samuel Lee	"Well Close"	82
	pt. "St. Clements Mannor"	105
John Bready	pt. "Baily's Rest"	100
	"Brady's Lot"	25

Peter Ford	pt. "St. Giles's"	81
	"Mount Pleasant"	100
	"May Pole"	96
	pt. "Strand"	91
Thomas Wheatly	"Wheatlys Plains"	204
John Chesley	pt. "Cragburn"	300
	"Cragburns Island"	13
	"Cragburns Swamp"	17½
	pt. "Indian Creek"	36
Thomas Greenfield	pt. "Indian Creek"	843
	pt. "Good Luck"	275
Thomas Bond	"Knotting"	100
39:1757:33 ...		
Rev. John Urquhart	pt. "Fawns Kirk"	250
	"Spring Blossom"	221
	pt. "Keith & Prices's Rest"	60
	"Hopewells Chance"	170
Benjamin Gristy	"Venture"	50
	"Gristy's Vein"	34½
Thomas Clark	pt. "Moffats Will"	69
Thomas Breeden	pt. "Moffat's Will"	69
John Biscoe	"Barren Wood"	46
Henry Winsatt	"Harberts Grief"	44
	pt. "Nuns Oake"	20
James Dickson	"Dickson's Venture" or "Haydens Fair"	115½
h/o Edward Pye	"Underwood"	300
John Adams	"Small Hope with Addition"	50
John Greaves	pt. "Greaves's Chance"	94
James Thompson (head of Chaptico)	pt. "St. Johns"	50
	"Harberts Swamp"	21
Joseph Stevens, Jr.	"Stevens's Chance"	46
	"Parnasses"	75
39:1757:34 ...		
Ignatius Greenwell	"Ignatius's Dread"	100
	"Addition"	25
Mary Fenwick	pt. "Fenwick Manor"	200

Daniel Watts	"Watts's Lodge"	160
John Plummer	pt. "Elizabeth Mannor"	300
Richard Shurly	"Shurly's Adventure"	150
Thomas Keen	"Keen's Rest"	49
Thomas Matthews	"Friends Conjunction"	72
Edward Aprice	pt. "St. Barbary's"	100
John Anderson	"Sothoron's Desire"	100
	pt. "Fox's Race"	52
Benjamin Bean	pt. "Friends Conjunction"	72
John Sykes	pt. "Friends Conjunction"	56
John Thompson	"Mitcham Meadows"	140
	"Thompson's Lott"	172
39:1757:35 ...		
h/o Mark Thomas	"Penancy"	100
	"Brewar's Woodhouse"	50
	"Luke's Hardship"	7
	"Marks Adventure"	36
Henry How	"White Land"	225
	"How's Fortune"	19
	"How's Adventure"	42
John Biscoe	pt. "Harrison's Rest"	80
	pt. "Williams's Fortune"	32
Dr. William Murray	"Indian Creek"	563
Peter Peake	pt. "Friends Goodwill"	100
Benjamin Fenwick	pt. "Fenwick Mannor"	200
Robert Henley	pt. "Massom"	150
	"John's Content"	93½
	"Keens Rest"	50
Robert Newgent	"Marking Place"	100
	"Fox Catch'd"	11
James Smith (cnp)	"Trinity", "St. Gabriel" & "St. Michael's Mannor"	3000
	"Pountly's Oversight"	198
	"Tripple Defence Rectifyd"	269
	"Addition to Tripple Defence Rectifyd"	34
	"Pine Land"	370
	pt. "Turvey"	201

	"Hazzard"	57
39:1757:36 ...		
Cornelius Wildman	"Brooke Chance"	81
	"Dyllion's Disappointment"	103
	"Williams Venture"	54
	"Goulding Grove"	153
	"Tavern"	100
Enoch Abell	pt. "Wheatly's Chance"	50
	"Abells Content"	113
	"Slipe"	24
John Medly Thompson	pt. "Scotland"	50
Thomas Barber	pt. "Burch Hanger"	20
Charles Greenwell	"Farther Adventure"	65½
Thomas Jordan	pt. "Macoome"	25
John Clark	"Evans's Quarter"	100
Michael Goldsmith	pt. "St. Clements Mannor"	86
	pt. "Bashford Mannor"	100
William Aude	pt. "Hanover"	30
John Shiercliffe	"Shiercliffe"	250
	"St. Williams"	90
	"Q Name"	100
	pt. "Linstead"	78
	pt. "Linstead Addition"	100
	"Coles Adventure"	150
39:1757:37 ...		
Richard Millard	"Little St. Thomas"	84
	pt. "St. Johns"	50
	"Turners Plains"	16
Thomas Pearce	pt. "Cortany's Fancy"	50
Kenelm Truman Greenfield	pt. "Trent Neck"	1519
Henry Lowes	"Warnett"	240
Henry Jarbeo	pt. "St. Peters Hills"	126
Henry Bryant	"Williams's Endeavour"	50
	pt. "Farther Adventure"	37
	"Greens Plott"	44
William Deacon, Esq. (cnp)	pt. "St. Peters"	50

	pt. "Chandlers Point"	112
	pt. "St. Mary's Freehold"	248
William Hicks	pt. "St. Peters"	100
	"Governours Fields" & "Popes Freeshold"	200
	"Chapple"	25
	pt. "St. Mary's Freehold"	7
John Miles	"Wastfield"	140
	"Somersett"	195
Edward Parsons	pt. "Guiberts Chance"	50
	"Small Addition"	19½
39:1757:38 ...		
Sabastian Thompson	"Thompson's Expence"	208
Joseph Jenkins	pt. "Truth & Trust"	400
William Heard	pt. "Wellfound"	106
	pt. "Fenwick Mannor"	175
George Plater, Esq.	pt. "St. Joseph's Mannor"	819
	"Bowles's Preservation"	695
	pt. "Fenwick Mannor"	400
	"Staffords Hope"	125
	"Resurrection Mannor"	4000
Richard Raper	"Maynards Comfort"	100
	pt. "Baily's Fortune"	45
	pt. "St. Clements Mannor"	50
	pt. "Bapt. Hope"	200
Thomas Doxey	pt. "Harrison's Rest"	70
Richard Brooke	"Delle Brooke Mannor"	2000
	"Two Brothers"	235
	pt. "Back Land"	400
Thomas Hobson	pt. "Weems"	100
Elizabeth Hulse	pt. "Westham"	150
Charles King	"Deptford"	300
	pt. "St. Joseph's Mannor"	200
Just. Greenwell	pt. "Kirby's Choice"	67
39:1757:39 ...		
William Williams (cnp)	"Drydocking"	100
	pt. "Stock Park"	76

	pt. "Roberts Neck" a/s "Medly"	95
	"Harberts Gift"	60
	pt. "Roberts Freehold"	75
Robert Fenwick	pt. "St. Joseph's Mannor"	126
John Mareman	pt. "Hopton Park"	197
	"Vowles's Purchase"	156
Samuel Jenifer	pt. "St. Joseph Mannor"	50
Leonard Green	pt. "Fenwick Mannor"	50
Thomas Manly	pt. "Elizabeth Mannor"	100
Thomas Bladen, Esq.	pt. "Elizabeth Mannor"	247
	pt. "Cross Mannor"	500
Stourton Edwards	"St. Thomas"	190
	"Doe Park"	69
	pt. "Hanover"	100
Thomas Brome	pt. "No Name"	250
John Lancaster	pt. "Hillelee"	250
	pt. "St. Clements Mannor"	400
Peter Gough	pt. "Lewgroes Plains"	100
39:1757:40 ...		
James Hagoe	pt. "Beaverdam"	59
John Abell	pt. "Wheatly's Chance"	31
	pt. "Kirby's Choice"	68
	pt. "St. Josephs Mannor"	56
Cuthbert Abell	"Wisemans Chance"	100
Benjamin Redman	"Small Hope"	50
Dennis Burn	pt. "Beckworths Lodge"	163
Joseph Walker	pt. "Gillmotts Hills"	100
	"Addition to Farthings Fortune"	140
Ignatius Baily	pt. "Little Yielding"	117
William Jones	"Salter's Hall"	83
	"Addition to Salter's Hall"	34
	"Jones's Conveniency"	35½
	pt. "Beckworths Lodge"	163
	"Jones's Lane"	1¾
	"Muggs Adventure"	52
John Jarbeo (cnp)	pt. "Hanover"	17

	pt. "Heards Security"	24
Thomas Warren	"Warren's Lot Rectified"	146
Matthias Nottingham	"Salmon"	50
39:1757:41 ...		
Ruth Jones	"Davis's Forrest"	50
Henry Spalding	pt. "Joseph"	152½
	"Two Brothers"	165
	pt. "Newcastle"	50
	pt. "Rich Neck"	98
Thomas Devaun	pt. "Partnership"	200
John Watson	pt. "Partnership"	65½
George Maxwell	pt. "Indian Creek with Addition"	461
Col. Abra. Barnes	"America Felix Secundus"	956
	pt. "Ranglefield"	40
	pt. "Forrest Harvey"	100
	"Westbury Mannor"	1250
	pt. "Forrest Lodge"	100
	pt. "Drapers Neck"	215
	"Walnut Point"	55
Capt. Zachariah Bond	pt. "St. Barbary's"	200
	pt. "Piles's Discovery"	112
William Doxey, Jr.	pt. "St. Patricks Hill"	50
Edmund Bowling	pt. "Collingwood"	25
John Morris	pt. "Collingwood"	25
Francis Knott	pt. "Hazzard"	56
39:1757:42 ...		
George Bowles	"Steplition Fortune"	200
	"Hazzard"	234
John Tippett	"Tippett's Purchase"	46
William Spalding	pt. "Rich Neck"	152
Mark Norris	pt. "Wheatly's Content"	118
	pt. "Burch Plains"	70
Ignatius Fenwick	"Hopton Hole"	350
	pt. "Hopton Hole"	70
John Holt	pt. "St. Clements Mannor"	167
Ignatius Wheeler	pt. "St. Clements Mannor"	250

John Lee	pt. "St. Clements Mannor"	200
John Haskins	pt. "St. Clements Mannor"	100
John Baptist Greenwell	pt. "Rochester"	100
John Bould	pt. "Cadle"	150
	"Addition to White Acre"	25
John Wimsatt	pt. "Hatfield Hills"	73
John Bullock	pt. "St. Clements Mannor"	100
Thomas Wherrett	"Hogg Neck"	100
39:1757:43 ...		
John Buchannan	"Fox Grape Barren"	106
David Downie	"Town Support"	81
	"Bary"	65
	3 lots in Leonard Town	3
James Jarbeo	"Denby"	250
Thomas Jenkins	"Poplar Point"	100
Benjamin Moulton	pt. "Bashford Mannor"	200
John Pike	"Forney Branch"	50
Clement Medley	pt. "Medley"	200
William Medley	pt. "Medley"	100
Basil Peake	pt. "Medley"	100
George Greenwell	pt. "Medley"	50
John Lewellin	pt. "St. Clements Mannor"	400
John Fenwick	pt. "Rivits Backside"	172
	pt. "Rivits"	151
	pt. "Chancellors Point"	112
	pt. "Crofts"	100
Bennett Neale	pt. "St. Clements Mannor"	200
Aust. Leigh Massey	"Plumb Point"	308
Elizabeth Lock	pt. "Cold Wells"	65½
39:1757:44 ...		
Stephen Chilton	pt. "Peter's Quay"	50
	"Fishing Creek Neck"	44
Richard Milburn	pt. "Halfhead Folley"	100
	pt. "Cortany's Neck"	82
	"Milburn's Chance with Addition"	246
John Smith	pt. "Mattapany"	289

Clement Spalding	"Spaldings Adventure"	729
John Eden	pt. "Bashford Mannor"	277
John Bond	pt. "St. Clements Mannor"	605
	pt. "Hopton Park"	400
	pt. "St. Johns"	438
	"Gardiners Chance"	155
	pt. "Burlington" or "St. Clements Mannor"	25
Richard Edelen	"Trumans Hunting Quarter"	200
	pt. "Hope"	64
Justinian Jordan	pt. "St. Clements Mannor"	200
George Backster	"Batchellors Comfort"	190
George Slye	pt. "St. Clements Mannor"	1000
	"Wee Bitt"	50
John Boult	pt. "St. Clements Mannor"	100
Edward Turner	pt. "Bashford Mannor"	200
39:1757:45 ...		
Charles Sewall	pt. "Little Eltonhead Mannor"	50
	"Friends Discovery"	117
John Blackiston	pt. "St. Clements Mannor"	550
	pt. "St. Clements Island"	100
John Mason	pt. "St. Clements Mannor"	450
Mary Tennison	pt. "St. Clements Mannor"	100
Kenelm Chiseldyne	pt. "St. Clements Mannor"	725
Cyrenius Chiseldyne	pt. "St. Clements Mannor"	25
Charles Carroll, Esq.	pt. "St. Clements Mannor"	1650
	pt. "St. Clements Mannor"	479
	"Oxford"	209
	pt. "Barbary's Addition"	250
	pt. "Loughborough"	150
	"Addition"	41
	"Temple Barr"	100
John Maddox	pt. "Bashford Mannor"	150
John Reshwick	pt. 2 tracts escheated land	47
Edward Welsh	"Ossfield"	72
John Attaway Clarke (cnp)	pt. "Poney Point"	750
	pt. "James Johnson's Neck"	200

	"Blake Creek"	50
	"Tower Hill"	25
Robert Hagoe	pt. "Truth & Trust"	100
39:1757:46 ...		
Nicholas Lewis Sewall	pt. "Mattapany"	911
	"Sewalls Discovery"	108
	"Fishing Point"	13
Leonard Davis	pt. "Desart"	62½
	"Thorn's Venture"	103
James Wheatly	"Kington" a/s "Newton Quit"	117
	pt. "Wheatly's Addition"	21
John Smith	pt. "Bashford Mannor"	200
Mary McWilliams	pt. "St. Clements Mannor"	300
Stourton Edwards, Jr.	"Taunton Dean"	164
Thomas Suite	pt. "Trent Fort"	84
	pt. "Horse Range"	100
James Mills	pt. "Bashford Mannor"	100
Leonard Mattingly	"Audly End"	190
Notly Goldsmith	pt. "Bashford Mannor"	100
Roger Smith	pt. "Notly's Addition"	275
Dent Suite	pt. "Horse Range"	100
Thomas Crane	"Dally" or "Waughops Walker"	100
	"Smoots Marsh"	31
John Ford (weaver)	"Pomphry Fields"	50
	"Ministerdam"	54
Henry Taylor	"Taylors Plains"	50½
39:1757:47 ...		
Thomas Suite, Jr.	pt. "Cold Wells"	100
Joseph Edwards	pt. "Cold Wells"	52
	pt. "Trent Fort"	8
Thomas Wyn Taylor	pt. "Wrighting"	100
Clement Medley, Sr.	"No Name"	100
John Somervell	pt. "St. Richards Mannor"	100
	"Clarke's Last Discovery"	99
	pt. "St. Jerom's Mannor"	200
John Waughop	"Waughop's Chance"	138

John Coode	pt. "St. Clements Mannor"	300
Anthony Roberts	"Whittenham"	200
Benjamin Burroughes	pt. "Trent Fort"	129
Peter Ford, Jr.	"Nuns Oake"	75
John Curlet	"Willingborough"	70
h/o James Heath	pt. "St. Jerom's Mannor"	5500
James Kindrick	"Kindrick's Lane"	80
John Reeves	pt. "Bashford Mannor"	100
John Kelley	"Kelley's Luck"	138
	"Kelley's Fortune"	182
39:1757:48 ...		
James Tarlton	pt. "Beaverdam"	59
	pt. "Elizabeth"	34
Samuel Swann	pt. "Swans Forrest"	40
	"Swann's Venture"	140
James Latimore	pt. "Hopewell"	89½
Leonard Payne	"Fox"	100
Rev. Arnold Livers	"Little Brittain"	750
	pt. "Brittains Outlet"	43
James Baily	pt. "St. Clements Mannor"	45
Thomas Yates, Jr.	pt. "St. Clements Mannor"	100
John Goldsmith	pt. "Bashford Mannor"	100
Samuel Maddox	pt. "Bashford Mannor"	38
Thomas Vowles	pt. "Vowles's Purchase"	50
Thomas Melton	pt. "Burch Hanger"	95
George Bullock	pt. "Burlington" or "St. Clements Mannor"	75
39:1757:49 ...		
Matthew Clarke	"Clark's Lott"	52
Joseph Edwards s/o John	"Lott"	22
John Wynn (PG)	"Addition to Hogg Neck"	16
Michael Lyon	"Pettits Addition"	27
	pt. "St. Margarets"	88
George Chilton	pt. "Forrest Lodge"	50
William Forgisson	"Copthall"	100
John Burch	"Burch's Forrest"	100
John Goodwin, Esq.	3 lots in Leonard Town	3

George Gordan	2 lots in Leonard Town	2
Col. Barnes	5 lots in Leonard Town	5
George Plater, Esq.	2 lots in Leonard Town	2
Philip Key, Esq.	1 lot in Leonard Town	1
(N) Greenfield	1 lot in Leonard Town	1
Court House	1 lot in Leonard Town	1
John Wheatly	pt. "Townhill"	43
John Somervell	"Addition to Fortune"	100
Cuthbert Fenwick	"Fenwicks Prevention"	58
William Hamersly	"Gore"	16
Cuthbert Clarke	"Clarkes Lott"	19

39:1758:1 ...		**Acres**
Daniel Clocker	"Clockers Freehold"	50
	"Lewis's Neck"	30
John Milburn (~~Elisabeth Clocker~~)	"St. Ann's Freehold"	70½
	"Clocker's Fancy"	56
Thomas Palmer Waughop	"Hunting Quarter"	150
	"Poiney Point"	750
	"Smoots Hollow"	150
Nicholas Sewall	pt. "Little Eltonhead Mannor" a/s "Rich Neck"	1590
Edward Digges	pt. "Little Elton Head Mannor" a/s "Rich Neck"	300
William Price	"Brick Hill"	217
	"Parks Addition"	110
Edward Horn	pt. "Halfheads Folly"	100
Ignatius Taylor	pt. "Little Eltonhead Mannor" a/s "Rich Neck"	60
James Daffron	"Coles Harbour"	150
George Aisquith	"Stinmore"	100
	"Inclosure"	30
	"Thomas & George in Company"	4½
John Roades	pt. "Jesbury Plains"	330
Isaac Pavatt	"Cow Ridge"	50
	pt. "Cross Mannor"	150
Robert Pearce	pt. "Cortanys Fancy"	50
	pt. "Prices Chance"	25
39:1758:2 ...		
Thomas Thorp	"Strife"	50
Fargus Keough	"Surgeons Folly"	50
	"Wills Swamp"	150
	"Readers Addition"	79
James Styles	pt. "Styles Chance"	59
	"What Care I"	28½
	pt. "Chance"	6
	pt. "Elizabeth"	43
John Price	"Grove"	50
	"Farnham"	83
Robert Greenwell (cnp)	pt. "Buckland Plains"	70
	pt. "Lamptons Pleasure"	117

	pt. "Greenwells Marsh"	49
Robert Vaulx	pt. "Massom"	100
Barnaby Egan	pt. "Massom"	100
	pt. "Hopewell"	100
	"Strife"	100
	"Harberts Begining"	50
	"Clockers Marsh"	100
	"Lordships Favour"	100
	"Dunbarr"	100
	"Addition" taken up by Mr. Debuts	20
Rev. Moses Tabbs	"Itchcombs Freehold"	340
James White	pt. "Fresh Pond Neck"	150
39:1758:3 ...		
Richard Barnhouse	pt. "Cross Mannor"	1000
	pt. "Elizabeth Mannor"	1000
John Cole (New Town)	pt. "Rivets Backside"	50
	"Nobles Victor"	50
	pt. "Harberts Gift"	43
	pt. "Shock Park"	24
John Mitchell	"Mitchells Choice"	47
Cornelius Barber	pt. "Luckland" a/s "Eastham"	470
	"Nicholl's Hope"	135
Baptist Barber	pt. "Wastham"	250
	pt. "Luckland" a/s "Eastham"	200
	"Leigh"	100
Elizabeth Donaldson	pt. "Mitcham Hills"	200
Philip Barton Key	pt. "Mitcham Hills"	100
George Latham	pt. "Mitcham Meadows"	100
Luke Russell	pt. "Brough"	50
James Gough	"St. Barnards"	100
	"St. Margarets"	200
	"Bacon Neck"	200
	"Proprietarys Gift" a/s "Lordships Favour"	50
	"Q Name" pt. "Lordships Favour"	50
	"St. Teresia"	100

William Morgan (St. Mich.)	"Hazzard"	73
	"Addition to White Birch Freehold"	53
	pt. "St. Patricks"	15
	"White Birch Freehold"	100
39:1758:4 ...		
William Sissell	pt. "Cadle"	50
Thomas Sissell	pt. "White Acre" or "No Name"	50
	pt. "Addition to White Acre"	18
John Thompson	pt. "Davis's Rest"	50
George Booth	pt. "Hopton Part"	56
Mary Greenwell	pt. "Green Hill"	221
Athan. Nottingham	"Nevits St. Annes"	100
Clement Stratford	"Leeith"	100
Thomas Hatton Combs	"Hattons Rest"	250
	"Addition to Hearts Delight"	152
John Heard	pt. "St. Lawrence Freehold"	193
	pt. "Heards Security"	43
	pt. "Hanover"	350
Peter Howard	pt. "Twitenham"	100
Mark Jarbeo	pt. "Heards Security"	40
	pt. "Hanover"	20
John Norris	"Shercliff"	300
John Bap. Carberry	"Hopton Park"	797
Edward Hill. Hebb	"Little Recovery of Birthright"	13
William Mattingly	pt. "Suttles Range"	80
39:1758:5 ...		
Matthew Heard	"Pole"	120
	"William Heards Purchase"	115
	"Ashmans Freehold"	150
	pt. "Hanover Addition"	123
	pt. "Heards Choice"	100
	pt. "Heards Security"	169
Mark Heard	"Thirds"	425
James Taylor (St. Mary's)	pt. "Snow Hill Manor"	100
Matthew Hebb	"Small Hope"	56
John French	pt. "Hopton Park"	160

John Hammond	pt. "Lewgroes Plains"	200
William Watts	"Bushels Rest" or "No Name"	150
John Gardiner (St. Georges)	"Timber Swamp"	100
	"Addition to Timber Swamp"	60
William Hebb	"Gardiners Purchase" or "No Name"	100
	"St. Williams"	114
	"Freehold"	75
	"Causin" or "No Name"	50
	"St. Georges Point"	50
	"No Name"	50
	pt. "Hibtons Hole"	280
	"Corbut" or "No Name"	100
	"Mackeys Point" (Neck)	50
	"Cross Mannor"	170
	"Wickahandick"	225
	"Gardiners Gore"	42
James Thompson	"Small Hope"	100
	pt. "Swamp & Island"	120
	"Farthings Fortune"	50
	"Addition"	10
	"Mills Meadows"	150
	pt. "Hounslow"	50
	"Prattlewell"	100
	"Small Hopes Addition"	78
	"Divided Hills"	51
	pt. "Hatfield Hills" for William Lake	75
Richard Brewer	pt. "Hounslow"	50
39:1758:6 ...		
Nicholas Mills	"Strife"	200
	"Strifes Addition"	109
	pt. "Wheatly's Chance"	150
	pt. "Squable"	50
	pt. "Meddle"	300
James Bromfield	"Coles Addition"	50
	"Roberts Freehold" or pt. "Medley"	90½
John Sanders Power	pt. "St. Barbarys"	200

h/o James Neale	pt. "St. Winnifreds Freehold"	30
h/o Roswell Neale	pt. "St. Winnifreds Freehold"	220
	"Surplus" pt. "St. Winnifreds Freehold"	452
Robert Cole	"Coles Purchase"	210
Edward Mattingly	pt. "St. Winnifreds Freehold"	250
Philip Tippet	pt. "Suttles Range" a/s "Rest"	74
William Warthen	pt. "Suttles Range" a/s "Rest"	80
William Ward	"Quainton"	100
Thomas Mattingly	"Mount Misery"	100
	pt. "St. Thomas"	150
	"Mattinglys Lane"	25
Vincent Taylor	pt. "St. Teresia"	100
	"Plains"	150
	"Engsbath"	400
	"Engsbath Addition"	140
Joshua Guibert	pt. "Dynard"	100
39:1758:7 ...		
Abel Simmonds	"Stratford"	100
	"Trophy"	100
James Wood	"Desart"	125
	"Arabia"	76
William Meekin	"Beards Choice"	150
	"St. Margrets Fields"	100
	"St. Margrets Forrest"	100
	"Sperwell" or "No Name"	100
John Thompson	pt. "Susquehannah Point"	100
	"Smith Discovery"	258
	"Q Name" or "Susquehannah Point"	195
John Suttle	pt. "Suttles Range"	136
Andrew Mills	"Woolverhampton"	150
Joseph Edelen	"New Design"	350
John Hilton	pt. "Hopewell"	146
John Edwards	"Prices Lott"	100
	"Plains of Jerecho"	93
	"Buck Park"	100
	"John Edwards's Discovery"	241

Thomas Aisquith	pt. "St. Richards Mannor"	350
	pt. "Hamstead"	100
	"Hunting Neck"	200
	"Hickory Hills"	100
	"Addition"	31
Cornelius Manning	pt. "Neales Lott"	209½
	"Broad Neck"	83
	"Rednor"	404
	pt. "Nuns Oake"	63
Elizabeth Wiseman	"Batchellors Hopewell Rectified"	374
	"Forced Putt"	100
	"Hopewell Delight"	200
	"Back Acres"	100
39:1758:8 ...		
William Stone	pt. "Graden"	100
Cuthbert Fenwick	pt. "Fenwick Mannor"	175
	"Fenwicks Prevention"	58
Joseph Hopewell	pt. "Massom"	300
	"Aisquiths Defence"	122
	"Gardiners Neck"	200
	"Hogpen Neck"	150
John Price Williams	pt. "Keith & Prices Rest"	190
James Heard	pt. "St. Clements Mannor"	150
	pt. "Fenwick Mannor"	175
	pt. "Heards Hardship"	147
	"Kenevits Beginning"	100
	"Two Friends"	131
	"Heards Addition"	58
John Sanner	pt. "Fresh Pond Neck"	150
Thomas Rabling	"Best Land"	50
John Thorn	pt. "Desart"	62½
	pt. "Jesham"	50
James Keech	pt. "Keech & Prices Rest"	200
	"Town Neck"	200
	"Satisfaction"	580
	"Remainder"	19

Absolom Tennison	"Phipes Fort"	100
	"Johns Fortune"	61
	"Guiberts Folly"	36
	pt. "St. Patricks ~~Hills~~"	13
	"Inclosure"	62
Meverell Lock	"Hulston"	100
	pt. "Trumans Lodge"	150
	pt. "Keith & Prices Rest"	58
Mary Clarke	"Addition"	100
39:1758:9 ...		
George Mills	pt. "St. Clements Mannor"	150
Hugh Hopewell	"Hopewells Adventure"	95
	"Addition to Hopewells Adventure"	52
	pt. "St. Richards Mannor"	500
John Arthurs	pt. "Underwoods Choice"	100
Anthony Smith	pt. "Underwoods Choice"	100
John Wilkinson	"Industry"	153
William Harrison	pt. "St. Margarets"	166
	"Wards Addition"	36
h/o Charles Ganyot	"Ganyots Lot"	50
	pt. "Yoke by Chance"	41
Mary Edwards	"Damonds Adventure"	110
	"Edwards Back Land"	52
Thomas Shanks	"Shanks Adventure"	101
	pt. "Clarker"	100
	pt. "St. Oswell"	100
	~~pt. "Cole Park" a/s~~ "Clarks West Discovery"	50
Clement Hayden	"Shanks's Risque"	102
John Morgan	pt. "Parish Beadle"	100
Joseph Dafforon	"Maids Delight"	78
John Welsh	pt. "Cortanys Neck"	68
39:1758:10 ...		
Dennis Tippet	pt. "Suttles Range"	60
	"St. Barbary's Addition"	120
George Vaudry	"Woods Inclosure"	344
Benedict Spalding (cnp)	"Hearts Delight"	200

	1 lot in Leonard Town	1
Clement Stratford	"Slipe"	69
	pt. "Bailys Fortune"	168
Ignatius Mattingly	"Clever"	155
James Mattenly	pt. "Mattinglys Hope"	130
	pt. "St. Johns"	50
Jesse Wharton	"Notly Hall" or pt. "St. Clements Mannor"	400
	"Neighbourhood" or pt. "St. Clements Mannor"	146
Thomas Vaughan	pt. "Beckworths Lodge" a/s "James Chance"	200
William Daft	pt. "Rockey Point" a/s "Curry Glass"	100
Stephen Greenwell	"Cole Brooke Level"	129
John Taylor	pt. "Frog Marsh"	100
	"Gillmuts Adventure"	123
	"Neglect"	53
	"Williams's Addition"	22
	"White House"	63
	pt. "Chancellors Point"	64
	"Taylors Chance"	53
39:1758:11 ...		
James Somerhill	pt. "Wastham"	100
Isabella Cooke	"Jones Fortune"	112
William Boarman	"St. Dorothy"	263
Mary Jordan	pt. "St. Clements Mannor"	211
William Morgan	pt. "Friends Conjunction"	50
Jeremiah Jordan	pt. "St. Clements Mannor"	85
William Jordan	pt. "St. Clements Mannor"	135
Thomas Reeder (cnp)	"Thomas Henry"	113
	pt. "Fawns Kirk"	165
	"Chance"	50
	"Rose Land with Addition"	133
	"Bogue Increase"	273
	pt. "St. Johns"	595
	"Workington Park"	932
	"Middle Ground"	102
	"Maidens Lott"	236
	~~"Addition to Rose Land"~~	~~83~~

	pt. "Hopes"	36
	pt. "Wastham"	87
	pt. "Dembury Hills"	100
	pt. "Trumans Lodge"	105
	"Inclosure"	14
	pt. "Faun Kirk"	87
	pt. "Parish Beadle"	100
	"Young Mans Venture"	130
	"Fourth Addition Rectifyed"	209
	pt. "St. Thomas"	100
	"Hipworth"	100
	pt. "Dynard"	100
	pt. "Bottom"	50
	"Wildmans Levells"	168½
	"Rooms Conveniency"	100
	pt. "Hopewell"	151
	pt. "St. Clements Mannor"	150
39:1758:12 ...		
William Hebb, Jr.	"White Cliff" or "No Name"	50
Thomas Sanner	"Salsbury Plains"	100
Samuel Ashcom	"No Name"	681
	"Ashcoms Marsh"	32
Thomas Reshwick	pt. 2 tracts escheat land	64
	pt. "White Acre" or "No Name"	50
Robert Lydell	"Synnets Chance"	56
Charles Dyllion	"Charles's Chance"	75
Mark Stephens	"Richards Fancy"	138
Dr. Thomas James	"Bacon Point" or "Beans Point"	106
	pt. "Revels"	151
	pt. "Fortune"	50
	"Taunton Dean"	40
	"Crooked Billet"	38
William Aisquith	"White Marsh"	93
Thomas Swann	"T.B."	119
James Roach	pt. "Medley"	100
	"Hucklebury Lane"	10

Elioner & Ann Groves	pt. "Hopewell"	131
	"Hardshipt"	50
	"Hardshift Addition"	186
John Oliver	pt. "Cornelius"	39
	"Fortune"	50
	"Pearth"	62
	"Britains Outlet"	16
	"Archies Hills"	65
39:1758:13 ...		
Elizabeth Nelson	pt. "Doe Park"	75
	~~pt. "Addition to~~ Doe Park"	50
George Graves	"Graves's Swamp"	108
Thomas Standage	pt. "Doe Park"	21
	"North Addition to Doe Park"	147
Samuel Ward	"Cannoe Neck"	100
Anthony Simms	"Wickohandick"	125
John Burroughs	pt. "Trent Fort"	129
	pt. "Remainder Charles Lott"	166½
William Cartwright	pt. "Remainder Charles Lott"	166½
John Cartwright	pt. "Long Look'd for Come at Last"	75
	"Cartwrights Pasture"	20
	pt. "Burrough's Gift"	40
George Burroughs	pt. "Long Looked for Come at Last"	400
George Dent	pt. "Freestone Point"	174
John Buckman	pt. "Freestone Point"	50
John Dent	pt. "Freestone Point"	100
James Crooke	"Ludgate"	50
Richard Sothoron	"Sothorons Desire"	125
39:1758:14 ...		
Samuel Sothoron	"Trumans Lott"	40
	"Little Worth"	25
	"Sothorns Supply"	21
Thomas Taney	"Green Meadows"	200
Thomas Norris	pt. "Lewgores Plains"	130
	pt. "Wheatlys Contentment"	95
	pt. "Heards Choice"	57

Free School	pt. "Hopton Park"	100
John Lynch	"Greenes Content"	100
	pt. "Plumb Point"	162
Robert Chesley	2 lots in Leonard Town	2
	"Vineyard"	343
	pt. "Pork Hall"	50
	"Charles's Park"	130
	"Towleys Last Shift"	100
	"Woodstock"	127
Henry Reily	"Saturdays Work"	100
	"Addition to Saturdays Work"	21
Peter Mills	pt. "St. Johns"	230
Thomas Biscoe	pt. "McKeys Neck"	50
Winnefred Rowson	"Maidens Lot"	100
	"Bare Waiscoat"	50
	"Winnefreds Chance"	36
William Hamersly	"Beverly"	380
	"Batchellors Hope" a/s "Bashford Mannor"	300
	"Gore"	16
Thomas Alstone	"Reeders Adventure"	380
	pt. "St. Clements Mannor"	200
39:1758:15 ...		
William Mills	pt. "Poplar Neck"	115
	"Anstruther"	30
John Johnson	"Peter Wills"	100
Peter Cartwright	pt. "Weston"	100
John Spalding	pt. "Batchellors Rest"	100
Martin Yates	pt. "Turvey"	93
Edmund Plowden	pt. "Tavern"	100
	"Farm"	500
	"Plowdens Discovery"	66
Isaac Shemwell	pt. "Devonshire"	50
	pt. "Trumania"	50
	"Derby Shire"	130
Thomas Spalding	pt. "Great St. Thomas"	200

Thomas Spalding (Leonard Town)	pt. "Cragburns Purchase"	100
	"Spaldings Addition"	42
	pt. "St. Giles's"	35
	"Spaldings Adventure"	207
	"Rich Neck"	150
Benjamin Branson	"Drayton"	57
	"Kennady" a/s "Hillfield"	96½
	"Keith & Prices Rest"	122
	"Best Land"	10
George Thompson	pt. "Hazard"	100
William Hall	pt. "Graden"	100
William Watson	"Edenborough"	100
39:1758:16 ...		
James Pike	"Forrest of Deane"	100
George Leigh	"Innis's Choice"	100
	"Gallowith" or "Betty Folly"	50
	"Innis's Reserve"	25
	"Paris"	150
	"Inclosure"	170
Peter Drury	pt. "Bottom"	50
Athanas. Ford	pt. "Strand"	91
William Thomas	"Waills"	200
	"Waills Addition"	91
	pt. "Boston"	100
	"Boggs"	19
George Warren	pt. "St. Johns"	68
	pt. "Birch Hanger"	75
Luke Mattingly	"Choice" pt. "Hazzard"	100
John Higgs	"Wednesdays Project"	98
	"Higgs's Purchase"	49
John Harbert	"Harberts Invention"	109
	"Good Yielding"	86
	"Good Yielding" on resurvey	67
Francis Ratcliff	pt. "Doe Park"	50
William Jenkins (cnp)	pt. "Truth & Trust"	273
	"Salem"	215

	"Croyden"	100
	"St. Thomas"	300
	"Addition"	103
	"Fox Range"	70
Thomas Watts	"Smoot"	50
	"Watts his Hazzard"	65
39:1758:17 ...		
William Martin	pt. "Hopewell"	74
	"Cracksons Rest"	50
	"Redmans Hardship"	50
	pt. "Hopeless"	11
Thomas Hall	pt. "Long Looked for Come at Last"	112
Peter Brown	pt. "White Acre"	222
Rev. James Ashby	"St. Innigoes Manner" & "St. Georges Island"	3000
Charles Beech	"Goslings Addition"	30
	pt. "Parting Path"	26
	pt. "Stiles Chance"	25
Elizabeth Gosling	pt. "Parting Path"	274
	"Garden Spott"	80
Henry Greenfield Sothoron	"Brotherhood"	140
	"Sothorons Hills"	50
	pt. "Wastham"	100
Matthew Guibert	pt. "Dynard"	81
Theodos. Jordan	pt. "St. Clements Mannor"	130
Philip Greenwell	"Honest Jones Inheritance"	150
Richard Fenwick, Jr.	pt. "Maynards Comfort"	100
	"Gannets Purchase" a/s pt. "Charles West Discovery"	40½
	"Fenwick's Gain"	55
Thomas Tippet	pt. "Suttles Range"	213
39:1758:18 ...		
William Lock	"Good Pennyworth"	50
	"Fair Field"	50
	"Locks Venture"	49
Horn Roberts	pt. "Fresh Pond Neck"	203
Thomas Morton	pt. "St. Johns"	100

Mrs. Dryden Forbes	"Orphans Gift"	400
	pt. "Holbrige Town"	130
	"Drayden"	483
Charles Ridghill	pt. "Inclosure"	50
John Ford, Sr.	pt. "Farthings Gift" a/s "Minsterdam"	10
	pt. "Durham"	100
	"Long in Dispence"	75
Mark Thompson	pt. "Hatsfield Hills"	25
Henry Cooper	pt. "Scotland"	150
John Sissell	pt. "Scotland"	50
Luke Sissell	pt. "Scotland"	50
James Sissell	"Sissells Venture"	88
Sarah Sissell	pt. "Bailys Rest"	150
James Brown	"Dry Docking Addition"	100
Alexander Fargisson	pt. "Small Hope with Addition"	9
	"Small Hope Addition"	42
	pt. "Blake Creek"	99
39:1758:19 ...		
Thomas Redman	pt. "Small Hope Addition"	100
Mark Taylor	"Branch"	50
Clement Spink	pt. "Guelmots Hills"	180
	"All Thats Left"	31¼
	pt. "Guelmots Hills"	150
John Tennison	pt. "Outlet"	50
John Mattingly	"Thames"	110
	"Mattinglys Addition"	50
Sarah Greenwell	"Holly Tree"	148
John Smith (New Town)	pt. "Nuns Oake"	142
William Howard	"Phomphret Fields"	100
Enoch Greenwell	"Hickory Hollows"	119
	"Farthings Adventure"	78
	pt. "Wheatlys Contentment" a/s "Backland"	55
Thomas Thompson	pt. "St. Johns Addition"	23
	pt. "Dynard"	13
	pt. "Chance"	89
John Key (cnp)	pt. "Weston"	100

	pt. "Notlys Addition"	175
	"Gardiners Gore" or "Landing"	100
James Smith (Rock Creek)	pt. "Outlet"	119
	"Fish Pond"	243
	"Mitcham Meadows"	100
	pt. "Hamstead"	100
	pt. "Blake Creek"	30
39:1758:20 ...		
John Horril	pt. "Weston Addition"	100
	pt. "Weston Addition"	13
	"Horrels Meadows"	10
George Thompson	pt. "Rockey Point"	50
Walter Davis	pt. "St. Williams Hermitage"	110
Richard Payne	pt. "Strife"	50
Clement Newton	"Newtons Rest"	63
	"Newtons Rest with Addition"	37
Samuel Johnson	pt. "Hopewell"	36
	"Addition" or "Pianas Grove"	19
Elizabeth Hayden	"Roaches Discovery"	251
	"Haydens Risque"	81
William Edley	pt. "Haydens Fair"	100
William Hayden	pt. "Haydens Fair"	100
Michael Wellman	pt. "Styles Chance"	100
Mary Watts	pt. "Jesbury Plains"	100
John Goss Lawrence	pt. "Frogg Marsh"	100
William Egerton	pt. "Punklys Marsh"	100
William Biggs	pt. "St. Clements Mannor"	100
Fran. Thompson	"Hard Fortune"	100
39:1758:21 ...		
Justinian Greenwell	pt. "Rochester"	100
Margret Plummer	"Asbustons Oak"	50
	"Hobsons Choice"	30
William Doxey	"Smiths Rest"	100
William Cavanagh	pt. "Massom"	250
	"Eyre"	328
h/o Richard Vowles (cnp)	pt. "Vowls's Purchase"	120

	pt. "Britains Outlet"	1
Robert Hammet	"Hammets Beginning"	34
	pt. "Birch Spring"	75
	pt. "Forrest Harvey"	100
	"Wildcat Neck"	104½
	"Hickory Flatt"	17½
	"Hammett & Chance"	69
Clement Mattingly	pt. "Vowles's Purchase"	239
h/o Peter Muggs	"Vowles's Addition"	80
	"St. Williams"	50
	pt. "Vowles's Purchase"	57
	pt. "Rockey Point"	50
James Greenwell	"Wheatlys Contentment"	75
Elizabeth King	pt. "Birch Springs"	50
James Biscoe, Jr.	"Hogg Neck"	100
39:1758:22 ...		
Joshua Milliard	"Neales Lott"	209
	pt. "Little St. Thomas"	16
	pt. "St. Johns"	134
Luke Norris	pt. "Wheatlys Contentment"	69
Ignatius Thompson	"Fibny"	100
Thomas Medley	"Barren Doe"	95
John Mills	"Little Yielding"	99
	pt. "Hopton Park"	80
Robert Drury	"Howards Mount"	40
Richard Cooper	pt. "Clarken"	100
	"Frightfull"	180
	"Clarken Addition"	94
	"Dynard"	100
	pt. "Hopewell"	65
	"Expence"	67
	pt. "Cragburns Purchase"	100
John Walter	pt. "Partnership"	65
Richard Burroughs	"Hold Fast"	76
	pt. "Long Look'd for Come at Last"	75
John Willson	"Indian Giant Sepulchre"	203

Abraham Hall	pt. "Gardiners Grove"	50
Thomas Hayes	pt. "Gardiners Grove"	197
	"Addition to Gardiners Grove"	82
39:1758:23 ...		
Edward Mahorney	pt. "Piles Discovery"	112
John Parsons	"Addition"	50
	pt. "Long Look'd for Come at Last"	112½
James Wattson	"Hedge Barron"	79
James Swann	pt. "Retirement"	63½
Stephen Caywood	pt. "Williamsons Purchase"	100
	"Westham"	200
	"Caywoods Expence"	157
Edward Barber	pt. "Swanns Forrest"	56
	pt. "Westham"	250
	pt. "Eastham" or "Luckland"	130
John Shanks	pt. "St. Oswell"	100
Joshua Greenwell	"Last Shift"	100
John Wiseman Greenwell	"This or None"	50
	"John Wiseman Greenwells Park"	49
	"Piles Wood Lane"	200
Hezekiah Briscoe	pt. "Retirement"	92
h/o Benjamin Gough	pt. "St. Margarets"	100
Charles Jarbeo	pt. "St. Peters Hills"	112
John Evans	pt. "Ishmaels Right"	165
39:1758:24 ...		
John Smith, Jr.	"Hap Hazzard"	304
John Wheatley	"Hickory Thicket"	48
	pt. "Hannover Addition"	45
John Knott	"Strapp"	44
John Hooper	"Ashcoms Greenfield"	100
Peter Paine	pt. "Howards Mount"	75
Thomas Spalding, Jr.	pt. "Great St. Thomas"	100
	pt. "Little St. Thomas"	100
William McWilliams	pt. "Batchellors Rest"	300
	pt. "St. Clements Manner"	100
	"Josias Plains"	16¾

William Peake	pt. "Hannover"	140
	pt. "Hannover Addition"	60
	pt. "Heards Security"	91
Henry Neale	pt. "Hillalee"	250
	pt. "St. Clements Mannor"	400
Thomas Hulston	pt. "Buckland Plains"	35
Richard Gardiner	"Poplar Hill"	200
	"Middle Ground"	50
	"Floods Quarter"	50
Thomas Graves	pt. "Graves Chance"	120
	pt. "Bap. Hope"	106
	"Hopewell"	99
	"Hardshift"	10
	"New Castle"	50
	pt. "Groves's Chance"	10
39:1758:25 ...		
John Ford (Co. House)	pt. "Lamptons Pleasure"	150
	"Fords Inclosure"	255
Richard Fenwick	"Chance Conclusion"	97
	"Addition to Chance Conclusion"	26
Mary Bright	pt. "Cold Wells"	65
Philip Key, Esq. (cnp)	"Bushwoods Lodge"	411
	pt. "Thames"	40
	"James Addition"	158
	pt. "St. Johns"	50
	"Addition to Peters Wills"	104
	pt. "Birch Hanger"	230
	"Cuckols Haven" & timberland	77
	pt. "Wems"	430
	"Woods Pleasure" & pt. "Chesham"	95
	pt. "Maiden Bower" or "St. Clements Mannor"	100
	pt. "Finchly"	102
	pt. "Boston"	98
	pt. "Westham"	87
	pt. "Boston" & "Peach Blossom"	55
	"Covent Garden" pt. "Luckland"	200

	pt. "Dynard"	119
	pt. "Suerance"	60
	"Yieldingbury"	15
	pt. "Yieldingbury"	88
	pt. "Milton Hope"	150
	pt. "Little Yielding"	35
	"Penryn" or "St. Clements Mannor"	192
Ignatius Greenwell	pt. "Wheatlys Meadows"	123
Mary Wheatly	pt. "Wheatlys Meadows"	153
Charles Daft	pt. "Medley"	200
39:1758:26 ...		
Peter Peake, Jr.	pt. "Hanover Addition"	50
John Melton	pt. "Burch Hanger"	94
Gilbert Irland	"Edenborough with Addition"	121
	pt. "St. Williams Hermitage"	73
	pt. "Hopton Park"	140
	pt. "Baptist Hope"	153
	pt. "Yieldingbury"	17
	pt. "Baptist Hope"	50
John Guither	pt. "Croft Rectified"	147
	"Saturday's Venture"	2½
	"Cornelius Swamp"	100
Ignatius Wheeler	pt. "Hopton Park"	50
Capt. Richard Ward Key	"Wolf Hole"	262
	"Addition to Guiberts Chance"	38
William Rodgers	"Rodgers's Venture"	50
Leah Ward	"Wards Defence"	100
Anthony Brown	"Clarks Rest"	300
Samuel Abell	pt. "Kirbys Choice"	118
	pt. "Squabble"	25
	"Scrubby Thicket"	25
	pt. "Wheatlys Chance"	41
Elioner Gardiner	pt. "St. Johns"	500
39:1758:27 ...		
Peter Oneal	pt. "Cragburns Purchase"	60
Kenelm Boult	pt. "Collicomb"	25

John Black	pt. "Massom"	200
	"Cadock Measure"	150
	"Court Freehold" or "Hearts Delight"	200
	"Fox Hall"	30
	"Ajoinder"	50
	"Gravelly Hill"	50
	"Oystershell Neck"	50
	"Newgents Venture"	50
	"Blumberry"	100
	"Dunbarr"	92
	"Long Neck" or "Butchers Slipe"	42
	"Poplar Point"	101
Barton Smoot	"Clarkes Range"	393
William Field	pt. "Batchellors Rest"	150
William Love	pt. "Partnership"	130
Enoch Fenwick, Jr.	pt. "St. Peters Hills"	150
	pt. "Cole Brooke Levell"	35
	"Spinks Rest"	65
Thomas Mooney	"St. Edward"	115
	"Tradesman Lott"	200
	pt. "Linstead"	18
	"Valentines Grove"	96
Daniel Harris	"Kingston"	50
	"Wheatlys"	38
39:1758:28 ...		
John Hynes	"Bite the Fox"	19
	"Hunters Hills"	150
James Anderson	pt. "Bakers Fancy"	78
	pt. "Cornelius"	39
	"Addition to Charles Park"	20
Charles Flower	pt. "St. Georges Point"	50
Benjamin Williams (cnp)	"Esquires Purchase"	37
	pt. "Muggs Adventure"	200
	"Fox Den"	89
	"Bakers Fancy"	25
	"New Fancy"	25

	pt. "Punklys Marsh"	100
John Tear	"Hollyday"	142
Enoch Fenwick	pt. "Fenwick Mannor"	175
Ignatius Heard	pt. "Well Found"	106
Sabina Truman Greenfield	"America Felix"	152
Thomas Newton	"Underwood" a/s "Newtons Property"	124
	"Greenwells Marsh"	19
Ann Greenfield	"Greenfields Discovery"	90
	"Trent Neck"	835
	"Stockbardolph"	75
39:1758:29 ...		
James Truman Greenfield	"Keech's Folly"	133
	"Lamby"	100
	"Punch Neck"	60
	pt. "Holbrige Town"	130
	pt. "Hopton Park"	120
Nathaniel Truman Greenfield	"Fork"	60
	"Addition"	78
	"White Haven"	164
	"Indian Creek & Addition"	491
	"Nighthood"	50
	"Bashford Mannor"	104
	"Thimblebee"	109
	"Fishing Place"	50
	pt. "Brough"	75
James Warwick	pt. "St. Johns"	150
John Dunbarr	"Chance"	240
Edward Castor	pt. "Redmans Hardship" for h/o (N) Redman	50
John Cole	"Jones Wood"	100
	"Addition to Jones Wood"	59½
Lydia Bright	pt. "Cold Wells"	65
John Michael Thomas Taney	pt. "Fenwicks Mannor"	450
Joseph Clarke	pt. "Mattinglys Hope"	70
	pt. "St. Johns"	300
	pt. "Coles Park" a/s "Clarks Discovery"	122
Sarah Carter	"Meer Chance"	113

39:1758:30 ...		
Mary Hamersly	"Carberys Discovery"	190
John Dant	"Hopewell"	100
	pt. "Yoke by Chance"	20
John Jones	"Poverty"	64
Thomas Yates	pt. "St. Peters Hills"	100
	pt. "Small Hopes with Addition"	30
	pt. "Hanover"	60
	pt. "Heards Security"	70
Enoch Combs	pt. "Pork Hall"	300
	"Grapnell"	200
	"Wilderpole"	300
John Wherret	pt. "Watts Lodge"	90
Thomas Cooke, Jr.	pt. "Brough"	68
Joseph Harding	pt. "Bailys Rest"	100
John McKey	pt. "McKeys Neck"	153
	pt. "St. Richards Mannor"	50
	pt. "Massom"	100
Samuel Belwood	pt. "Ishmaels Right"	165
	"Belwoods Grove"	128
	pt. "Styles's Chance"	16
Fairfax Compton	pt. "Honnard Mount"	75
39:1758:31 ...		
George Rodgers	pt. "Well Close"	100
	"Brothers Dread"	135
John Norris	"Goughs Levells"	42
	"Goughs Conveniency"	48
	"Britains Bay"	150
William Roach	pt. "St. Johns Landing"	117
	pt. "St. Johns Addition"	167
William Guither	"Maids Right"	100
	pt. "Smoot"	100
Cuthbert Clarke	"Chesley"	100
	"Clarks Lott"	19
William Taylor	"Poplar Hill"	63
	"Taylors Lot"	22

John Baker (Bay Side)	pt. "Drapers Neck"	285
Fran. Wheatly	pt. "Wheatlys Contentment"	66
	pt. "Buckland Plain"	50
Leonard Greenwell	pt. "Hannover Addition"	87
George Would	pt. "Hanover"	103
John Thomas	"Hampton"	100
39:1758:32 ...		
Clement Norris	"Tants Mark"	168
	"Norris's Frolick"	3½
Thomas Howard	pt. "Gillmots Hills"	75
Joseph Stephens	pt. "Devonshire"	50
	"Trumania"	50
	"Josephs Venture"	54
Samuel Lee	pt. "Well Close"	82
	pt. "St. Clements Mannor"	105
John Bready	pt. "Bailys Rest"	100
	"Bradys Lot"	25
Peter Ford	pt. "St. Giles's"	81
	"Mount Pleasant"	100
	"May Pole"	96
	pt. "Strand"	91
Thomas Wheatly	"Wheatlys Plains"	20
John Chesley	pt. "Cragburn"	300
	"Cragburns Island"	13
	"Cragburns Marsh"	17½
	pt. "Indian Creek"	36
Thomas Greenfield	pt. "Indian Creek with Addition"	843
	pt. "Good Luck"	275
Thomas Bond	"Knotting"	100
39:1758:33 ...		
Rev. John Urquhart	pt. "Faunskirk"	250
	"Spring Blossom"	221
	pt. "Keith & Prices Rest"	60
	"Hopewells Chance"	170
Benjamin Gristy	"Venture"	50
	"Gristys View"	34½

Thomas Clarke	pt. "Moffats Wills"	69
Thomas Breeden	pt. "Moffats Wells"	69
John Biscoe	"Barren Wood"	46
Henry Winsatt	pt. "Harberts Grief"	44
	pt. "Nuns Oak"	20
James Dickson	"Dicksons Venture" or "Haydens Fair"	115½
h/o Edward Pye	"Underwood"	300
John Adams	"Small Hope with Addition"	50
John Graves	pt. "Graves's Chance"	94
James Thompson (head Chaptico)	pt. "St. Johns"	50
	"Harberts Swamp"	21
Joseph Stephens, Jr.	"Stephens's Chance"	46
	"Parnasses"	75
39:1758:34 ...		
Ignatius Fenwick	"St. Ignatius"	100
	"Addition"	25
Mary Fenwick	pt. "Fenwick Mannor"	200
Daniel Watts	pt. "Watts's Lodge"	160
John Plummer	pt. "Elizabeth Mannor"	300
Richard Shurly	"Shurlys Adventure"	150
Thomas Keen	"Keens Rest"	49
Thomas Matthews	pt. "Friends Conjunction"	72
Edward Aprice	pt. "St. Barbarys"	100
John Anderson	"Sothorons Desire"	100
	pt. "Fox Race"	52
Benjamin Bean	pt. "Friends Conjunction"	72
John Sykes	pt. "Friends Conjunction"	56
John Thompson	pt. "Micham Meadows"	100
	"Thompsons Lott"	172
39:1758:35 ...		
h/o Mark Thomas	"Penamser"	100
	"Brown Wood House"	50
	"Lukes Hardship"	7
	"Marks Adventure"	36
Henry How (cnp)	"White Land"	225
	"Hows Fortune"	19

	"Hows Adventure"	42
John Biscoe	pt. "William Fortune" a/s "Harrisons Rest"	80
	pt. "Williams's Fortune"	32
Dr. William Murray	"Indian Creek"	563
Peter Peake	pt. "Fenwick Mannor"	200
Robert Henly	pt. "Massom"	150
	"Johns Content"	93½
	"Keens Rest"	50
Robert Nugent	"Marking Place"	100
	"Fox Hatch'd"	11
James Smith	"Trinity Mannor", "St. Gabriels Mannor" & "St. Michaels Mannor"	3000
	"Pountlys Oversight Rectified"	198
	"Tripple Defence Rectified"	206
	"Addition to Tripple Defence Rectified"	34
	"Pine Land"	370
	pt. "Turvey"	201
	pt. "Hazzard"	57
39:1758:36 ...		
Cornelius Wildman	"Brooke Chance"	81
	"Dyllions Disappointment"	103
	"Williams Venture"	54
	"Goulding Grove"	153
	"Tavern"	100
Enoch Abell	pt. "Wheatlys Chance"	50
	"Abels Content"	113
	"Slipe"	24
John Medley Thompson	pt. "Scotland"	50
Thomas Barber	pt. "Burch Hanger"	20
Charles Greenwell	"Farthing Adventure"	65½
Thomas Jordan	pt. "Collicomb"	25
John Clarke	"Evans Quarter"	100
Michael Goldsmith	pt. "St. Clements Mannor"	86
	pt. "Bashford Mannor"	100
William Aude	pt. "Hannover"	30
James Chizzam	pt. "Bakers Fancy"	100

John Shercliff	"Shercliff"	250
	"St. Williams"	90
	"No Name"	100
	pt. "Linstead Addition"	100
	pt. "Linstead No Name"	78
	"Coles Adventure"	150
39:1758:37 ...		
Richard Milliard	"Little St. Thomas"	84
	pt. "St. Johns"	50
	"Turners Plains"	16
Thomas Pearce	pt. "Cortanys Fancy"	50
Kenelm Truman Greenfield	pt. "Trent Neck"	1519
Henry Lowes	"Warnell"	240
Henry Jarbeo	pt. "St. Peters Hills"	126
Henry Bryant	"Williams Endeavours"	50
	pt. "Farthings Adventure"	37
	"Greens Plott"	44
William Deacon, Esq.	pt. "St. Peters"	50
	pt. "Chancellers Point"	112
	pt. "St. Marys Freehold" a/s "No Name"	248
William Hicks	pt. "St. Peters"	100
	"Governors Fields"	100
	"Popes Freehold"	100
	"Chapple Freehold" a/s "No Name"	25
	pt. "St. Marys Freehold" a/s "No Name"	7
John Miles	"Waistfield"	140
	"Somerset"	195
Edward Parsons	pt. "Guiberts Chance"	50
	"Small Addition"	19½
39:1758:38 ...		
Sabastian Thompson	"Thomas Expence" or "Thompsons Expence"	208
Joseph Jenkins	pt. "Truth & Trust"	400
William Heard	pt. "Wellfound"	106
	pt. "Fenwick Mannor"	175
George Plator, Esq. (cnp)	pt. "St. Josephs Mannor"	81
	"Bowls's Preservation"	890

	pt. "Fenwick Mannor"	400
	"Stewarts Hope"	125
	"Resurrection Mannor"	4000
Richard Raper	"Maynards Comfort"	100
	pt. "Bailys Fortune"	45
	pt. "St. Clements Mannor"	50
	pt. "Bap. Hope"	100
Thomas Doxey	pt. "Harrisons Rest" a/d "Williams Fortune"	70
Richard Brooke	"Delle Brooke Mannor"	2000
	"Two Brothers"	235
	"Backland"	400
Thomas Hobson	pt. "Wems"	100
Elizabeth Hulse	pt. "Westham"	150
Charles King	"Deptford"	300
	pt. "St. Josephs Mannor"	200
Justinian Greenwell	pt. "Kirbys Choice"	67
39:1758:39 ...		
William Williams	"Dry Docking"	100
	pt. "Shock Park"	76
	pt. "Roberts Neck" a/s "Medly"	95
	pt. "Harberts Grief"	60
	pt. "Roberts Freehold" a/s "Medly"	75
Robert Fenwick	pt. "St. Josephs Mannor"	126
John Mareman	pt. "Hopton Park"	197
	"Vowles's Purchase"	156
Samuel Jenefer	pt. "St. Josephs Mannor"	50
Leonard Green	pt. "Fenwick Mannor"	50
Thomas Manly	pt. "Elizabeth Mannor"	100
Thomas Bladen, Esq.	pt. "Elizabeth Mannor"	247
	pt. "Cross Mannor" a/s "Cornelius Cross"	500
Stourton Edwards	"St. Thomas"	190
	"Doe Park"	69
	pt. "Hanover"	100
Thomas Brome	pt. "No Name"	250
John Lancaster	pt. "Hillalee"	250
	pt. "St. Clements Mannor"	400

Peter Gough	pt. "Lewgroes Plains"	100
39:1758:40 ...		
James Hagoe	pt. "Beaverdam"	59
John Abell	pt. "Wheatlys Chance"	31
	pt. "Kirbys Choice"	88
	pt. "St. Josephs Mannor"	56
	"Last Part of the Ripe"	100
	"Johns Guess"	170
Cuthbert Abell	"Wisemans Chance"	100
Benjamin Redman	"Small Hope with Addition"	50
Dennis Burn	pt. "Beckworths Lodge"	81½
Joseph Walker	pt. "Gillmots Hills"	100
	"Addition to Farthings Fortune"	140
Ignatius Bailey	pt. "Little Yielding"	117
William Jones	"Salters Hall"	83
	"Addition to Salters Hall"	34
	"Jones's Conveniency"	35½
	pt. "Beckworths Lodge"	81½
	"Jones's Lane"	1¾
	pt. "Muggs Adventure"	52
John Jarbeo	pt. "Hanover"	17
	pt. "Heards Security"	24
Thomas Warren	"Warrens Lott Rectified"	116
Matthias Nottingham	"Salmon"	50
39:1758:41 ...		
Ruth Jones	"Davis's Forrest"	50
Henry Spalding	"St. Joseph"	152½
	"Two Brothers"	165
	pt. "New Castle"	50
	pt. "Rich Neck"	98
Thomas Devaun	pt. "Partnership"	200
John Wattson	pt. "Partnership"	65½
George Maxwell	pt. "Indian Creek with Addition"	461
Col. Abraham Barnes (cnp)	"America Felix Secundus"	956
	pt. "Banglefield"	40
	pt. "Forrest Harvey"	100

	"Westbury Mannor"	1250
	pt. "Forrest Lodge"	100
	pt. "Drapers Neck"	215
	"Walnut Point"	55
Capt. Zacharia Bond	pt. "St. Barbarys"	200
	pt. "Piles's Discovery"	112
William Doxey, Jr.	pt. "St. Patricks Hills"	50
Edmond Bowling	pt. "Collingwood"	25
John Morris	pt. "Collingwood"	25
Fran. Knott	pt. "Hazzard"	56
39:1758:42 ...		
George Bowles	"Steplihon Fortune"	200
	"Hazzard"	234
John Tippett	"Tippets Purchase"	46
William Spalding	pt. "Rich Neck"	152
Mark Norris	pt. "Wheatlys Content"	118
	pt. "Buckland Plains"	70
Ignatius Fenwick	pt. "Hebdonshole" or "No Name"	350
	pt. "Hebdonshole" or "No Name"	70
John Holt	pt. "St. Clements Mannor"	167
Ignatius Wheelor	pt. "St. Clements Mannor"	250
John Lee	pt. "St. Clements Mannor"	200
John Haskins	pt. "St. Clements Mannor"	100
John Baptist Greenwell	pt. "Rochester"	100
John Bould	pt. "Cadle"	150
	"Addition to White Acre"	25
John Wimsatt	pt. "Hatfield Hills"	75
John Bullock	pt. "St. Clements Mannor"	100
Thomas Wherret	"Hogg Neck"	100
39:1758:43 ...		
John Buchannon	"Fox Grape Barren"	106
David Downie	"Town Support"	81
	"Barry"	65
	3 lots	3
James Jarbeo	"Denby"	250
Thomas Jenkins	"Poplar Point"	100

Benjamin Moulton	pt. "Bashford Mannor"	200
John Pike	"Torney Branch"	50
Clement Medley	pt. "Medley"	200
William Medley	pt. "Medley"	100
Basil Peake	pt. "Medley"	100
George Greenwell	pt. "Medley"	50
John Lewellin	pt. "St. Clements Mannor"	400
John Fenwick	pt. "Rivets Backside"	172
	pt. "Rivets"	151
	pt. "Chancellors Point"	112
	pt. "Crofts Rectified"	100
Bennet Neale	pt. "St. Clements Mannor"	200
Austin Leigh Massey	pt. "Plumb Point"	308
Elizabeth Lock	pt. "Cold Wells"	65½
39:1758:44 ...		
Stephen Chilton	pt. "Peters Quay"	50
	"Fishing Creek Neck"	44
Richard Milburn	pt. "Halfhead Folly"	100
	pt. "Cortanys Neck"	82
	"Milburns Chance with Addition"	246
John Smith	pt. "Mattapany Sewall"	289
John Eden	pt. "Bashford Mannor"	277
John Bond	pt. "St. Clements Mannor"	605
	pt. "Hopton Park"	400
	pt. "St. Johns"	438
	"Gardiners Chance"	155
	pt. "Burlington" or "St. Clements Mannor"	25
Richard Edelen	"Trumans Hunting Quarter"	200
	pt. "Hope"	64
Justinian Jordan	pt. "St. Clements Mannor"	200
George Backster	"Batchellors Comfort"	190
George Lee	pt. "St. Clements Mannor"	1000
	"Wee Bit"	50
John Boult	pt. "St. Clements Mannor"	100
Edward Turner	pt. "Bashford Mannor"	200
39:1758:45 ...		

Charles Sewall	pt. "Little Eltonhead Mannor" a/s "Rich Neck"	50
	"Friends Discovery"	117
John Blackiston	pt. "St. Clements Mannor"	550
	pt. "St. Clements Island" pt. "Manor"	100
John Mason	pt. "St. Clements Mannor"	450
Mary Tennison	pt. "St. Clements Mannor"	100
Kenelm Chiseldyne	pt. "St. Clements Mannor"	720
Cyrenus Chiseldyne	pt. "St. Clements Mannor"	25
Charles Carrol, Esq.	pt. "St. Clemments Mannor"	1650
	pt. "St. Clemments Mannor"	479
	"Oxford"	209
	"St. Barbarys Addition"	250
	pt. "Loughborough"	150
	"Addition"	41
	"Temple Barr"	100
John Madox	pt. "Bashford Mannor"	150
John Reshwick	pt. 2 tracts of escheat land	47
Edward Welsh	"Ossfield"	72
John Attaway Clarke	pt. "Piney Point"	750
	"Poplar Hill"	200
	pt. "Blake Creek"	50
	"Tower Hill"	25
Robert Hagoe	pt. "Truth & Trust"	100
39:1758:46 ...		
Nicholas Lewis Sewal	pt. "Mattapany"	911
	"Sewals Discovery"	108
	"Fishing Point"	13
Leonard Davis	pt. "Desart"	62½
	"Thorns Venture"	103
James Wheatley	"Kington" a/s "Ninto Quit"	117
	pt. "Wheatlys Addition"	21
John Smith	pt. "Bashford Mannor"	200
Mary McWilliams	pt. "St. Clements Mannor"	300
Stourton Edwards, Jr.	"Taunton Dean"	164
Thomas Suite	pt. "Trent Fort"	84
	pt. "Horse Range"	100

James Mills	pt. "Bashford Mannor"	100
Leonard Mattingly	"Audly End"	190
Notly Goldsmith	pt. "Bashford Mannor"	100
Rodger Smith	pt. "Notlys Addition"	275
Dent Suite	pt. "Horse Range"	100
Thomas Crane	"Dally"	100
	"Smoots Marsh"	31
John Ford (weaver)	pt. "Pomphry Fields"	50
	"Minsterdam"	54
Henry Taylor	"Taylors Plains"	50½
39:1758:47 ...		
Thomas Suite, Jr.	pt. "Cold Wells"	100
Joseph Edwards	pt. "Cold Wells"	52
	pt. "Trenfort"	8
Thomas Wyn Taylor	pt. "Writing"	100
John Somervell	pt. "St. Richards Mannor"	100
	"Clarks East Discovery"	99
	pt. "St. Jeroms Discovery"	200
	"Addition to Fortune"	100
Clement Medly, Sr.	"No Name"	100
John Waughop	"Waughops Chance"	138
John Coode	pt. "St. Clements Mannor"	300
Anthony Roberts	pt. "Twitnam"	200
Benjamin Burroughs	pt. "Trent Fort"	129
Peter Ford, Jr.	"Nuns Oake"	75
John Curlet a/s John Corbet	"Willingborrough"	70
h/o James Heath	pt. "St. Jeroms Mannor"	5500
James Kindrick	"Kindricks Lane"	80
John Reeves	pt. "Bashford Mannor"	100
John Kelly	"Kellys Luck"	138
	"Kellys Fortune"	182
39:1758:48 ...		
James Tarlton	pt. "Beaverdam"	59
	pt. "Elizabeth"	34
Samuel Swann	pt. "Swans Forrest"	40
	"Swans Venture"	140

James Latimore	pt. "Hopewell"	89½
Leonard Payne	"Fox"	100
Rev. Arnold Livers	"Little Brittain" or "No Name"	750
	pt. "Brittains Outlet"	43
James Bailey	pt. "St. Clements Mannor"	45
Thomas Yates, Jr.	pt. "St. Clements Mannor"	100
John Goldsmith	pt. "Bashford Mannor"	100
Samuel Maddox	pt. "Bashford Mannor"	38
Thomas Vowls	pt. "Vowls's Purchase"	50
Thomas Melton	pt. "Burch Hanger"	95
George Bullock	pt. "Burlington" or "St. Clements Mannor"	75
39:1758:49 ...		
John Wynn (PG)	"Addition to Hogg Neck"	16
Michael Lyon	"Pettits Addition"	27
	pt. "St. Margarets"	88
George Chilton	pt. "Forrest Lodge"	50
William Forgisson	"Copthall"	100
John Burch	"Burch's Forrest"	100
John Wheatly	pt. "Tower Hill"	43
John Goodwin, Esq.	3 lots in Leonard Town	3
George Gordan	2 lots in Leonard Town	2
Col. Barnes	5 lots in Leonard Town	5
George Plater, Esq.	2 lots in Leonard Town	2
Philip Key, Esq.	1 lot in Leonard Town	1
(N) Greenfield	1 lot in Leonard Town	1
(N) Bright	1 lot in Leonard Town	1
Court House	1 lot in Leonard Town	1
39:1758:50-51 **index**		
39:1758:52 ...		
Fargus Keough	"Reeders Addition"	<n/g>
William & Mary Parish	"Jenifers Gift"	100
John Thompson	pt. "Davis Forest"	50
~~James Smith~~	~~pt. "Turvey"~~	~~201~~
Peter Cartwright	pt. "Weston Addition"	100
James Thompson	"Swamp & Island"	120
Joseph Clarke	pt. "St. Johns"	300

Robert Vaulx	pt. "Massom"	100
John Mackey	pt. "Massom"	100
John Baker	pt. "Drapers Neck"	185
Ignatius Jarbo	pt. "Hickory Hills"	105
Peter Oneall	"Hard Fortune"	62
~~William Norris~~	~~"Readers Addition"~~	~~77~~

40:1759:1 ...		Acres
Daniel Clocker	"Clockers Freehold"	50
	"Lewis Neck"	30
Elizabeth Clocker	pt. "St. Ann's Freehold"	70½
	"Clockers Fancy"	56
Thomas Palmer Waughop	"Hunting Quarter"	150
	"Piney Point"	750
	"Smoots Hollow"	150
Nicholas Sewall	pt. "Little Eltonhead Manor" a/s "Rich Neck"	1590
Edward Digges	pt. "Little Eltonhead Manor"	300
William Price	"Buckhill"	217
	"Park's Addition"	110
Edward Howe	pt. "Halfhead Folly"	100
Ignatius Taylor	pt. "Little Eltonhead Manor" a/s "Rich Neck"	60
James Dafferon	"Cole Harbour"	150
George Aisquith	"Stinmore"	100
	"Inclosure"	33
	"Thomas & George in Company"	4½
John Roades	pt. "Jesbury Plaines"	330
Isaac Peavatt	"Cow Ridge"	50
	pt. "Cross Manor"	150
Robert Pearce	pt. "Cortanys Fancy"	50
	pt. "Prices Chance"	25
Thomas Thorpe	"Strife"	50
Fargus Kough	"Surgeon's Folly"	50
	"Wills & Swamp"	150
	"Reader's Addition"	79
James Stiles	pt. "Styles Chance"	59
	pt. "What Care I"	28½
	pt. "Chance"	6
	pt. "Elizabeth's Manor"	43
John Price	"Grove"	50
	"Farnhans"	83
Robert Greenwell	pt. "Buck Land Plains"	70
	pt. "Lampton's Pleasure"	117
	pt. "Greenwell's Marsh"	49

40:1759:2 ...		
Robert Vaulx	pt. "Massom"	100
Barnaby Egan	pt. "Massom"	100
	pt. "Hopewell"	100
	"Strife"	100
	"Harberts Beginning"	50
	"Clockers Marsh"	100
	"Lordships Favour"	100
	"Dunbarr"	100
	"Addition" taken up by Mr. Debutts	20
Rev. Moses Tabb	"Itchcombs Freehold"	340
James White	pt. "Fresh Pond Neck"	150
Richard Barnhouse	pt. "Cross Manor"	1000
	pt. "Elizabeth Manor"	1000
John Cole (New Town)	pt. "Rivets Backside"	50
	"Nobles Victor"	50
	"Harberts Gift"	48
	pt. "Shock Park"	24
John Mitchell	"Mitchell Choice"	47
Cornelius Barber	pt. "Luckland"	470
	"Nicholl's Hope"	185
Baptist Barber	pt. "Westham"	250
	pt. "Luckland"	200
	"Leighe"	100
Elizabeth Donaldson	pt. "Mitcham Hills"	200
Philip Barton Key	pt. "Mitcham Hills"	100
George Latham	pt. "Mitcham Meadows"	100
Luke Russell	pt. "Brough"	50
James Gough	"St. Bernards"	100
	"St. Margarets"	200
	"Bacon Neck"	200
	"Proprietary's Gift"	50
	"Q Name"	50
	"St. Teresia"	100

William Morgan (St. Michael)	"Hazard"	73
	"Addition to White Burch Freehold"	53
	pt. "St. Patricks Hills"	15
	"White Burch Freehold"	100
40:1759:3 ...		
William Sissell	pt. "Cadle"	50
Thomas Yeats	pt. "Whiteacre"	50
	"Addition to Whiteacre"	18
John Thompson	pt. "Davis's Forrest"	50
George Booth, Jr.	pt. "Hopton Park"	56
Mary Greenwell	pt. "Green Hill"	221
Athanasius Nottingham	"Nevitts Saint Ann"	100
Clement Stratford	"Leeing"	100
Thomas Hatton Combs	"Hattons Rest"	250
	"Addition to Heart's Delight"	152
John Heard	pt. "St. Laurences Freehold"	193
	pt. "Heards Security"	43
	pt. "Hanover"	350
Peter Howard	"Twittenham"	100
Mark Jarbeo	pt. "Heards Security"	40
	pt. "Hanover"	20
John Norris	"Shircliff"	300
John B. Carbery	pt. "Hopton Park"	797
Edward Hillard Hebb	"Little Resurvey of Birth Right"	13
William Mattingley	pt. "Suttles Rest"	80
Mathew Heard	"Pole"	122
	"William Heards Purchase"	115
	"Ashcombs Freehold"	150
	pt. "Hanover Addition"	123
	"Heards Choice"	100
	pt. "Heards Security"	169
Mark Heard	"Thirds"	425
James Taylor (St. Mary's)	pt. "Snow Hill"	100
40:1759:4 ...		
Matthew Hebb	pt. "Small Hopes"	56
John French	pt. "Hopton Park"	160

John Hammond	pt. "Lewgroves Plaines"	200
William Wales	"Bushells Rest"	150
John Gardiner (St. Georges)	"Timber Swamp"	100
	"Addition to Timber Swamp"	60
William Hebb	"Gardiners Purchase"	100
	"St. Williams"	114
	"Freehold"	75
	"Cousin"	50
	"St. Georges"	50
	"No Name"	50
	"Hibton's Hole"	280
	"Hunting Corbet"	100
	"Macky's Point"	50
	"Cross Manor"	170
	"Wichahandwick"	225
	"Gardiners Gore"	42
James Thompson	"Small Hope"	100
	"Swamp & Island"	120
	"Farthings Fortune & Addition"	60
	"Mill Meadows"	150
	pt. "Hounslow"	50
	"Prattlewell"	100
	"Small Hopes Addition"	78
	"Davis's Hills"	51
	pt. "Hatfield Hills" for William Lake	75
Nicholas Mills	"Strife"	200
	"Strife's Addition"	109
	pt. "Wheatleys Chance"	150
	pt. "Squabble"	50
	pt. "Medly"	300
Richard Brewer	pt. "Hounslow"	50
James Broomfield	"Cole's Addition"	50
	"Roberts Freehold"	90¾
John Sanders Power	pt. "St. Barbara's"	200
h/o James Neal	pt. "St. Wineferts Freehold"	30
40:1759:5 ...		

h/o Roswell Neale	pt. "St. Winefreds Freehold"	220
	"Surplust"	432
Robert Cole	"Coles Purchase"	209
Edward Mattingley	pt. "St. Winefreds Freehold"	250
Philip Tippett	pt. "Suttles Range" a/s "Rest"	74
William Warthen	pt. "Suttles Range" a/s "Rest"	80
William Wood	"Quainton"	103
Thomas Mattingley	"Mount Misery"	100
	pt. "St. Thomas"	150
	pt. "St. Johns" a/s "Mattingleys Land"	25
Vincent Taylor	pt. "St. Teresia"	100
	"Plains"	130
	"Englebeth"	300
	"Englebeth Addition"	140
Joshua Guibert	pt. "Dynard"	100
Abell Simmons	"Stratford"	100
	"Trophy"	100
James Wood	"Desart"	125
	"Arabia"	78
William Meekin	"Beards Choice"	150
	"St. Margarets Fields"	100
	"St. Margarets Forrest"	100
	"Speedwell"	100
John Thompson	pt. "Susquehanna Point"	100
	"Smiths Discovery"	258
	"Q Namc"	195
John Suttle	pt. "Suttles Range" a/s "Rest"	136
Andrew Miller	"Wolverhampton"	150
Joseph Edelen	pt. "New Design"	350
John Hatton	pt. "Hopewell"	146
40:1759:6 ...		
John Edwards	"Prices Lott"	100
	"Plaines of Jericho"	93
	"Buck Park"	100
	"John Edwards Discovery"	241
Thomas Aisquith (cnp)	pt. "St. Richards Manor"	350

	pt. "Hamstead"	100
	"Hunting Neck"	200
	"Hickory Hills"	100
Cornelius Manning	"Neales Lot"	209½
	"Broad Neck"	83
	"Rednor"	404
	pt. "Nun's Oak"	63
Elizabeth Wiseman	"Batchellors Hopewell"	374
	"Force Putt"	100
	"Hopewells Delight"	200
	"Back Acres"	100
William Stone	pt. "Graden"	100
Cuthbert Fenwick	pt. "Fenwick Manor"	175
Joseph Hopewell	pt. "Massom"	300
	"Aisquiths Defence"	122
	"Gardiner's Neck"	200
	"Hogpen Neck"	150
John Price Williams	pt. "Keith & Prices Rest"	190
James Heard	pt. "St. Clements Manor"	150
	pt. "Fenwick Manor"	175
	pt. "Hardship"	147
	"Knevitts Beginning"	100
	"Two Friends"	131
	"Heards Addition"	58
John Sanner	pt. "Fresh Pond Neck"	150
Thomas Rabling	"Best Land"	50
John Thorn	pt. "Desart"	62½
	pt. "Jesham"	50
40:1759:7 ...		
James Keech	pt. "Keech & Prices Rest"	200
	"Town Neck"	200
	"Satisfaction"	580
	"Remainder"	19
Absolom Tennison (cnp)	"Phips's Fort"	100
	"John's Fortune"	61
	"Guiberts Folly"	36

	pt. "Patricks Hills"	13
	"Inclosure"	62
Meverell Lock	"Hulston"	100
	pt. "Trumans Lodge"	150
	pt. "Keech & Prices Rest"	58
Mary Clarke	"Addition"	100
Hugh Hopewell	"Hopewells Adventure"	95
	"Addition to Hopewells Adventure"	52
	pt. "St. Richards Manor"	500
George Mills	pt. "St. Clements Manor"	150
John Arthurs	pt. "Underwoods Choice"	100
Anthony Smith	pt. "Underwood"	100
John Wilkinson	"Industry"	153
William Harrison	pt. "St. Margarets"	166
	"Woods Addition"	38
h/o Charles Ganyott	"Ganyotts Lott"	50
	pt. "Yoke by Chance"	41
Mary Edwards	"Damond's Adventure"	110
	"Edwards Backland"	52
Thomas Shanks, Jr.	"Shank's Adventure"	101
	pt. "Clarker"	100
	pt. "St. Osswell"	100
	pt. "Cole Park" a/s "Charles W. Discovery"	30
Clement Hayden	"Shank's Risk"	102
40:1759:8 ...		
John Morgan	pt. "Parish Beadle"	100
Joseph Dafferon	"Marks Delight"	78
John Welch	pt. "Cortany's Neck"	68
Dennis Tippett	pt. "Suttles Range"	60
	pt. "St. Barbaras Addition"	120
George Vaudry	"Underwood" a/s "Wood Land" now called "Woods Pleasure"	344
Benedict Spalding	"Hearts Delight"	200
	1 lot in Leonard Town	1
Clement Stratford	"Slipe"	69
	pt. "Bailys Fortune"	168

Ignatius Mattingley	"Clever"	155
James Mattingley	pt. "Mattingleys Hope"	130
	pt. "St. Johns"	50
Jesse Wharton	"Notley Hall" or pt. "St. Clements Manor"	400
	"Neighbourhood" or pt. "St. Clements Manor"	146
Thomas Vaughon	pt. "Beckworths Lodge" a/s "James's Chance"	200
William Daft	pt. "Rocky Point" a/s "Curry Glass"	100
Stephen Greenwell	"Colebrook Levell"	120
John Taylor	pt. "Frog Marsh"	100
	"Milmots Adventure"	123
	"Neglect"	53
	"Williams's Addition"	22
	"White House"	63
	pt. "Chancellors Point"	64
	"Taylors Chance"	53
40:1759:9 ...		
James Somerhill	pt. "Wastham"	100
Isabella Cooke	"Jones Fortune"	112
William Boarman	"St. Dorothy"	263
Mary Jordan	pt. "St. Clements Manor"	211
William Morgan	pt. "Friends Conjunction"	50
Jeremiah Jordan	pt. "St. Clements Manor"	85
William Jordan	pt. "St. Clements Manor"	135
Thomas Reeder (cnp)	"Thomas & Henry"	113
	pt. "Fawnskirk"	165
	"Chance"	50
	"Rose Land"	50
	"Bogan's Increase"	273
	pt. "St. John's"	595
	"Workington Park"	932
	"Middle Grounds"	102
	pt. "Burroughs's Gift"	60
	"Maiden's Lott"	236
	"Addition to Rose Land"	83
	pt. "Hope"	36
	pt. "Wastham"	87

	pt. "Denbury Hills"	100
	pt. "Truman's Lodge"	105
	"Inclosure"	14
	pt. "Fawnskirk"	87
	pt. "Parish Beadle"	100
	"Young Mans Venture"	130
	"Fourth Addition"	83
	pt. "Great St. Thomas"	100
	"Hipworth"	100
	pt. "Dynard"	100
	pt. "Bottom"	50
	"Wildmans Levells"	168½
	"Rooms Conveniency"	100
	pt. "Hopewell"	151
	pt. "St. Clements Manor"	150
40:1759:10 ...		
William Hebb, Jr.	"White Cliff"	59
Thomas Sanner	"Salisbury Plains"	100
Samuel Ashcom	"No Name"	881
	"Ashcoms Marsh"	32
Thomas Reshwick	pt. 2 tracts escheat land	64
	pt. "White Acre"	50
Robert Lydell	"Synetts Chance"	56
Charles Dillion	"Charles's Chance"	75
Mark Stevens	"Richards Fancy"	38
Dr. Thomas James	"Bacon Point"	100
	pt. "Rivitts"	151
	pt. "Fortune"	30
	"Taunton"	40
	"Crooked Billet"	38
William Aisquith	"White Marsh"	93
Thomas Swann	"T.B."	119
James Roach	pt. "Medley"	100
	"Huckleberry Lane"	10
Eleanor & Ann Graves (cnp)	"Hopewell"	131
	"Hardshift"	50

	"Hardshift Addition"	186
John Olliver	pt. "Cornelius"	39
	"Fortune"	50
	"Pearth"	62
	"Fortune Outlett"	16
	"Archies Hills"	65
Elizabeth Nelson	pt. "Doe Park"	75
	pt. "Addition to Doe Park"	50
George Graves	"Grave's Swamp"	108
Thomas Standage	pt. "Doe Park"	21
	"North Addition to Doe Park"	147
40:1759:11 ...		
Samuel Wood	"Cannoe Neck"	100
Anthony Simms	"Wickhohandrick"	125
John Burroughs	pt. "Trent Fort"	129
	pt. "Remainder Charles's Lot"	166½
William Cartwright	pt. "Remainder Charles's Lot"	166½
	"Ridge"	50
John Cartwright	pt. "Long Look for Come at Last"	75
	"Cartwrights Pasture"	20
	pt. "Burrough's Gift"	40
George Burroughs	pt. "Long Look for Come at Last"	100
George Dent	pt. "Free Stone Point"	174
John Buckman	pt. "Free Stone Point"	50
John Dant	pt. "Free Stone Point"	100
James Crooke	"Ludgate"	50
Richard Sothoron	"Sothoron's Desire"	125
Samuel Sothoron	"Trumans Lott"	40
	"Littleworth"	25
	"Sothoron's Supply"	21
Thomas Taney	"Green Meadows"	200
Thomas Norris	pt. "Lewgrows Plains"	133
	pt. "Wheatlys Content"	95
	pt. "Heards Choice"	57
Free School	pt. "Hopton Park"	100
John Lynch (cnp)	"Granes Content"	100

	"Plumb Point"	162
Robert Chesley	2 lots in Leonard Town	2
	"Vineyard"	343
	pt. "Pork Hall"	50
	"Charles Park"	130
	"Tobys Last Shift"	100
	"Wood Stock"	127
40:1759:12 ...		
Henry Reiley	"Saturdays Work"	100
	"Addition to Saturdays Work"	21
Peter Mills	pt. "St. Johns"	230
Thomas Biscoe	pt. "Mackays Neck"	50
Winefred Rowen	"Maidens Lott"	100
	"Bare Waiscoat"	50
	"Winefred Chance"	36
William Hamersley	"Beverly"	380
	"Batchellors Hope"	300
Thomas Allstone	"Reeders Adventure"	350
	pt. "St. Clements Manor"	200
William Mills	pt. "Poplar Neck"	115
	"Ansterday"	30
John Johnson	"Peters Wells"	100
Peter Cartwright	pt. "Waston Addition"	100
John Spalding	"Batchellors Rest"	100
Martin Yates	pt. "Turvey"	93
Edmond Plowden	pt. "Tavern"	100
	"Farm"	500
	"Plowdens Discovery"	66
Isaac Shemwell	pt. "Devonshire"	50
	pt. "Trumania"	50
	"Derbyshire"	130
Thomas Spalding	pt. "St. Thomas"	200
Thomas Spalding (L.T.) (cnp)	pt. "Cragburns Purchase"	100
	"Spaldings Addition"	42
	pt. "St. Giles"	35
	"Spaldings Adventure"	207

	"Rich Neck"	150
Benjamin Branson	"Drayton"	57
	"Kennaday" a/s "Kielfield"	96½
	"Keech & Prices Rest"	122
	pt. "Best Land"	10
40:1759:13 ...		
George Thompson	pt. "Hazard"	100
William Hall	pt. "Gradin"	100
William Watson	"Edinburgh"	100
James Pike	"Forrest Dunn"	100
George Leigh	"Innis's Reserve"	100
	"Gallowith"	50
	"Innis's Reserve"	25
	"Pearth"	150
	"Inclosure"	170
Peter Drury	pt. "Bottom"	50
Athanatius Ford	pt. "Strand"	91
William Thomas	"Wails"	200
	"Wail's Addition"	91
	pt. "Boston"	50
	"Boggs"	19
George Warren	pt. "St. John's"	68
	pt. "Burch Hanger"	75
Luke Mattingley	pt. "Hazard"	100
John Higgs	"Wednesdays Project"	98
	"Higg's Purchase"	49
John Harbert	"Harberts Invention"	109
	"Good Yielding"	86
	"Good Yielding" on resurvey	67
Francis Ratcliff	pt. "Doe Parke"	50
William Jenkins	pt. "Truth & Trust"	273
	"Salem"	215
	"Croyden"	100
	"St. Thomas"	300
	"Addition"	103
	"Fox Range"	70

Thomas Watts	"Smoot"	50
	"Watts his Hazard"	65
40:1759:14 ...		
William Martin	pt. "Hopewell"	74
	"Cracksons Rest"	30
	"Redmans Hardship"	50
	pt. "Hopeless"	11
Thomas Hall	pt. "Long Look For Come at Last"	112
Peter Brown	pt. "White Acre"	222
Rev. James Ashby	pt. "St. Inigoes Manor" & "St. George's Island"	3000
Charles Beech	"Goslings Addition"	30
	pt. "Parting Path"	26
	"Stiles Chance"	25
Elizabeth Gosling	pt. "Parting Path"	274
	"Garden Spot"	80
Henry Greenfield Sothoron	"Sothorons Hills"	50
	pt. "Brotherhood"	140
	pt. "Wastham"	100
Matthew Guibert	pt. "Dynard"	81
Theodorus Jordan	pt. "St. Clements Manor"	130
Philip Greenwell	"Honest Jones's Inheritance"	150
Richard Fenwick, Jr.	"Maynard Comfort"	100
	"Ganeth's Purchase" a/s "Charles's West Discovery"	40½
	"Fenwicks Gain"	55
Thomas Tippett	pt. "Suttles Range"	213
William Lock	"Good Pennyworth"	30
	"Fairfield"	50
	"Locks Venture"	49
Horn Roberts	pt. "Fresh Pond Neck"	233
Thomas Morton	pt. "St. Johns"	100
Dryden Forbes	"Orphans Gift"	400
	"Holbridge Town"	133
	"Drayden"	483
40:1759:15 ...		
Charles Ridgell	"Joynture"	50

John Ford, Sr.	pt. "Farthings Gift" a/s <n/g>	10
	pt. "Durham"	100
	pt. "Long in Dispence"	75
Mark Thompson	pt. "Hatfield Hills"	25
Henry Cooper	pt. "Scotland"	150
John Sissell	pt. "Scotland"	150
Luke Sissell	pt. "Scotland"	50
James Sissell	"Sissells Venture"	88
James Brown	"Drydocking Addition"	100
Alexander Forguson	pt. "Small Hope"	9
	"Small Hope Addition"	42
	pt. "Black Creek"	99
Thomas Redman	pt. "Small Hopes Addition"	100
Mark Tyler	"Branch"	50
Clement Spink	pt. "Guelmots Hills"	180
	"All Thats Left"	31¼
	pt. "Guilmots Hills"	150
John Tennison	pt. "Outlett"	50
John Mattingley	"Thames"	110
	"Mattingleys Addition"	50
Sarah Greenwell	"Holly Tree"	148
John Smith (New Town)	pt. "Nuns Oak"	142
William Howard	"Pumpharys Fields"	100
Enoch Greenwell	"Hickory Hollows"	119
	"Farthings Adventure"	78
	pt. "Wheatlys Content" a/s "Back Land"	55
40:1759:16 ...		
Thomas Thompson	"Adjoinder" a/s "St. Johns Addition"	23
	pt. "Dynard"	13
	pt. "Chance"	89
John Key	pt. "Weston"	100
	pt. "Knotleys Addition"	175
	"Gardiners Landing"	100
James Smith (Rock Creek) (cnp)	pt. "Outlet"	119
	"Fresh Pond"	243
	"Mitcham Meadows"	100

	pt. "Hamstead"	100
	pt. "Black Creek"	30
John Horrell	pt. "Weston Addition"	100
	pt. "Weston Addition"	12
	"Horrells Meadows"	10
George Thompson	pt. "Rockey Point"	50
Walter Davis	"St. Williams Hermitage"	110
Richard Payne	pt. "Strife"	50
Clement Newton	"Newtons Rest"	63
	"Newtons Rest with Addition"	37
Samuel Johnson	pt. "Hopewell"	36
	"Addition" or "Pianas Grove"	19
Elizabeth Hayden	"Roaches Discovery"	251
	"Haydens Risk"	81
William Edley	pt. "Haydens Fair"	100
William Hayden	pt. "Haydens Fair"	100
Michael Wellman	pt. "Stiles Chance"	100
Mary Watts	pt. "Jesbury Plaines"	100
John Goss Laurence	"Frog Marsh"	100
William Edgerton	pt. "Punkleys Marsh"	100
40:1759:17 ...		
William Biggs	pt. "St. Clements Manor"	100
Francis Thompson	"Hard Fortune"	100
Justinian Greenwell	pt. "Rochester"	100
Margaret Plummer	"Orbustons Oak"	50
	"Hobsons Choice"	30
William Doxey	"Smiths Rest"	100
William Cavenough	pt. "Massom"	250
	"Eyre"	328
h/o Richard Vowles	pt. "Vowles's Purchase"	120
	pt. "Brittains Outlett"	1
Robert Hammett (cnp)	"Hammets Beginning"	34
	pt. "Burch Spring"	75
	pt. "Forrest Harvey"	100
	"Wild Catt Neck"	104½
	"Hicory Flatt"	17½

	"Hammett & Chance"	64
Clement Mattingley	pt. "Vowle's Purchase"	239
h/o Peter Muggs	pt. "Vowles's Addition"	80
	"St. Williams"	50
	pt. "Vowles Purchase"	57
	pt. "Rockey Point"	50
James Greenwell	"Wheatleys Content"	75
Elizabeth King	pt. "Burch Springs"	50
James Biscoe, Jr.	pt. "Hog Neck"	100
Joshua Millard	"Neale's Lott"	289
	pt. "Little St. Thomas"	16
	pt. "St. Johns"	136
Luke Norris	pt. "Wheatleys Content"	69
40:1759:18 ...		
Ignatius Thompson	"Tibny"	100
Thomas Medley	"Barren Doe"	95
John Mills	"Yielding Bury"	99
	pt. "Hopton Park"	80
Robert Drury	"Honnards Mount"	40
Richard Cooper	pt. "Clarker"	100
	"Frightful"	180
	"Coopers Addition"	94
	"Dynard"	100
	"Hopewell"	65
	"Expense"	67
	pt. "Cragburns Purchase"	100
John Walter	pt. "Partnership"	85
Richard Burroughs	"Hold Fast"	76
	pt. "Long Look for Come at Last"	75
John Wilson	"Indian Giant Sepulcher"	203
Abraham Hall	pt. "Gardiners Grove"	50
Thomas Hayes	pt. "Gardiners Grove"	197
	"Addition to Gardiners Grove"	82
Edward Mahoney	"Piles Discovery"	112
John Parsons	"Addition"	50
	pt. "Long Look for Come at Last"	112½

James Watson	"Hedge Barren"	79
Stephen Cawood	pt. "Williamsons Purchase"	100
	"Westham"	200
	"Cawoods Expence"	157
Edward Barber	pt. "Swanns Forrest"	56
	pt. "Westham"	250
	pt. "Luckland"	130
James Swann	pt. "Retirement"	63½
40:1759:19 ...		
John Shanks	pt. "St. Oswell"	100
Joshua Greenwell	"Last Shift"	100
John Wiseman Greenwell	"This or None"	50
	"John Wiseman Greenwell Park"	49
	"Piles's Wood Lane"	200
Hezekiah Briscoe	pt. "Retirement"	92
h/o Benjamin Gough	pt. "St. Margarets"	100
Charles Jarbeo	pt. "St. Peters Hills"	112
John Evans	pt. "Ishmaels Right"	165
John Smith, Jr.	"Hazhazard"	304
John Wheatley	"Hickory Thickett"	48
	pt. "Hanover Addition"	45
John Knott	"Sharp"	44
John Hooper	"Ashcombs Greenfield"	100
Peter Payne	pt. "Howards Mount"	75
Thomas Spalding, Jr.	pt. "Great St. Thomas"	100
	pt. "Little St. Thomas"	100
William McWilliams	pt. "Batchellors Rest"	300
	pt. "St. Clements Manor"	100
	"Josias Plaines"	16¾
William Peake	pt. "Hanover"	140
	pt. "Hanover Addition"	60
	pt. "Heards Security"	91
Henry Neale	pt. "Hillalee"	250
	pt. "St. Clements Manor"	400
Thomas Hulston	pt. "Buck Land"	35
Richard Gardiner (cnp)	"Poplar Hills"	200

	"Middle Ground"	50
	"Floods Quarter"	50
40:1759:20 ...		
Thomas Graves	pt. "Graves Chance"	120
	pt. "Baptist Hope"	106
	"Hopewell"	99
	"Hardshift"	11
	"Prince William New Castle"	50
	pt. "Graves Chance"	16
John Ford (Court House)	pt. "Lamptons Pleasure"	150
	"Fords Inclosure"	255
Richard Fenwick	"Chance Conclusion"	97
	"Addition to Chance Conclusion"	26
Mary Bright	pt. "Cold Wells"	65
Philip Key, Esq.	"Bushwoods Lodge"	411
	pt. "Thames"	40
	"James Addition"	158
	pt. "St. John's"	50
	"Addition to Peters Wills"	104
	pt. "Burch Hanger"	230
	"Cuckold Haven" & timberland	77
	pt. "Wems"	430
	"Woods Pleasure" & pt. "Chesham"	95
	pt. "Maiden Bower"	100
	pt. "Finchly"	102
	"Boston"	98
	pt. "Westham"	87
	pt. "Boston" & pt. "Blossom"	55
	"Luckland"	200
	pt. "Dynard"	119
	pt. "Shurance" & "Yieldingbury"	75
	pt. "Yieldingbury"	88
	pt. "Milton Hope"	150
	pt. "Little Yielding"	35
	"Penryn" or pt. "St. Clements Manor"	192
Ignatius Greenwell	pt. "Wheatleys Meadows"	123

Mary Wheatley	pt. "Wheatleys Meadows"	153
Charles Daft	pt. "Medley"	200
Peter Peake, Jr.	pt. "Hanover Addition"	50
John Melton	pt. "Burch Hanger"	94
40:1759:21 ...		
Gilbert Ireland	"Edinburgh with Addition"	121½
	pt. "Hermitage"	23
	pt. "Hopton Park"	140
	pt. "Baptist Hope"	153
	pt. "Yieldingbury"	17
	"Evans Lott" a/s "Hamstead" a/s "Baptist Hope"	50
John Guyther	pt. "Croft"	147
	"Saturdays Venture"	2½
	"Cornelius's Swamp"	100
Ignatius Wheeler	pt. "Hopton Park"	50
Capt. Richard Ward Key	"Wolf Hole"	262
	"Addition to Guiberts Chance"	37
William Rogers	"Roger's Venture"	50
Eleanor Gardiner	pt. "St. Johns"	500
Sarah Ward	"Wards Defence"	100
Anthony Brown	"Charles Rest"	300
Samuel Abell	pt. "Kirbys Choice"	118
	pt. "Squabble"	25
	"Scrubby Thickett"	25
	pt. "Wheatleys Chance"	41
Peter Oncalc	pt. "Cragburns Purchase"	60
Kenelm Boult	pt. "Collingwood"	25
John Black (cnp)	pt. "Massom"	200
	"Cadocks Measure"	150
	"Court Freehold" or "Hearts Hall"	200
	"Fox Hall"	30
	"Adjoinder"	50
	"Gravelly Hill"	50
	"Oyster Hill Neck"	50
	"Newgents Venture"	50
	"Blumbury"	100

	"Dunbar"	92
	"Batchelors Hope" or "Long Neck"	42
	"Poplar Point"	101
40:1759:22 ...		
Barton Smoot	"Clarkes Range"	393
Walter Fields	pt. "Batchellors Rest"	100
William Love	pt. "Partnership"	100
Enoch Fenwick, Jr.	pt. "St. Peters Hills"	150
	"Colebrooke Levell"	35
	"Spink's Rest"	65
Thomas Mooney	pt. "St. Edwards"	115
	"Tradesman Lott"	200
	pt. "Linsteed"	18
	pt. "Valentines Grove"	96
Daniel Harris	"Kingston"	50
	"Wheatleys"	38
John Hynes	"Bite the Fox"	19
	"Hunters Hills"	150
James Anderson	pt. "Balkers Fancy"	78
	pt. "Cornelius"	39
	"Addition to Charles's Parke"	20
Charles Flower	pt. "St. Georges"	50
Benjamin Williams	"Esquire's Purchase"	37
	pt. "Muggs Adventure"	200
	"Fox Denn"	89
	"Baker's Fancy"	25
	"New Fancy"	25
	pt. "Punkley's Marsh"	100
John Tear	"Hollyday"	142
Enoch Fenwick	pt. "Fenwick Manor"	175
Ignatius Heard	pt. "Well Found"	106
40:1759:23 ...		
Sabina Truman Greenfield	"America Felix"	152
Thomas Newton	"Underwood"a/s "Newtons Propriety"	124
	pt. "Greenwells Marsh"	19
Ann Greenfield (cnp)	"Greenfields Discovery"	90

	"Trent Neck"	835
	"Stock Bardolph"	75
James Truman Greenfield	"Keeches Folly"	133
	"Lamly"	100
	"Punk Neck"	60
	"Holbridge Town"	130
	pt. "Hopton Park"	120
Nathaniel Truman Greenfield	"Fork"	60
	"Addition"	78
	"Whitehouse"	164
	"Indian Creek" & "Addition"	491
	"Nighthood" & "Bashford"	154
	"Thimblebe"	109
	"Fishing Place"	50
	"Brough Lane"	75
James Warwick	pt. "St. John's"	150
John Dunbarr	"Chance"	240
Edward Caster for h/o (N) Redman	"Redmans Hardship"	50
John Cole	"Jones's Wood"	100
	"Addition to Jones's Wood"	59½
Lydia Bright	pt. "Cold Wells"	65
John Michael Thomas Taney	pt. "Fenwick Manor"	450
Joseph Clarke	"Mattingleys Hope"	70
	pt. "St. John's"	300
	pt. "Charles's West Discovery"	122
40:1759:24 ...		
Sarah Carter	"Meer Chance"	113
Mary Hemersly	"Carburys Discovery"	190
John Dant	"Hopewell"	100
	pt. "Yoak by Chance"	25
John Jones	"Poverty"	64
Thomas Yates	pt. "St. Peters Hills"	100
	pt. "Small Hope"	30
	pt. "Hanover"	60
	pt. "Heards Security"	70

Enoch Combs	pt. "Pork Hall"	300
	"Grape Hill"	200
	"Wilderpoole"	300
John Wherret	pt. "Watt's Lodge"	90
Thomas Cooke, Jr.	pt. "Brough"	68
Joseph Harding	"Baileys Rest"	100
John McKey	pt. "McKeys Neck"	153
	pt. "St. Richards Manor"	50
	pt. "Massom"	100
Samuel Belwood	"Ismaels Right"	165
	"Belwoods Grove"	128
	pt. "Stiles Chance"	16
Fairfax Compton	pt. "Honnards Mount"	75
George Rogers	pt. "Well Close"	100
	"Brothers Dread"	135
40:1759:25 ...		
John Norris	"Goughs Levels"	42
	"Gauphs Conveniency"	48
	"Brittain Bay"	150
William Roach	pt. "St. Johns Landing"	217
	pt. "John's Addition"	167
William Guither	"Maids Delight"	100
	pt. "Smoot"	100
Cuthbert Clarke	"Chesley"	100
William Taylor	"Poplar Hill"	63
	"Taylor Lott"	22
John Baker (B.S.)	pt. "Drapers Neck"	285
Francis Wheatly	pt. "Wheatleys Content"	66
	pt. "Buck Land"	30
Leonard Greenwell	pt. "Hanover Addition"	87
George Would	pt. "Hanover"	103
John Thomas	"Hampton"	100
Clement Norris	"Tants Mark"	168
	"Norris Frolick"	3½
Thomas Howard	pt. "Guilmots Hills"	75
Joseph Stevens (cnp)	pt. "Devonshire"	50

	"Trumania"	55
	"Joseph's Venture"	54
40:1759:26 ...		
Samuel Lee	"Welclose"	82
	pt. "St. Clements Manor"	105
John Brady	pt. "Bailys Rest"	100
	"Bradys Lott"	25
Peter Ford	pt. "St. Giles's"	81
	"Mount Pleasant"	100
	"May Pole"	96
	pt. "Strand"	91
Thomas Wheatly	"Wheatly's Plaines"	204
John Chesley	pt. "Cragburne"	300
	"Cragburns Island"	13
	"Cragburnes Swamp"	17½
	pt. "Indian Creek"	36
Thomas Greenfield	pt. "Indian Creek"	843
	pt. "Good Luck"	275
Thomas Bond	"Knotting"	100
Rev. John Urquhart	pt. "Fawnskirk"	250
	"Spring Blossom"	221
	pt. "Keeth & Prices Rest"	60
	"Hopewells Chance"	170
Benjamin Gristie	"Venture"	50
	"Gristy's Vein"	34½
Thomas Clarke	pt. "Moffatts Will"	69
Thomas Breeden	pt. "Moffatts Will"	69
40:1759:27 ...		
John Biscoe	"Barren Wood"	46
Henry Wimsatt	"Harberts Grief"	44
	pt. "Nuns Oak"	20
James Dickson	"Dickson's Venture" or "Hadens Fair"	115½
h/o Edward Pye	"Underwood"	300
John Adams	"Small Hope with Addition"	50
John Graves	pt. "Graves Chance"	94
James Thomson (cnp)	pt. "St. John's"	50

	"Harberts Swamp"	21
Joseph Stevens, Jr.	"Stevens' Chance"	46
	"Parnasses"	75
Ignatius Greenwell	"Ignatius Dread"	100
	"Addition"	25
Mary Fenwick	pt. "Fenwick Manor"	200
Daniel Watts	"Watt's his Lodge"	160
John Plummer	pt. "Elizabeth Manor"	300
Richard Shurley	"Shurleys Adventure"	150
Thomas Keen	"Keen's Rest"	49
Thomas Matthews	"Friends Conjunction"	72
40:1759:28 ...		
Edward Aprice	pt. "St. Barbara's"	100
John Anderson	"Sothorons Desire"	100
	pt. "Fox Race"	52
Benjamin Been	pt. "Friends Conjunction"	72
John Stiles	pt. "Friends Conjunction"	106
John Thompson	"Mitcham Meadows"	100
	"Thompsons Lott"	172
h/o Mark Thomas	"Penancy"	100
	"Brown Woodhouse"	50
	"Lukes Hardship"	7
	"Marks Adventure"	34
Henry How	"White Land"	225
	"How's Fortune"	19
	"How's Adventure"	42
John Biscoe	pt. "Harrison's Rest"	80
	pt. "William's Fortune"	32
Dr. William Murray	"Indian Creek"	563
Peter Peake	pt. "Friends Goodwill"	100
Benjamin Fenwick	pt. "Fenwick Manor"	250
Robert Henley	pt. "Massom"	150
	"John's Content"	93½
	"Keene's Rest"	50
Robert Newgent	"Marking Place"	100
	"Fox Catched"	11

40:1759:29 ...		
James Smith	"Trinity Manor", "St. Gabriels Manor", "St. Michael's Manor"	3000
	"Pountleys Oversight"	198
	"Tripple Defence Rectified"	259
	"Addition to Tripple Defence Rectified"	34
	"Pineland"	370
	pt. "Tarvey"	201
	"Hazzard"	57
Cornelius Wildman	"Brook Chance"	81
	"Tailors Disappointment"	103
	"Williams Venture"	54
	"Golding Grove"	153
	"Tavern"	100
Enoch Abell	pt. "Wheatlys Chance"	50
	"Abell's Intent"	113
	"Slipe"	24
John Medley Thompson	pt. "Scotland"	50
Thomas Barber	pt. "Burch Hanger"	20
Charles Greenwell	"Farther Adventure"	65½
Thomas Jordan	pt. "Callicome"	25
John Clarke	"Evans's Quarter"	100
Michael Goldsmith	pt. "St. Clements Manor"	86
	pt. "Bashford Manor"	100
William Aude	pt. "Hanover"	30
James Chizzam	"Bakers Fancy"	111
40:1759:30 ...		
John Shircliffe	"Shircliff"	250
	"St. Williams"	90
	"Q Name"	100
	pt. "Linstead"	78
	pt. "Linstead Addition"	100
	"Coles Adventure"	150
Richard Millard	"Little St. Thomas"	84
	pt. "St. Johns"	50
	"Turner's Plaines"	16

Thomas Pearce	pt. "Cortany's Fancy"	53
Kenelm Truman Greenfield	pt. "Trent Neck"	1519
Henry Lowes	"Warnett"	240
Henry Jarbo	pt. "St. Peters Hills"	126
Henry Bryant	"Williams's Pleasures"	50
	pt. "Farther Adventure"	37
	"Green's Plott"	44
William Deacon, Esq.	pt. "St. Peters"	50
	pt. "Chancellors Point"	112
	pt. "St. Marys Freehold"	248
William Hicks	pt. "St. Peters"	100
	"Governors Field" & "Popes Freehold"	250
	"Chapple"	25
	pt. "St. Marys Freehold"	7
John Miles	"Westfield"	140
	"Somersett"	195
Edward Parsons	pt. "Guiberts Chance"	50
	"Small Addition"	19½
40:1759:31 ...		
Arther Thompson	"Thompsons Expence"	200
Joseph Jenkins	pt. "Truth & Trust"	400
William Heard	pt. "Well Found"	101
	pt. "Fenwick Manor"	175
George Plater, Esq.	pt. "St. Joseph's Manor"	819
	"Boules's Preservation"	890
	pt. "Fenwick Manor"	400
	"Staffords Hope"	125
	"Resurrection Manor"	4000
Richard Raper	"Maynards Comfort"	100
	pt. "Baileys Fortune"	45
	pt. "St. Clements Manor"	50
	pt. "Baptist Hope"	100
Thomas Doxey	pt. "Harrison's Rest"	70
Richard Brooke	"De la Brooke Manor"	2000
	"Two Brothers"	235
	pt. "Buck Land"	400

Thomas Hobson	pt. "Weems"	100
Elizabeth Hulse	pt. "Westham"	150
Charles King	"Deptford"	300
	pt. "St. Joseph's Manor"	200
Justinian Greenwell	pt. "Kirbys Choice"	67
40:1759:32 ...		
William Williams	"Drydocking"	100
	pt. "Shock Park"	76
	pt. "Roberts Neck" a/s "Medly"	45
	"Harberts Gift"	60
	pt. "Roberts Freehold"	75
Robert Fenwick	pt. "St. Josephs Manor"	126
John Mareman	pt. "Hopton Park"	197
	"Vowles's Purchase"	156
Samuel Jenefer	pt. "St. Joseph's Manor"	50
Leonard Green	pt. "Fenwick Manor"	50
Thomas Manly	pt. "Elizabeth Manor"	100
Thomas Bladen, Esq.	pt. "Elizabeth Manor"	247
	pt. "Cross Manor"	500
Sturton Edwards	"St. Thomas"	190
	"Doe Park"	69
	pt. "Hanover"	100
Thomas Broome	pt. "No Name"	250
John Lancaster	pt. "Hillalee"	250
	pt. "St. Clements Manor"	400
Peter Gough	pt. "Lewgroes Plaines"	100
James Hagoe	pt. "Beaverdam"	59
40:1759:33 ...		
John Abell	pt. "Wheatlys Chance"	31
	pt. "Kirbys Chance"	88
	pt. "St. Josephs Manor"	56
Cuthbert Abell	"Wisemans Chance"	100
Benjamin Redman	"Small Hope"	50
Dennis Burns	pt. "Beckworths Lodge"	81½
Joseph Walker	pt. "Guilmots Hills"	100
	"Addition to Farthings Fortune"	140

Ignatius Bailey	pt. "Little Yielding"	117
William Jones	"Salters Hall"	143
	"Addition to Salters Hall"	34
	"Jones's Conveniency"	35½
	pt. "Beckworths Lodge"	163
	"Jones's Lane"	1¾
	"Mugg's Adventure"	52
John Jarbeo	pt. "Hanover"	17
	pt. "Heards Security"	24
Thomas Warren	"Warrens Lott Rectified"	116
Mathias Nottingham	"Salmon"	50
Ruth Jones	"Davis's Forrest"	50
Henry Spalding	pt. "Joseph"	182½
	"Two Brothers"	165
	pt. "Newcastle"	50
	pt. "Rich Neck"	98
40:1759:34 ...		
Thomas Devaun	pt. "Partnership"	200
John Watson	pt. "Partnership"	65½
George Maxwell	pt. "Indian Creek with Addition"	461
Col. Abraham Barnes	"America Felix Secundus"	956
	pt. "Ranglefield"	40
	pt. "Forrest Harvey"	100
	"Wastbury Manor"	1258
	pt. "Forrest Lodge"	100
	pt. "Drapers Neck"	215
	"Walnut Point"	55
Capt. Zachariah Bond	pt. "St. Barbara's"	200
	pt. "Piles Discovery"	112
William Doxey, Jr.	pt. "St. Patricks Hills"	50
Edmund Bowling	pt. "Collingwood"	25
John Morris	pt. "Collingwood"	25
Francis Knott	pt. "Hazzard"	56
George Bowles	"Steplehon Fortune"	200
	"Hazzard"	234
John Tippett	"Tippetts Purchase"	46

William Spalding	pt. "Rich Neck"	152
Mark Norris	pt. "Wheatleys Content"	118
	pt. "Buck Plaines"	70
40:1759:35 ...		
Ignatius Fenwick	"Hopton Hole"	350
	pt. "Hopton Hole"	70
John Holt	pt. "St. Clements Manor"	167
Ignatius Wheeler	pt. "St. Clements Manor"	250
John Lee	pt. "St. Clements Manor"	200
John Hoskins	pt. "St. Clements Manor"	100
John Baptist Greenwell	pt. "Rochester"	100
John Bold	pt. "Cadle"	150
	"Addition to White Acre"	25
John Wimsatt	pt. "Hatfield Hills"	73
John Bullock	pt. "St. Clements Manor"	100
Thomas Wherrett	"Hogg Neck"	100
John Buchannan	"Fox Grape Barren"	106
David Downie	"Town Support"	81
	"Bary"	65
	3 lots in Leonard Town	3
James Jarbeo	"Denby"	250
Thomas Jenkins	"Poplar Point"	100
Benjamin Moulton	pt. "Bashford Manor"	200
40:1759:36 ...		
John Pike	"Forney Branch"	50
Clement Medley	pt. "Medley"	200
William Medley	pt. "Medley"	100
Basil Peake	pt. "Medley"	100
George Greenwell	pt. "Medley"	50
John Llewellin	pt. "St. Clements Manor"	400
John Fenwick	pt. "Rivitts Backside"	172
	pt. "Rivitts"	151
	pt. "Chancellors Point"	112
	pt. "Crofts"	100
Bennett Neale	pt. "St. Clements Manor"	200
Austin Leigh Massey	"Plumb Point"	308

Elizabeth Lock	pt. "Cold Wells"	65½
Stephen Chilton	pt. "Peter Quay"	50
	"Fishing Creek Neck"	44
Richard Milburne	pt. "Halfhead Folly"	100
	pt. "Cortany's Neck"	82
	"Milburne Chance with Addition"	246
John Smith	pt. "Matapany"	289
40:1759:37 ...		
John Eden	pt. "Bashford Manor"	277
John Bould	pt. "St. Clements Manor"	605
	pt. "Hopton Park"	400
	pt. "St. John's"	438
	"Gardiner's Chance"	155
	pt. "Burlington" or "St. Clements Manor"	25
Richard Edelen	"Trumans Hunting Quarter"	200
	pt. "Hope"	64
Justinian Jordan	pt. "St. Clements Manor"	200
George Baxter	"Batchellors Comfort"	190
George Slye	pt. "St. Clements Manor"	1000
	"Wee Bitt"	50
John Boult	pt. "St. Clements Manor"	100
Edward Turner	pt. "Bashford Manor"	200
Charles Sewall	pt. "Little Eltonhead Manor"	50
	"Friends Discovery"	117
John Blackistone	pt. "St. Clements Manor"	550
	pt. "St. Clements Island"	100
John Mason	pt. "St. Clements Manor"	450
Mary Tennison	pt. "St. Clements Manor"	100
Kenelm Cheseldyne	pt. "St. Clements Manor"	725
40:1759:38 ...		
Cyrenius Cheseldine	pt. "St. Clements Manor"	25
Charles Carroll (cnp)	pt. "St. Clements Manor"	1000
	pt. "St. Clements Manor"	199
	"Oxford"	209
	pt. "Barbara's Addition"	250
	pt. "Laughborough"	150

	"Addition"	41
	"Temple Barr"	100
John Maddox	pt. "Bashford Manor"	150
John Reshwick	pt. 2 tracts of escheat land	47
Edward Welch	"Ossfield"	72
John Attaway Clarke	pt. "Piny Point"	750
	pt. "James Johnson's Neck"	200
	"Blake Creek"	50
	"Tower Hill"	25
Robert Payne	pt. "Truth & Trust"	100
Nicholas L. Sewall	pt. "Mattapany"	911
	"Sewalls Discovery"	108
	"Fishing Point"	13
Leonard Davis	pt. "Desart"	62½
	"Thorne's Pasture"	103
James Wheatley	"Kington" a/s "Newton Quit"	117
	pt. "Wheatleys Addition"	21
John Smith	pt. "Bashford Manor"	200
40:1759:39 ...		
Mary McWilliams	pt. "St. Clements Manor"	300
Sturton Edwards, Jr.	"Taunton Dean"	154
Thomas Sute	pt. "Trent Fort"	84
	pt. "Horse Range"	100
James Mills	pt. "Basford Manor"	100
Leonard Mattingley	"Audley End"	190
Notley Goldsmith	pt. "Bashford Manor"	100
Roger Smith	pt. "Notleys Addition"	275
Dant Suite	pt. "Horse Range"	100
Thomas Crane	"Dally" or "Waughop Walker"	100
	"Smoots Marsh"	31
John Ford (weaver)	"Pomphry Fields"	50
	"Minsterdam"	54
Henry Taylor	"Taylors Plains"	50½
Thomas Suite, Jr.	pt. "Cold Wells"	100
Joseph Edwards	pt. "Cold Wells"	52
	pt. "Trent Fort"	8

Thomas Wyn Taylor	pt. "Weighting"	100
Clement Medly, Sr.	"No Name"	100
40:1759:40 ...		
John Somervell	pt. "St. Richards Manor"	100
	"Charles West Discovery"	99
	pt. "St. Jerome's Manor"	200
John Waughop	"Waughops Chance"	130
John Coode	pt. "St. Clements Manor"	300
Anthony Roberts	"Whittenham"	200
Benjamin Burroughs	pt. "Trent Fort"	129
Peter Ford, Jr.	"Nuns Oake"	73
John Curlet	"Willingborough"	70
h/o James Heath	pt. "St. Jerome's Manor"	5500
James Kindricks	"Kindrick's Lane"	80
John Reeves	pt. "Bashford Manor"	100
John Kelly	"Kelly's Luck"	138
	"Kelly's Fortune"	182
James Tarlton	pt. "Beaverdam"	59
	pt. "Elizabeth"	34
Samuel Swann	pt. "Swann's Forest"	40
	"Swann's Venture"	140
40:1759:41 ...		
James Latimore	pt. "Hopewell"	89
Leonard Payne	"Fox"	100
Rev. Arnold Livers	"Little Brittain"	750
	pt. "Brittains Outlett"	43
James Baily	pt. "St. Clements Manor"	45
Thomas Yates, Jr.	pt. "St. Clements Manor"	100
John Goldsmith	pt. "Bashford Manor"	100
Samuel Maddox	pt. "Bashford"	38
Thomas Vowles	pt. "Vowles's Purchase"	50
Thomas Melton	pt. "Burch Hanger"	95
George Bullock	pt. "Burlington" or "St. Clements Manor"	75
Matthew Clarke	"Clarke's Lott"	52
Joseph Edwards s/o J.	"Lott"	22
John Wynn (PG)	"Addition to Hog Neck"	16

Michael Lyon	"Pettits Addition"	27
	pt. "St. Margarets"	88
George Chilton	pt. "Forrest Lodge"	50
40:1759:42 ...		
William Forgison	"Copthall"	100
John Burch	"Burches Forrest"	100
John Goodwin, Esq.	3 lots in Leonard Town	3
George Gordon	2 lots in Leonard Town	2
Col. A. Barnes	5 lots in Leonard Town	5
George Plater, Esq.	2 lots in Leonard Town	2
Philip Key, Esq.	1 lot in Leonard Town	1
(N) Greenfield	1 lot in Leonard Town	1
(N) Bright	1 lot in Leonard Town	1
Court House	1 lot in Leonard Town	1
John Wheatly	pt. "Towerhill"	43
John Somerville	"Addition to Fortune"	100
Cuthbert Clarke	"Clarkes Lott"	19
Cuthbert Fenwick	"Fenwicks Prevention"	58
William Hamersley	"Gore"	16
John Abell	"Last Part of the Ripe"	100
	"Johns Guess"	170
Thomas Aisquith	"Addition"	31
Sarah Sissell	pt. "Baileys Rest"	150
40:1759:43 ...		
~~John Cartwright~~	~~"Addition to Cartwrights Pasture"~~	~~14~~
~~Thomas James~~	~~"Coles Addition"~~	~~71~~
	~~"Pasture Ground"~~	~~12~~
~~Jesse Tennison~~	~~"Foxes Hall"~~	~~10~~
~~John Norriss~~	~~"Buck Neck"~~	~~53~~
~~William Hebb~~	~~"Pasture Ground"~~	~~18~~
~~John Railey~~	~~"Hammer"~~	~~16~~
~~Thomas Bond~~	~~"Strife"~~	~~7~~
~~Thomas Jeans~~	~~"Pleasant Springs"~~	~~100~~
~~John Henley~~	~~"Henleys Addition"~~	~~23~~
~~Stephen Chilton~~	~~"Bill"~~	~~9~~
~~John Ford s/o P.~~	~~"Primus"~~	~~11~~

~~John Tippitt~~	~~"Addition"~~	~~65~~
~~John Bassett~~	~~"Bassetts Plains"~~	~~66½~~
~~Richard Burroughs~~	~~"Burroughs Lott"~~	~~33~~
40:1759:44 ...		
~~Philip Key~~	~~"Miltons Hope Rectified"~~	~~144~~
~~Anthony Roberts~~	~~"Leeth's Marsh"~~	~~12~~
~~Philip Key~~	~~"Wems"~~	~~517~~
~~Col. Abraham Barnes~~	~~"Addition"~~	~~86~~
40:1759:45-6 ...		
40:1759:47 from Rent Rolls		
John Cartwright	"Cartwrights Pasture"	34
Philip Key, Esq.	"Miltons Hope Rectified"	144
	"Weems"	517
Thomas James	"Coles Addition"	71
	"Pasture Ground"	12
Anthony Roberts	"Leeths Marsh"	12
Jesse Tennison	"Foxes Hall"	18
John Norris	"Buck Neck"	53
Col. Abraham Barnes	"Addition"	86
William Hebb	"Pasture Ground"	18
John Railey	"Hammer"	16
Thomas Bond	"Strife"	7
Thomas Jeanes	"Pleasant Springs"	100
John Henly	"Henlys Addition"	23
Stephen Chilton	"Bilt"	94
John Ford	"Primus"	11
John Tippit	"Addition"	65
40:1759:48 ...		
John Basset	"Bassets Plaines"	66½
Richard Burroughs	"Burroughs Lott"	33

www.ingramcontent.com/pod-product-compliance
Lightning Source LLC
Chambersburg PA
CBHW060155280326
41932CB00012B/1769